The Tactile Eye

Touch and the Cinematic Experience

JENNIFER M. BARKER

University of California Press

BERKELEY   LOS ANGELES   LONDON

University of California Press, one of the most distinguished university presses in the United States, enriches lives around the world by advancing scholarship in the humanities, social sciences, and natural sciences. Its activities are supported by the UC Press Foundation and by philanthropic contributions from individuals and institutions. For more information, visit www.ucpress.edu.

University of California Press
Berkeley and Los Angeles, California

University of California Press, Ltd.
London, England

Library of Congress Cataloging-in-Publication Data
Barker, Jennifer M., 1969–.
    The tactile eye : touch and the cinematic experience / Jennifer M. Barker.
        p.   cm.
    Includes bibliographical references and index.
    ISBN 978–0-520–25840–2 (cloth : alk. paper)
    ISBN 978–0-520–25842–6 (pbk. : alk. paper)
    1. Body, Human—In motion pictures.   2. Motion pictures—Psychological aspects.   3. Motion picture audiences — Psychology.
I. Title.

PN1995.9.B62B35   2009
791.43′6561—dc22   2008034392

18   17   16   15   14   13   12   11   10   09
10   9   8   7   6   5   4   3   2   1

For my family and friends

Contents

Illustrations

Acknowledgments

This project began as a series of questions regarding an aspect of the cinema experience that moves me profoundly but which I couldn't quite put my finger on. I am grateful to all the teachers, fellow students, colleagues, family, and friends who lent a hand over the years as I felt my way toward a vocabulary for it.

For her intellectual generosity and unflagging encouragement, special thanks go to Vivian Sobchack, who has supported this project from its first incarnation as a dissertation in UCLA's Critical Studies program. She encouraged me to follow my gut instincts, to take seriously my knee-jerk reactions, to embrace the touchy-feely, and to investigate all these things rigorously and with purpose, rather than dismiss them out of hand. I could not have asked for a more intrepid tour guide on what has been a fantastic voyage through the study of embodied, sensual cinema spectatorship.

Thanks also to Laura Marks, who kindly offered suggestions as I embarked on this project and continues to do so, and whose work has significantly shaped my thinking about haptic visuality. I am grateful to Laura as well as to Elena del Río and an anonymous reader for insightful and incisive comments that greatly improved the final work. Several people deserve my thanks, too, who provided valuable feedback on early drafts, including Steve Mamber, Peter Wollen, Dudley Andrew, and Linda Williams.

In the last stages of writing and editing, colleague Michele Schreiber's friendship kept my spirits up and my glass at least half-full. That, combined with the moral support and moviegoing companionship of Jennifer Henderson, Amy Sperling, Cathy Coppolillo, and Alison Byrne, saw me through to the finish. As for beginnings, I thank Boppa for instilling me with a love of the movies and the rest of my family for indulging it.

Naomi Shersty cheerfully agreed to help with the illustrations, to my great relief, and thanks finally to my editor Mary Francis at University of California Press, for her editorial guidance and support, and to her assistant, Kalicia Pivirotto. They have expertly steered the book along its journey from digital to tangible form.

Introduction

Eye Contact

Film is the greatest teacher because it teaches not only through the
brain but through the whole body.
VSEVOLOD PUDOVKIN

TACTILITY

> Concentrate! Your attention is on your hands. Your hands are becom-
> ing tense. You are concentrating your will, your great desire to succeed,
> on your hands. . . . Look at your fingers. They're becoming tense. . . .
> I'll remove the tension now and you will speak clearly and effortlessly.
> You will speak loudly and clearly all your life. One. Two. Three!

Thus begins Andrey Tarkovsky's *Mirror* (1975). This brief preamble, in
which a hypnotherapist attempts to cure a young man's stutter, immediately announces its concern with vision and touch and its insistence on the
meaningful, material link between mind and body. The therapist touches
the boy repeatedly, pushing, pulling, and palpating his temples, shoulders,
back, face, and hands. By drawing the tension from his mind into his hands,
she says, she can remove that physical tension and, with it, the mental tension that stifles his speech. The premise of this therapy session is that any
stark division between mind and body is a false one, and that there is
instead a fluid connection between the two.

Although her focus is resolutely on the hands (his and hers), the tension
moves throughout the boy's entire body. He stumbles and is drawn toward
the therapist or pushed away, and the muscles of his face tighten as she holds
him in this hypnotic trance. The hands, then, are only the beginning, the
contact point, of a mutual engagement of body and mind that extends deep
into the body, involving the muscles and tendons as surely as the fingers.

Throughout Tarkovsky's film, emotion is inextricably bound up with
motion and materiality. Love, desire, loss, nostalgia, and joy are perceived and
expressed in fundamentally tactile ways, not only by characters but also, even
more profoundly, by film and viewer. These embodied, emotional experiences

1

may begin in and on the surface of the body, but they come to involve the entire body and to register as movement, comportment, tension, internal rhythms, and a full-bodied engagement with the materiality of the world.

This book follows that deepening of touch from surface to depth, from haptic touch to total immersion. Its argument is that touch is not just skin-deep but is experienced at the body's surface, in its depths, and everywhere in between. The book begins at the surface and moves on through three regions—skin, musculature, viscera—to end with a kind of immersion and inspiration that traverses all three at once. I hope to show that touch is a "style of being" shared by both film and viewer, and that particular structures of human touch correspond to particular structures of the cinematic experience. In other words, the forms of tactility that filmgoers experience at the movies are shared—in complex, not always comfortable ways—by both spectator and film.

Exploring cinema's tactility thus opens up the possibility of cinema as an *intimate* experience and of our relationship with cinema as a *close* connection, rather than as a distant experience of observation, which the notion of cinema as a purely visual medium presumes. To say that we are touched by cinema indicates that it has significance for us, that it comes close to us, and that it literally occupies our sphere. We *share* things with it: texture, spatial orientation, comportment, rhythm, and vitality.

Touch need not be linked explicitly to a single organ such as the skin but is enacted and felt throughout the body, for "the body is borne towards tactile experience by all its surfaces and all its organs simultaneously, and carries with it a certain typical structure of the tactile 'world.'"[1] As a material mode of perception and expression, then, cinematic tactility occurs not only at the skin or the screen, but traverses all the organs of the spectator's body and the film's body. As J. J. Gibson wrote, "vision is kinaesthetic in that it registers movements of the body just as much as does the muscle-joint-skin system and the inner-ear system."[2] Tension, balance, energy, inertia, languor, velocity, rhythm—this book considers all of these to be "tactile," though none manifests itself solely, or even primarily, at the surface of the body.

In this book, "touch" comes to mean not simply contact, but rather a profound manner of being, a mode through which the body—human or cinematic—presents and expresses itself to the world and through which it perceives that same world as sensible. Maurice Merleau-Ponty's approach to the general meaningfulness of matter, summarized here by Glen Mazis, bears on my description of tactility as a "style" or mode of being in and at the world:

> A "manner of being" emerges as giving identity to a thing and the
> person(s) perceived in the "coition, so to speak, of our body with

things." This "manner of being" indicates what Merleau-Ponty calls "style." . . . It emerges as the thread running through all the properties of the thing and in my interaction with the thing. . . . The glasslike feel, brittleness, tinkling sound [of a drinking glass], and such have an accent, an atmosphere, that also encompasses the over-glass-sliding-movement-of-the-finger or the bent-shooting-out-finger-striking-tinkling-evoking-flick movement of the hand. Both perceived and perceiver are joined in that style of intercourse from which their identity emerges.[3]

Tactility is a mode of perception and expression wherein all parts of the body commit themselves to, or are drawn into, a relationship with the world that is at once a mutual and intimate relation of contact. The intimate and close contact between touching and touched, as well as the relationship of mutual, reciprocal significance that exists between them, are universal structures. Within those general structures, tactility contains the possibility for an infinite variety of particular themes or patterns: caressing, striking, startling, pummeling, grasping, embracing, pushing, pulling, palpation, immersion, and inspiration, for example, are all tactile behaviors.

Cinematic tactility, then, is a general attitude toward the cinema that the human body enacts in particular ways: haptically, at the tender surface of the body; kinaesthetically and muscularly, in the middle dimension of muscles, tendons, and bones that reach toward and through cinematic space; and viscerally, in the murky recesses of the body, where heart, lungs, pulsing fluids, and firing synapses receive, respond to, and reenact the rhythms of cinema. The film's body also adopts toward the world a tactile attitude of intimacy and reciprocity that is played out across its nonhuman body: haptically, at the screen's surface, with the caress of shimmering nitrate and the scratch of dust and fiber on celluloid; kinaesthetically, through the contours of on- and off-screen space and of the bodies, both human and mechanical, that inhabit or escape those spaces; and viscerally, with the film's rush through a projector's gate and the "breathing" of lenses. The following three chapters seek out the resonance and reverberation of tactile patterns between the human body and the cinema at these corporeal locales.

In recent years, there has been a new appreciation for the sensual dimension of the cinematic experience, as many media scholars have turned their attention toward embodied spectatorship, examining the historical and theoretical implications of the viewer's (and in some cases, the cinema's) particular forms of embodiment. My own study builds on this trend in media studies toward what Paul Stoller calls "sensuous scholarship."[4] It also draws considerably on the work of Vivian Sobchack, whose *The Address of the Eye* set out a framework for a distinctly existential phenomenological approach to the cinema, one that grounds its description of the reversible and reciprocal correlation between film and viewer in the notion that consciousness is materially embodied.[5] Sobchack reminds us that

> as film theorists, we are not exempt from sensual being at the movies—nor, let's admit it, would we wish to be. As "lived bodies" (to use a phenomenological term that insists on "the" objective body as always also lived subjectively as "my" body, diacritically invested and active in making sense and meaning in and of the world), our vision is always already "fleshed out"—and even at the movies it is "in-formed" and given meaning by our other sensory means of access to the world: our capacity not only to hear, but also to touch, to smell, to taste, and always to proprioceptively feel our dimension and movement in the world. In sum, the film experience is meaningful *not to the side of our bodies but because of our bodies.*[6]

In this book, I seek to elicit and examine the specifically tactile structures of embodied cinematic perception and expression that are taken up by on-screen bodies (human or otherwise), filmgoers, and films themselves. Close analysis of sound and image will reveal certain patterns of texture, space, and rhythm enacted by films and viewers. Attention to these embodied structures and patterns allows for a sensually formed (and informed) understanding of the ways that meaning and significance emerge in and are articulated through the fleshy, muscular, and visceral engagement that occurs between films' and viewer's bodies.

THE FILM'S BODY

Mirror's opening scene, with the stuttering boy and therapist, is at once intellectually, emotionally, and physically discomforting. This is in part because it is unclear exactly how the episode "fits" into the film as a whole. It begins abruptly, before the credits have started, and provides no narrative context or character identification; indeed, over the course of the film, we never return to either of these characters. However, more pressing, quite literally, is the question of how we viewers "fit" into the scene: we are drawn too close *not* to be involved somehow in the intensely charged encounter between the therapist and the boy, but the terms of our involvement are ambiguous, even contradictory. The scene's unsettling and unpredictable use of camera movement and framing establishes an intimate, tactile, and complex contact between three types of bodies—the characters', the viewer's, and the film's—that continues throughout the entire film.

The scene begins in color, as a young boy in a well-appointed apartment switches on a black-and-white television set. As he steps back to watch the

1. *Mirror* (Andrey Tarkovsky, U.S.S.R., 1975)

screen, the camera tracks with him, closing in on the back of his head. The movement leads us to expect that we might soon share his point of view, but the film cuts abruptly to a much closer framing of the scene; this shot eliminates the television set and screen altogether. We have no time to prepare for that cut, nor do we find a safe landing spot once we are plunged into the scene. The first shot we get of the scene is a close-up of a woman (the therapist) that is both too close and too quick for us to get our bearings: the camera barely glances over her face before panning swiftly in the direction of her gaze, moving rightward across a blank wall to land on a similarly tight close-up of an adolescent boy.

Facing the camera, the boy answers a series of questions asked by the therapist, who remains off screen for the time being. After this brief interview, the therapist announces, "We'll begin now." The boy turns right to face her, his movement setting into motion the camera's own slow pan to the left. The camera pans away from his body, across the expanse of gray wall behind them, and comes to rest on the woman, who urges the boy to "look right into my eyes." She touches her fingertip to the bridge of her nose, then positions it a hand's width from her face. As she begins to move it slowly, almost imperceptibly, toward her face (and to our left), the camera pans slowly in the opposite direction. Only when the panning camera meets up with the boy do we discover that he is also moving, or being moved: he tilts forward in the opposite direction, very slowly, drawn toward her just as the camera is drawn away. She seems to exert a kinetic force on both the boy's body and the camera, albeit in opposite directions.

Something in this set of movements is physically and perceptually disorienting. At the moment that camera and boy cross paths, it is difficult to tell the difference between his movement to the left and the camera's movement to the right. This is not unlike the experience of being seated on an eastbound train, looking out the window at a westbound train and, when one train lurches into motion, being unable to tell who is actually moving, "us" or "them."

Moments later, the therapist stands and turns the boy away from her, placing her hand on the back of his head. "Concentrate on my hand," she says. "My hand is pulling you back." At this point, the boy is not yet moving: the therapist is merely setting up the scenario, indicating what he *will* do. But the camera (and with it, the viewer) is already doing it: the camera zooms out slowly to a long shot of both figures, as she speaks and the boy stands still. Occasionally, too, the camera will move in ways not clearly motivated by the therapist's instructions, zooming slowly in and out seemingly driven by its own intention and attention, without instruction from her. The camera's behavior throughout this scene, and the odd relationship between it and our viewing bodies, again begs the question, "who's moving?" or even "who's being moved?"

The unsettling nature of the scene derives from the fact that our experience of it is intimate, tactile, and kinetic in multiple directions at once. Tarkovsky's framing and camera movements place us too close to the characters for us not to be intimately involved in the scene, and yet it refuses us an "anchor" and a single direction that our intention and attention might take. Extreme close-ups of the boy and the therapist draw us toward them, but we're at the same time moved by the camera along its own path of attention, which is quite often away from the characters. We are immersed and involved in the space and time of the events of the film, but without a single body with whom to align ourselves unequivocally—be it a character in the scene or a neutral camera—we are moved, both emotionally and physically, in two directions at once. We are rendered conceptually and physically *ambi-valent*, drawn in two opposing directions at once.

If the scene makes us uneasy, then, it is because it refuses any easy identification, either physical or emotional, between viewers and characters. It does this by drawing attention to another body in the equation, which exists in every cinematic experience but is rarely so visible and explicitly announced: here, the film's body is a palpable, if elusive, presence to be reckoned with. As the scene unfolds through a series of slow, seemingly unmotivated but intensely felt camera movements and cuts, the film's body makes its presence known. As the therapist speaks of tension, kinetic forces, bodily movements, and flowing speech, the film's body itself enacts these, leaving us to wonder whether she is addressing the boy or the film itself.

Earlier I had called this opening scene "discomforting," but "discomfiting" may be more apt: with its root in the Latin *conficere*, "put together," that term more accurately describes the way we and the characters are simultaneously aligned with one another and pulled apart. The easy separation we might ordinarily assume between human and cinematic bodies is impossible here. Seated in the theater but invested bodily in the actions on (and *of*) the screen, we must ask, "where are we in this picture?" The film complicates the notion of character identification and "objective" observation by calling into question, without entirely collapsing, the boundaries between "here" and "there," and between "us" (the viewers), "them" (the characters), and "it" (the film).

This sensual and structural ambivalence provoked Gilles Deleuze to call the film a "turning crystal."[7] As he writes, "the crystal-image, or crystalline description, has two definite sides which are not to be confused. For the confusion of the real and the imaginary is a simple error of fact, and does not affect their discernibility: the confusion is produced solely 'in someone's head.' But indiscernibility constitutes an objective illusion; it does not suppress the distinction between the two sides, but makes it unattributable, each side taking the other's role in a relation which we must describe as reciprocal presupposition, or reversibility."[8]

I will draw again upon *Mirror*, in this chapter and in the conclusion, using it in precisely this way, as a "turning crystal" that allows me to reflect upon and think through the reversibility at play between films and viewers and between various dimensions of the body, both cinematic and human.

David MacDougall neatly outlines a range of ways in which films have been said to "be" or "be like" bodies, symbolically speaking, then asks, "to whose body do they correspond? Is it the body of the subject? Is it the body of the spectator or the filmmaker? Or is it an 'open' body capable of receiving all of these?"[9] My usage of the term throughout this project will be neither symbolic nor completely "open," neither a Vertovian *kino-eye* nor a Deleuzian body without organs, for example. For me, the "film's body" is a concrete but distinctly cinematic lived-body, neither equated to nor encompassing the viewer's or filmmaker's body, but engaged with both of these even as it takes up its own intentional projects in the world.

In *The Address of the Eye*, Sobchack mobilizes Merleau-Ponty's philosophy of perception to demonstrate that a film does indeed live an embodied existence in the world, and that, like the other whom we recognize through the gaze and through our mutual inhabitation of a certain mode of material being, the film's body shares with us certain modes of visual perception.[10] She argues that both film and viewer are simultaneously and mutually engaged in the intentional acts of perception and expression, although the means by which they *enact* these will of course be different. "Watching a film," she writes, "we can see the seeing as well as the seen, hear the hearing as well as the heard, and feel the movement as well as see the moved."[11]

She explains that a film is at the same time a *subject of* experience and an *object for* experience, an active participant of both perception and expression. As Sobchack puts it in her own reading of Merleau-Ponty, to perceive expression is to experience the world's significance, and to express perception is to signify. To exist in a lived-body is always to do both, and so the film is, essentially, perception and expression in motion. There need not be reflection about these correlated acts; indeed, reflection is an after-the-fact distancing from the whole of this dynamic behavior. In experience, perception and expression are in a dynamic relation of reversibility (i.e., expression is the visible gesture of perception), so that a lived-body is always in the act of perceiving expression *and* expressing perception.[12] That perpetual behavior constitutes the lived-body's active and mobile existence in the world among others. Gabrielle Hezekiah summarizes the unique role of the film's body this way: "It is presented to us as a technologically mediated consciousness of experience and to itself as an immediate experience of consciousness."[13]

As a lived-body in and for the world, then, "the cinema uses *modes of embodied existence* (seeing, hearing, physical and reflective movement) as the vehicle, the 'stuff,' the substance of its language."[14] Thus, both film and viewer might engage in the act of looking closely, exhibiting doubt, or becoming enthralled, dizzy, or agitated, but each would enact those behaviors in a different way, because the "technologies" that enable those behaviors (e.g., the camera and the cornea, the zoom lens and the inner ear) are different, biological in the case of the viewer and mechanical in the case of the film. Viewer and film share certain ways of being in, seeing, and grasping the world, despite their vast differences as human and machine, one blood and tissue, the other light and celluloid.

Perhaps the most striking evidence of the film's body in Tarkovsky's opening scene is the shadow of the boom microphone, visible on the upper-left corner of the wall behind the stuttering boy in the latter half of the scene. That shadow is a visible sign of the film's body performing its own attention and attitude as actively as actors and viewers do theirs. As the therapist tells the boy to concentrate on his hands and speaks of the tension he carries in his fingers, the microphone's shadow quivers slightly: the film's body, in this moment, *perceives* (by listening and attending to) the characters' tense concentration and *expresses* tense concentration in its own embodied movements, in a visible quiver. As the boom microphone "stands at attention," the film's body both perceives and expresses tension and attention in tactile, muscular, and distinctly cinematic terms.

Sobchack is careful to point out that the film's body is not identical to the human body, filmmaker's or viewer's, and that it is not an anthropomorphic concept. Instead, her description of the film's body is built upon Merleau-Ponty's notion of a primordial subjectivity that acts in embodied, material, and irreducible relation with the world. The film's body that Sobchack posits is a lived-body (but not a human one) capable of the perception of expression and the expression of perception: the film certainly perceives, experiences, is immersed in, and has a vantage point on the world, and without a doubt the film signifies, or otherwise there would be nothing at all for us to see, hear, feel, or interpret.

It is important to differentiate between the "film's body" and the body of the boom operator or the cameraperson, for example. Although those individuals are certainly responsible for the quivering shadow and the unpredictable zooms, the quiver and the zooms taken together are behaviors of the film's own lived body, which is unified in time and space and which performs its own perception (of the world) and expression (to the world) in embodied ways that are muscular, tactile, and distinctly cinematic.

The film is more than a representation of the filmmaker's vision—or the boom operator's or cameraperson's—because what we see when we "see a film" is not merely a record and product of what the filmmaker saw at a given moment in a given space: that would be a photograph. Nor is it identical to the human filmmaker's own bodily forms of vision, because a filmmaker doesn't see the world in close-up in quite the same way that the film does, for example.[15] What we do see is *the film seeing:* we see its own (if humanly enabled) process of perception and expression unfolding in space and time.[16]

In that same way, the film is also always more than a representation constituted by the spectator. Our experience of the film is not the film's experience of itself. The camera perceives and expresses through dolly tracks, tripod, wide-angle lens, and so forth; viewers do so by means of posture, muscle tension, visual concentration, facial expressions, and human gestures. As the film pulls us toward and away from the scene of therapist and stuttering boy through tracking and zooming, for example, the viewer may move with or against the film's movements by squinting at the screen to counteract the shift in focal point, or leaning forward to resist the pull away from the increasingly distant figures. The point, though, is that all these bodies—characters', actors', viewers', and film's—are entities whose attitudes and intentions are expressed by embodied behavior.

Neither can the film be equated with or reduced to its physical body, any more than the viewer can. The technological body (or enabling mechanism) of the film is no more a *visible* mediator in the experience of a film than are the producers, directors, and camera operators who initiate it. The film's body is the mechanism through which its intentional projects in the world take shape. That enabling body is generally transparent: we see the perception and expression that it makes possible, but not the body itself. The film's subjectivity can be, and often is, foregrounded by particular films or filmmakers, but the fact of a film's subjectivity does not depend upon the film's being self-consciously aware of it or remarking upon it, although that possibility certainly exists.[17]

I'd like to point out a provocative difference between the microphone's shadow and unpredictable zooms in Tarkovsky's film and, for example, the sudden appearance of film catching fire in a projector's gate in *Persona* (Ingmar Bergman, 1966), or *Fight Club*'s momentary glimpse of sprocket holes and projectionist's cues (David Fincher, 1999). In those cases, the films self-consciously shift our attention (and their own) directly toward one aspect of their mechanical bodies that enables their perception and expression: the celluloid. In contrast, *Mirror*'s quivering shadow of the boom and its wandering zooms are *indirect* signs of the microphone and the camera lens, which partly constitute the film's body. The zoom is not the camera; it is the film's embodied expression of an attitude (perhaps discomfort or distraction) that is enabled by the camera. The quivering shadow is not the boom itself, but a visible enactment of the film's tension and attention that is made possible by the boom and visible by the camera, optical printer, and projector. Even in these moments of reflexivity, the film refuses to let us see its mirror image: we get only a shadow, a movement caught in the corner of our eye.

The film's body is a ghostly entity in Tarkovsky's film, more explicitly announced than in most narrative cinema but more elusive than in other blatantly reflexive films. Perhaps it would be better to say, though, that it behaves in ghostly ways, eluding our direct gaze, slipping through our fingers, skirting past us as we approach it. Just as characters slip from the edges of frames, as the past slips into the present, and as memory slips into dream, the film's body slips from our grasp. In this way, a scene that seems to have no direct narrative relevance to the film turns out to foreshadow the precise embodied, tactile patterns by which the film will evoke and express its poignant theme of lost time, lost places, and lost love forever out of reach.

Phenomenological description seeks to identify the underlying structures of the phenomenon at hand by studying its intimate entailment with the intentional act of perception to which the phenomenon is present. When we approach a film experience this way, it is helpful to recall Mikel Dufrenne's point, that "aesthetic objects . . . call for a certain attitude and use on the part of the body—witness again the cathedral that regulates the step and gait, the painting that guides the eye, that poem that disciplines the voice."[18] In these examples, the artwork's ways of being in the world resonate meaningfully with its beholder's ways of moving, looking, listening, and speaking.

I've suggested that, in a way that is thematically relevant, *Mirror* draws us toward but also pulls us away from on-screen characters, places, and events, leaving us always off balance, neither "here" nor "there." By shifting the focus to the embodied behaviors of the film itself—its ambivalent tracking and zooming, its tense quivering, its aimless wandering—I hope it becomes clear that this compelling, complex structure describes not only our relationship to characters and events but also, more profoundly, our embodied relationship to the viewing/viewed body of the film itself.

In his book *Sculpting in Time*, Tarkovsky recalls viewer responses to *Mirror*, which ranged from hostile bafflement to awed reverence. He quotes a letter written by a young woman attempting to explain just how and why the film affects her so profoundly. "There's another kind of language," she writes,

> another form of communication: by means of feelings, and images. That is the contact that stops people being separated from each other, that brings down barriers. Will, feeling, emotion—these remove obstacles from between people who otherwise stand on opposite sides of a mirror, on opposite sides of a door. . . . The frames of the screen move out, and the world which used to be partitioned off comes into us, becomes something real . . . And this doesn't happen through little Andrey, it's Tarkovsky himself addressing the audience directly, as they sit on *the other side of* the screen.[19]

Of course, Tarkovsky does not address the audience directly, but *through* the film's body. Otherwise, though, the letter-writer's description of the intimate engagement between viewers and images is quite apt. She speaks of communication "by means of feelings and images" as a contact that occurs between images and viewers. Chapter 1 will investigate the skin-to-skin contact between viewers and moving images and seek to understand exactly how it "brings down barriers." Her description of how "the frames of the screen move out, and the world which used to be partitioned off comes into us" suggests that the encounter has something to do with body contours and "frames" (both human and cinematic), something I discuss at length in chapter 2.

For now, I'd like to consider the letter-writer's notion that the film somehow addresses viewers "directly, as they sit *on the other side of* the screen." Her description astutely points to the way that cinematic perception is both direct and distant at the same time. For existential phenomenology, perception always involves the coexistence of distance and proximity. As Hezekiah writes, "For Merleau-Ponty, vision is enabled by a certain *distance* between the seer and the thing. This distance constitutes the medium of access to vision."[20]

Even when the distance and difference between film's body and viewer's body registers less strongly than in the experience of *Mirror*, the film's body is not easily or completely aligned with the viewer's body, despite the fact that the two take up similar structures of perception and expression. The relationship involves a mimetic relationship that is immediate, tangible, and yet tenuous; the possibility of tension, slippage, and resistance inheres.

Tarkovsky's admiring fan alternately describes the meeting place of film and viewer as a mirror, a screen, and a door. No one metaphor sticks, perhaps for two reasons. First, the "stuff" of the contact between film and viewer is too permeable and flexible to be described in quite these rigid terms. Second, what keeps us separate from the film isn't a "thing" at all, but our bodies' own surfaces and contours. Merleau-Ponty's "flesh" may be a better metaphor: the material contact between viewer and viewed is less a hard edge or a solid barrier placed between us—a mirror, a door— than a liminal space in which film and viewer can emerge as co-constituted, individualized but related, embodied entities.[21]

Watching a film, we are certainly not *in* the film, but we are not entirely *outside* it, either. We exist and move and feel in that space of contact where our surfaces mingle and our musculatures entangle. Jennifer Deger refers to this contact of image, imaged, and viewer as the "transformative space of betweenness."[22] This sense of fleshy, muscular, visceral contact seriously undermines the rigidity of the opposition between viewer and film, inviting us to think of them as intimately related but not identical, caught up in a relationship of intersubjectivity and co-constitution, rather than as subject and object positioned on opposite sides of the screen. Thus the cinematic experience involves what Anne Rutherford describes as a "movement or displacement of the self" that

> is not conceived as a physical movement across a physical space: no empirical measurement can discern it, nor can an optical model define it. This is a movement interior to both the gritty materiality of the body's location in space, and simultaneously to the carnality of an idea or experience. It is a movement of the entire embodied being towards a corporeal appropriation of or immersion in a space, an experience, a moment. It is a movement away from the self, yes, but away from the self conceived as the subject, in so far as this concept is a cognitive or disembodied one—a movement out of the constraints of the definable, knowable—a groping towards a connection, a link-up with the carnality of the idea, the affect of the body, the sensible resonances of experience.[23]

MOVING PICTURES

Our first glimpse of the field that surrounds the childhood home of Tarkovsky's narrator, to which he and the film will retreat in dreams and recollections, begins with a long shot of a fence that stretches horizontally across the frame. Seated serenely on the fence with her back to the camera is a woman, soon to be identified as the mother of the narrator, smoking a cigarette as she looks off into the distance across a green field. A man approaches in the distance. The camera tracks toward the fence and the woman, its slow, steady approach echoing her leisurely movements. Just as she lowers her cigarette, the forward-tracking camera performs a barely perceptible reverse zoom. Both movements, forward and reverse, continue for a brief few seconds, as the camera passes the woman and she disappears from the edge of the frame. Precisely at the same instant, the man in the field passes behind a distant tree, and we are momentarily set adrift, left for a brief instant without any*body* whose solid presence might allow us to get our bearings. Finally, the camera comes to a stop, and all we can do is wait for the still-distant visitor to arrive. The slowness of the forward tracking motion and the slightness of the reverse zoom yield an effect that, though subtle, is dizzying.

Whereas the camera approaches the field in that first shot, it retreats from the field in the film's final shot, in which an old woman fetches the children home from the field. As they walk amidst the tall grasses, the camera takes up a position in the adjacent forest. The human figures move in and out of our vision as they pass behind trees, as the male figure had done in the opening shot. As the woman and children walk toward the left of the screen, the camera tracks leftward alongside them, and backward, away from them, at the same time, pulling us further into the forest. Suddenly, and without provocation or narrative motivation, there's a brief but dramatic forward zoom. The trees seem to expand in front of us, bringing us perceptually closer even as we move physically further away from the human figures. Stranger still is the backward zoom that follows almost immediately on the heels of the forward zoom, this one much slower than the first. The camera continues to track gracefully backward throughout both these shifts in focal length. The effect is not only dizzying, but also poignant. It is as if the film's body acts on behalf of the (now silent) narrator, reaching forward even as it is pulled back, in a brief and unsuccessful attempt to grasp the human figures as they pass into the distance.

Describing the actress Margarita Terekhova's simultaneous "capacity at once to enchant and repel" in her dual roles as the narrator's mother and wife, Tarkovsky wrote, "It is not possible to catch the moment at which the positive goes over into its opposite, or when the negative starts moving towards the positive. Infinity is germane, inherent in the very structure of the image."[24] He may as well be describing these strangely compelling gestures of the camera: they move very slowly in opposite directions and, for a few moments, dwell in a space in between, in the utter absence of a human frame of reference. Like the actress's performance, these images are impossible to dismember, because each one is all things at once.

The in-betweenness elicited by that shift in camera distance and focal length allows a fleeting glimpse at a something beneath, beyond, and within any one figure—field, fence, man, woman, child, camera, spectator—caught up in it. It may be a "presencing" of Being in a Heideggerian sense, or an instance of Deleuzian "becoming," or an evocation of what Merleau-Ponty calls the "intertwining." It is ontologically provocative and at the same time thematically relevant; indeed, it suggests that those two things are inseparable. By drawing us at once toward and away from the field and the figures passing through it, the dolly-zooms make "past" and "home"—the hallmarks of Tarkovsky's film—familiar and strange, elusive and palpably present at the same time. These two extraordinarily delicate gestures of the camera express through embodied motion the film's own ambivalent, emotional, and existential relationship to passing time, as well as to things and bodies in the world, including its viewer and itself. Indeed, the same pattern marks the film as a whole: it experiences and expresses emotion through motion, drawing us temporally, spatially, viscerally, and emotion-ally back and forth, toward and away, so that we exist in a state of tension between here and there, now and then, presence and absence, body and spirit, memory and dream, childhood and adulthood. These brief scenes are but one example of the way meaning and affect emerge in the fleshy, visceral encounter between films and viewers.

In *The Cultural Politics of Emotion*, Sara Ahmed emphasizes the way "emotions shape the very surface of bodies, which take shape through the repetition of actions over time, as well as through orientations towards and away from others."[25] Thus, love is lived as specific inflections of a general "towardness," hate as an "againstness," fear as an "aboutness," disgust as recoil away from something or someone. The figures of the loved, the hated, the feared, and the disgusting do not in themselves possess qualities that make them the objects of these emotions; instead, they are shaped in and by these very movements toward, against, about, and away from them.

In her discussion of the discourse of multiculturalism, for example, Ahmed describes a humanist fantasy of universal love that is articulated as a hope for a distinct pattern and direction of movement: *"If only we got closer we would be as one."* "Getting closer" is desired as a mutual move-ment of one toward the other, such that "at one level, love comes into being as a form of reciprocity; the lover wants to be loved back, wants their love returned." I share Ahmed's interest in "affective economies, where feelings do not reside in subjects or objects, but are produced as effects of circula-tion,"[26] and throughout this book I consider meaning and emotion not as residing in films or viewers, but as emerging in the intimate, tactile encounter between them. That encounter is a conduit of sorts, manifested as specific gestures and styles of behavior (film's and viewer's). I'll consider the active, embodied encounter between film and viewer as a means of grasping the emotional, intellectual, and thematic aspects of any given cin-ematic experience.

So, for example, just as the film's narrator attempts to negotiate the dis-tance created by the passing of time, the film itself also repeatedly expresses, enacts, and elicits that simultaneous longing for an intimate, mutual towardness and return in its own gesture of reaching out toward something—a there, a then—even as it pulls itself away. The perplexing, incongruous but simultaneous movements of the film toward and away from its object are one of many iterations of a gesture akin to a child's game of *fort-da*, which Sigmund Freud described as a means of coping with loss by reassuring oneself that what is lost (the mother or mother-substi-tute) can be brought back.[27] In its immediate gestures (tracking motions that oppose zooms, for example) as well as in its larger narrative shift between a remembered past and the lived present, *the film* pushes away the past, brings it forward, and sends it away again. These ambivalent trajectories may be the film's own performance of love as a desire for a "getting closer" that is impossible; in this way, the film enacts anxieties and desires associated with time's passing.

Mirror thus moves and touches us emotionally precisely because it does so physically. Even before we can invest ourselves in the story of a man haunted by memories of his childhood home, peacetime, and a mother's love, we are *pulled* into a style of engagement with the film that palpably, viscerally produces those feelings—love, loss, desire, regret—as a simultaneous tug in opposite directions. Ultimately we feel and understand love and loss more profoundly by being immersed *in* and inspired by them than merely by thinking *about* them. The final chapter will discuss this inspiration in the double sense—being inspired creatively or emotionally as well as being in-spired, breathed in—as a way of thinking about film's and viewer's mutual embeddedness in something larger, something that moves beyond, beneath, and through both of them.

By emphasizing not bodies themselves but the contact between them, Ahmed understands emotions as emerging in and through that encounter.[28] They are not preexisting emotions brought into *contact*; rather, they are brought into *being* and given shape by the contact itself. It is through forms of movement, alignment, approach and retreat, for example, that the character of "loved," "feared," and "hated" objects is produced. Love isn't something a lover "has" for a loved one, but something that emerges in the encounter between lover and loved, just as "fear" isn't "in" someone fearful, but emerges in the contact between two entities, in which they take up a certain temporal and physical orientation toward one another. One cannot even say, as Ahmed shows, that this contact is between a "fearful" person and a "fearsome" object, because the object of love, hate, fear, and other emotions does not preexist the encounter as "loveable," "hateful," or "fearsome," nor even as an "object" separate from the "subject" who feels love, hatred, or fear toward the other. Instead, "emotions create the very effect of the surfaces and boundaries that allow us to distinguish an inside and an outside in the first place. So emotions are not simply something 'I' or 'we' have. Rather, it is through emotions, or how we respond to objects and others, that surfaces and boundaries are made: the 'I' and the 'we' are shaped by, and even take the shape of, contact with others."[29]

Ahmed's approach incorporates a phenomenological emphasis on intentionality, which is the dynamic and directional organization of consciousness such that it always irreducibly refers to and is correlated with something. Consciousness is always consciousness *of* something, and phenomenology insists that to describe any phenomenon it is necessary to describe *both* the objective and subjective aspects of this intentional structure; that is, we must attend not only to the object itself, but also to the conscious act through which we perceive it. Rather than examining just the structure of the object, or just the subjective act of our own looking or touching, we examine both together, with the understanding that they cannot exist separately. In this way, existential phenomenology recognizes "the role of subjective experience in co-constituting objects in the world."[30]

Existential phenomenology shifted the focus from Edmund Husserl's "lived-world" and the structures of consciousness toward embodied experience. Merleau-Ponty, in particular, emphasized the notion of the lived body and its reciprocal, intimate relationship with the world: "Our own body is in the world as the heart is in the organism: it keeps the visible spectacle constantly alive, it breathes life into it and sustains it inwardly, and with it forms a system."[31] He held that it is the body that mediates between the interior world of consciousness and the exterior world of objects. The body is always at once a subject engaged in conscious projects of the mind and an object in the material world. Merleau-Ponty centered his philosophy around the body as the means by which we are inserted into the world and the means by which we relate to it and make sense of it. This is not to say that the lived body *constitutes* the world around it, or that it is acted upon by a world that is always already determined. Rather, the body is "meaning-giving" and "sense-bestowing"; that is, it makes possible my relations with the world.[32] It is the context (historical and cultural, as well as material) within which I inhabit, interpret, and interact with a world that exists before "I" come into it, but to which my own and others' presence gives meaning.

In *Phenomenology of Perception*, Merleau-Ponty maintained that all perception is embodied perception, so that vision does not and cannot occur apart from the body that enables it, but is necessarily informed by the fleshy, corporeal, and historically specific structures of the way we live in and through our bodies and in and through the world. The reciprocal relationship between viewer and viewed is a hallmark of his philosophy: "Like Heidegger, Merleau-Ponty suggests that objects of vision are co-constituted by subject and object. . . . But for Merleau-Ponty, the object responds."[33] Existential phenomenology and its method thus not only invite us to attend to the material, lived world in order to better understand the lived structures of the emotional, the social, and the historical, but also give us a means of embodied analysis that respects the co-constitutive, reciprocal relationship between the perceiver and the perceived.

Merleau-Ponty's description of perception insists on its pre-personal nature. Though it is the means by which I express my subjectivity, the phenomenal body precedes my knowledge of myself *as* a subject. In his view, "perception is not something I do or something that happens to me—because the I is the product of reflection and perception is older, more primordial than reflection."[34] Perception takes place in the world of phenomena; we are immersed in it as we are immersed in materiality. It does not require a will and desire on our part as subjects to put it into play.

In seeking to describe the reciprocal relationship between subjects and objects in the world, Merleau-Ponty wrote extensively on the relationship between artist or viewer and the work of art. Perhaps his most famous example is the painter whose "gestures, the paths which he alone can trace and which will be revelations to others . . . seem to emanate from the things themselves. . . . Inevitably the roles between him and the visible are reversed," so that the painter feels himself to be seen by the trees he paints.[35] Philosopher Mikel Dufrenne applies these ideas of reversibility and intertwining to the interaction between perceiver and artwork, as well, where he also places the emphasis on prereflective experience. He writes that "objects do not exist primarily for my thought but for my body," and argues for the notion of a "corporeal intellection" that enables the perceiver to make sense of the work of art. "What I experience as expressed by the aesthetic object possesses a meaning and can be identified," he argues, "because of the echo it awakens within me—which . . . is not the work of an act of reflection."[36] Moreover, Dufrenne insists that artwork and spectator not be considered as isolated entities, but as mutually invested in one another, so that to understand the work of art, it is necessary to study the aesthetic experience constituted by the intimate relationship between its subject and object.

In his only essay on cinema, Merleau-Ponty wrote, "for the movies as for modern psychology dizziness, pleasure, grief, love and hate are ways of behaving."[37] These feelings and sensations are not perceived, expressed, and made meaningful first through mindful reflection, but through the viewer's and film's embodied enactment of them. A phenomenological approach to the cinematic experience, then, focuses neither solely on the formal or narrative features of the film itself, nor solely on the spectator's psychic identification with characters or cognitive interpretation of the film. Instead, phenomenological film analysis approaches the film and the viewer as acting together, correlationally, along an axis that would itself constitute the object of study.

In *Phenomenology of Perception,* Merleau-Ponty articulated the notion of reversibility in distinctly tactile terms by using the image of a person's one hand touching the other. When I touch one hand with the other, he explained, each hand plays the role of both the touching and the touched, but my experience of touching and being touched is not quite simultaneous.[38] *Either* I feel one hand touching the other as an object, *or* I feel subjectively one hand being touched by the other, but I can't feel both at once. The two hands are never identical, nor is my experience of them confused. Instead, they each vacillate between the role of touching and touched, just as the self and other alternate between the role of seer and seen. This structure of reversibility does not collapse the distinction between the two hands or between self and other, nor is it simultaneous. It involves a shifting of attention and intentionality from one aspect of the encounter to another.

"I am always on the same side of my body," Merleau-Ponty wrote, even as I recognize that there is an other perceiving me from another perspective with the same organs of vision that I have, or that one hand is touching the other in the same manner but from a different place.[39] The relationship is one of difference within identity; there is always slippage that prevents the two entities from eliding or collapsing their material boundaries altogether, even as both touching and touched, seer and seen, take up the same modes of being and each are immersed in the same constant flux of materiality. For Merleau-Ponty this double sensation provoked by one hand touching the other is the archetype for the subject/object relations in the world: irreducible one to the other, but embedded in a constantly mutual experience, constituted of the same "stuff."

This book holds that the film and viewer are in such a relationship of reversibility and that we inhabit and enact embodied structures—tactile structures—that are not the same, but intimately related and reversible. We do not "lose ourselves" in the film, so much as we exist—emerge, really—in the contact between our body and the film's body. It is not a matter simply of identifying with the characters on screen, or with the body of the director or camera operator, for example. Rather, we are in a relationship of intimate, tactile, reversible contact with the film's body—a complex relationship that is marked as often by tension as by alignment, by repulsion as often as by attraction. We are embedded in a constantly mutual experience with the film, so that the cinematic experience is the experience of being both "in" our bodies and "in" the liminal space created by that contact.

In his unfinished final work, *The Visible and the Invisible,* Merleau-Ponty offered the terms "intertwining," "chiasm," and "flesh" to refer to the primordial materiality in which we and all phenomenal objects are immersed in that relation of reversibility. "Flesh" is a precondition of difference, value, and subjectivity. Though "flesh" is not literally human flesh, Merleau-Ponty's choice of this term indicates the crucial role of materiality and touch in the overall concept of reversibility and pre-personal intersubjectivity toward which he had been moving from his earliest projects.[40]

In the chiasm, subjects and objects mingle but never lose their identity. M. C. Dillon sums up the notion of a tactile reversibility within the chiasm:

> Merleau-Ponty claims that there is a continuity between my body and the things surrounding me in the world I inhabit. Indeed, I can touch worldly things precisely because I am myself a worldly thing. If I were an incorporeal being, I could not palpate the things around me or interrogate the world with my hands. My hand "takes its place among the things it touches, is in a sense one of them, opens finally upon a tangible thing of which it is a part." For me to touch the table, I must be touched by the table. Yet, there is also a difference: touching the table and being touched by it is not the same as touching my right hand with my left and feeling with my right hand the pressure of my left. Reversibility obtains in both cases, but I cannot experience the table touching me in the same way the hand touched can take up the role of touching. The plain fact of the matter is that the table is neither part of my body nor sentient in the way my body is. [41]

I take very seriously the tactile model with which Merleau-Ponty's career began and ended, and that model informs my description of the relation between the spectator's lived-body and that of the film. They are in a relation of reversibility and sensual connection that exists somewhere between that of hand-touching-table and right-hand-touching-left-hand. That relationship is nowhere more evident or deeply felt than in the experience of *Mirror's* unusual opening scene, which highlights the fully embodied reversibility between film and viewer and provides ample material for a clearer understanding of the film's body as an entity intimately engaged with the bodies of characters, filmmakers, and viewers.

TOUCH AND GO

In order to explore this tactile, reversible relationship, *The Tactile Eye* identifies and describes very specific styles or modes of tactility experienced by filmgoers and shared by films, however tenuously or problematically. Each of the three central chapters illustrates a few of these modes of tactile behavior as they occur within three locales of the spectator's body and the film itself: the skin, the musculature, and the viscera. (These terms are not used here metaphorically, but are stretched beyond their literal, biological meanings to encompass their more phenomenological significance.) These categories helpfully lead us through a complicated terrain, but their boundaries are pliable and permeable. Sensations and behaviors constantly bleed, vibrate, dissolve, cut, infect, meander, or muscle their way from one dimension into the next.

Chapter 1 ("The Skin") discusses caressing, flaying, pricking or piercing, shock, texture and temperature, some of which may involve what Laura Marks has termed the "haptic" qualities of cinematic perception: "Haptic looking tends to rest on the surface of its object rather than to plunge into depth, not to distinguish form so much as to discern texture."[42] Chapter 2 ("The Musculature") addresses things like gripping, grasping, holding, clenching, leaning forward in one's seat or pulling away, and being physically startled by the images. I'm interested here in what David MacDougall refers to as a "'prehensile' vision" called for by the cinema, which Michael Taussig describes as a kind of "sentient contact that is another mode of seeing, the gaze *grasping* where the touch falters."[43] Chapter 3 ("The Viscera") describes a tension between continuity and discontinuity in the internal rhythms of film's and viewer's bodies (heartbeat, breathing, and film's motion through the projector's gate, for example). Following Walter Benjamin's metaphor of the cinema and the surgeon's hand, Taussig eloquently describes the phenomenon that is the focus of this section: "the new form of vision, of tactile knowing, is like the surgeon's hand cutting into and entering the body of reality to palpate the palpitating masses enclosed therein. . . . It comes to share in those turbulent internal rhythms of surging intermittencies and peristaltic unwindings."[44]

Like Tarkovsky's film, Michel Gondry's *The Science of Sleep* (2006) insists on the union between mind and body, and between vision and touch, albeit in a more exuberantly, irreverently playful way. The film's hero is a frustrated artist with a penchant for quirky handmade objects and stop-motion animation. He falls in love with a woman who, though annoyed by his childish approach to romantic relationships, indulges his sense of child's play. Gael García Bernal's lovestruck Stéphane has one particularly provocative speech that encapsulates the question I seek to answer in this book: "I love her because she makes things, with her hands. It's as if her synapses were married directly to her fingers. Like this," he says, staring at his own waggling fingers in amazement, "in this way." This comment aptly describes his artistically inclined love interest, but it could as easily be applied to the stuttering boy in Tarkovsky's opening sequence, or even to the hypnotist who cures him.

More important, though, this line is perfectly suited as a description of the spectator, not just of these two films but also of moving pictures in general. I will argue that synapses and fingers *are* married—as are mind and body, and vision and touch more generally—in the experience of cinema. I also argue that to think, to speak, to feel, to love, to perceive the world and to express one's perception of that world are not solely cognitive or emotional acts taken up by viewers and films, but always already *embodied* ones that are enabled, inflected, and shaped by an intimate, tactile engagement with and orientation toward others (things, bodies, objects, subjects) in the world. If these things are married in the experience of cinema, my challenge is to describe exactly *how so*. This book winds its way through the skin, the musculature, and the viscera, hoping to show that vision is married to touch "like *this*, in *this* way."

1. Skin

If I find a film dull, I find it infinitely more entertaining to watch
the scratches.

NORMAN MCLAREN

Carolee Schneemann's hand-touched experimental film *Fuses* (1967) is a
political treatise on the pleasures of tactility that actually uses tactility to
make its political statement. The film revels in texture, celebrating "the ordi-
nariness of surroundings in an intense erotic, domestic tactility."[1] Images of
the filmmaker and her lover making love are interspersed with serenely beautiful shots of sunlight streaming through windows and a cat watching placidly
from a windowsill, for example. More than these representational images,
however, what's most affecting and inviting are the layers upon layers of tick-
lish textures, such as specks of dust, scratches, and paint applied to the surface
of the film. While its subjects are in the throes of orgasm, the film throws
itself orgiastically into a world of materiality. This film is, like the act of sex
itself, a delirious tumult of smooth, rough, soft, hard, cool, hot, and wet.

The experience of *Fuses* is erotic not simply because the bodies on screen
are behaving erotically, but because the film and viewer are erotically
engaged with each other. As Caroline Koebel has noted, "*Fuses* exists in
folds, concealing, revealing, and repeating itself."[2] The film obscures its
objects, not prudishly but playfully, using shadows and superimpositions,
among other things, to make vision difficult and thus to invite the viewer
to feel rather than see the film, to make contact with its skin. And we
respond accordingly, touching back, concealing and revealing ourselves to
the film and pressing ourselves against it. Our eyes skitter over the film,
enjoying the textures we can't identify but can only feel; or we squint and
try to hold the film in place, try to look past the fluttering specks of dust
and cat hair in order to get a clearer view. It is in the meeting of the film's
skin and the viewer's skin that this film becomes meaningful.

Fuses is most often discussed as a political act, a reclaiming of female pleasure in the face of a long history of images in which women have been depicted as objects of male desire rather than subjects of their own. Schneemann asserts female sexuality not only by directing herself in a film that celebrates the female orgasm, but also through a sensuously tactile filmic image. Laura Marks sees "the haptic as a visual strategy that can be used to describe alternative visual traditions, including women's and feminist practices, rather than a feminine quality in particular."[3] That's just what's happening in *Fuses*. Schneemann's images emphasize surface rather than depth, a caressing touch rather than a penetrating gaze. The array of textures—rough scratches, tickling fur and dust speckles, dappled light and color, smooth dissolves and fluttery, quick cutting—expresses the point of the film as eloquently as Schneemann's directorial role and choice of subject do: that female desire is amorphous, intense, playful, and many-layered. It is a clever kind of political activism, in that it invites us not only to consider from a distance the film's feminist celebration of female desire but also, and more important, to partake in it, to experience this desire for ourselves in the act of watching the film. The power of the film's feminist political statement is thus not merely rhetorical, but profoundly tactile.

"As a painter, paint is the power of extending whatever you see or feel, of intensifying it, or reshaping it," said Schneemann of the film. "So I wanted the bodies to be turning into tactile sensations of flickers. And . . . you get lost in the frame—to move the body in and out of its own frame, to move the eye in and out of the body so it could see everything it wanted to, but would also be in a state of dissolution, optically, resembling some aspect of the erotic sensation in the body which is not a literal translation. It is a painterly, tactile translation edited as a music of frames."[4]

Her reference to painting draws on Schneemann's own work in that medium and calls to mind critical essays by Merleau-Ponty, Richard Shiff, Steven Connor, and others on painters such as Paul Cézanne and Pierre Bonnard, in whose work tactility plays a crucial part.[5] Perhaps more to the point, however, it recalls art theorist James Elkins's claim that the significant (if not signifying) tactility of a painting need not be limited to the intentional and representational aspects of the picture, such as color, composition, and brushstroke, but also includes extra-textual, even accidental, qualities including scratches or stains on the surface of a painting or print. (One can imagine that stray cat hair might fall into this category, as it fell into Schneemann's film.) After all, he writes,

> What is a figure? A faint webbing of paper fibers and remnants of chalk; a morass of sticky oil. . . . To speak *only* of what must exist in

spite of the marks against which it struggles—only of the figure, or the represented thing—is to capitulate to a concept of pictures that imagines there is a gap between marks and signs and that believes the way to come to terms with it is to omit both the gap and everything that comes before it. To elide the crucial moments of darkness, when the picture, in all its incomprehensible, nonlinguistic opacity, confronts us as something *illegible,* is to hope that pictures can deliquesce into sense.[6]

This chapter attempts to address the importance of texture in textual film analysis by using examples from films that pluck familiar objects from their everyday surroundings and from the safety net of narrative, rendering them unfamiliar to the eyes and newly perceptible to the fingertips. If these films refuse at times to "deliquesce into sense," visually speaking, they make sense on the surface of the skin. The chapter proceeds by way of several "textural analyses"—not "readings" of films so much as "handlings"—in order to demonstrate the ways in which careful attention to the tactile surfaces and textures involved in the film experience might illuminate complexities and significance that might be overlooked by a focus on visual, aural, or narrative aspects. Even those films that seem dominated by narrative and cognitive concerns might possess secrets that we miss at first glance, secrets we may only discover when we begin to scratch the surface with a more tactile form of analysis. My approach considers texture as something we and the film engage in mutually, rather than something presented *by* the films *to* their passive and anonymous viewers; in other words, I try to avoid reducing films to "texts" and viewers to passive receivers of them.

For a great deal of film analysis, the gaze—of characters, the camera, and the viewer, as it is mobilized and exchanged and imbued with power—has been of prime concern. We've learned to ask questions about who is looking, at what or whom, and under what circumstances. But what about touch? What forms does touch take in the cinema, or in a particular sequence, film, or genre? How do characters or the camera or the viewer perform particular kinds of touch, and what kinds of relationships among them do particular styles of touch imply? In this chapter, I will supplant traditional film theory's focus on such things as point-of-view shots, exchanged glances, and relationships as they are defined by a web of gazes with a feel for touch and movement, temperatures and textures, and the ways that materiality permeates the film experience. Rather than dwell in and on films' *visual and visible* patterns of difference and repetition, I attempt to put my finger on the *tactile and tangible* patterns and structures of significance.

By getting one's hands dirty in the process of film analysis, one may come away with a better impression—in the physical as well as intellectual sense—of what and how these films mean. The kinds of touch that occur between film and viewer shape, inflect, even infuse the meanings of films and the nature of the relationship we have with them, for as Siegfried Kracauer wrote, cinema "communicates less as a whole with consciousness than in a fragmentary manner with the corporeal material layers."[7]

FILM'S SKIN

For Antonin Artaud, "the human skin of things, the epidermis of real- ity . . . is the primary raw material of cinema."[8] Kracauer insisted that part of cinema's uniqueness as an art form derives from the fact that film "addresses its viewer as a 'corporeal-material being'; it seizes the 'human being with skin and hair': 'The material layers of the human being: his nerves, his senses, his entire physiological substance.'"[9] These two state- ments suggest that film perceives the skin of the world ("the epidermis of reality") and addresses itself to the skin of the viewer. Both things are true, but if the film has a body, it must also have a skin of its own. And yet, what might that mean? If we take "skin" to mean the literal fleshy covering of a human or animal body, then a film couldn't possibly have a skin. But if, as Merleau-Ponty said of touch, "skin" also denotes a general style of being in the world, and if skin is not merely a biological or material entity but also a mode of perception and expression that forms the surface of a body, then film can indeed be said to have a skin.

Merleau-Ponty's concept of "flesh," discussed in the introduction, may be helpful in coming to a definition of the film's skin. He extends the term's significance beyond biology, using it to describe the reversible and recipro- cal relationship between self and other. Patterns of movement, particular shapes and forms, habits, and goals thus reverberate even between viewer and viewed, subject and object, even between the inanimate thing and the animate body, creating an indissoluble connection between them.

Flesh is the possibility for being that surrounds any one thing, any one emergence of a fact or figure within the field. Within the flesh, visible and tangible qualities are not so much abstract qualities as they are differences set against the background of a general visibility. The red that I see in a print on my wall is not merely or generally red, but is "a punctuation in the field of red things"; it is itself because it is not the red of tiled roof tops, or of particular French terrains, or of a bishop's robe, to cite Merleau- Ponty's examples. He writes: "A naked color, and in general a visible, is not a chunk of absolutely hard, indivisible being . . . but is rather . . . a momentary crystallization of colored being or of visibility. Between the alleged colors and visibles, we would find anew the tissue that lines them, sustains them, nourishes them, and which for its part is not a thing, but a possibility, a latency, and a *flesh* of things."[10]

Merleau-Ponty's notion of flesh implies an equivocation of body and things, such that they are *of* each other, neither raised above the other, both related and interdependent. Flesh resolutely refuses the possibility of either absolute distance or absolute proximity. "What there is then are not things first identical with themselves, which would then offer themselves to the seer, nor is there a seer who is first empty and who, afterward, would open himself to them—but something to which we could not be closer than by palpating it with our look, things we could not dream of seeing 'all naked' because the gaze itself envelops them, clothes them with its own flesh."[11]

To apply Merleau-Ponty's concept of flesh to film theory is to contest the notion of either an ideal spectator, who accepts a meaning that is already intended by the film, or an empirical spectator, for whom the meaning of the film is determined solely by personal, cultural, and historical circumstances. Flesh insists on a spectator who is both at once, who joins the film in the act of making meaning. "That the presence of the world is precisely the presence of its flesh to my flesh, that I 'am of the world' and that I am not it, is what is no sooner said than forgotten," Merleau-Ponty reminds us.[12] Replacing "world" with "film" in his statement would give us a sense of the permanent intertwining of film and viewer.

In short, the "flesh" of the world (also called the "chiasm" in the philosopher's later work) is not human skin, film's skin, or specific matter in any way. It is not a tangible, but rather a field of tangibility that makes the tangibles possible. My definition of human skin and the film's skin draws upon Merleau-Ponty's discussion of flesh, but "skin" and his notion of "flesh" are not quite the same thing. The skin is not a field of possibilities; it is a specific tangible.[13] However, it does display the trait of reciprocity and reversibility that is a hallmark of flesh.

The skin is a meeting place for exchange and traversal because it connects the inside with the outside, the self with the other. It also constantly enacts both the perception of expression and the expression of perception; in other words, it perceives the world as the world objectively expresses itself, and it expresses its own act of perception to the world by touching it. The skin, for example, perceives a chill in the air and expresses that perception as visible goose bumps. This reciprocity and reversibility between body and world may be most visible upon the skin, but it is not limited only to the surface of the body. The musculature, for example, is in a "fleshy" relation with the world insofar as it perceives the space around it and expresses that perception in a muscular form: touched by a cool breeze, the body shivers. The viscera too perceive the body's surroundings, or at least get a sense of those surroundings from the signals sent to them by the skin and the musculature, and respond, with a bone-deep internal chill.

Although musculature and viscera share with skin this reciprocity and reversibility with the world, the uniqueness of skin lies in its location at (and constitution of) the boundary between the body and the world. "Where are we to put the limit between the body and the world, since the world is flesh?" Merleau-Ponty asks.[14] That limit is the skin, which is not actually a limit at all but a place of constant contact between the outside and the inside. Two-layered, the human skin's dermis connects with the blood and muscle of the inner body, while its epidermis connects with the surfaces of the world. Musculature and viscera can have no discernible, realizable texture until they are exposed in trauma (broken bones poking through skin, for example, or a lost lunch, or open-heart surgery) or death (inner organs palpated in autopsy). Skin alone constitutes the objective texture of the body, those surface qualities that are touchable by the world with which it comes into contact.

As the edge between the body and the world, then, the skin functions always as both a covering and an uncovering, because of its simultaneous proximity to the public world and to the secretive inner body. It covers the body's secrets by clothing us in a placid smoothness that hides the murky movements within. But the skin displays those secrets as well, expressing them on its surface so that we are also always naked in it. The skin *conceals:* without it, the pulsing liquid and muscle of our inner body would be laid open and visible (and, of course, unable to function without their container). But it also *reveals* corporeal conditions that in themselves are invisible to the naked eye: internal diseases render it visibly disturbed, puffy, jaundiced; nausea appears as a greenish tint; measles and smallpox erupt upon and scar the skin; embarrassment manifests itself as a blush.

From a phenomenological perspective, then, the skin is complicated, defined here as a functional boundary and mingling place between the inside and outside of a body, in addition to its role as a biological object. Just as the human skin is irreducible to merely biological "stuff," neither is the film's skin a solely mechanical entity. The film's skin must not be reduced to the screen, for example; if it were, to touch the film would be simply to mimic the child's caress of his mother's face on the film screen in *Persona* (Ingmar Bergman, 1966), which is too literal a touch to account for the full range of tactility we experience while watching a film. Nor is the film's skin reducible to celluloid, though that is an admittedly tempting idea. After all, celluloid is the material that serves as the boundary between the film and the world. It is used both by the camera, as it perceives the world, and by the projector, as it expresses that perception to the audience. Even the two-sided structure of celluloid as emulsion and base—one side soft and vulnerable, the other shiny and firm—could correspond to the dermis (the inner surface of the skin: soft, wet, and in contact with the internal organs) and the epidermis (the skin's outer surface: harder, tougher, providing a protective and touchable covering). However, celluloid is only one part of the film's body that is involved in the film's act of perception and expression. It enables, but does not encompass, the camera's perception of the world and the projector's expression of that perception back to the world, for example. The function of the film's skin as the perceptive and expressive boundary between self and other is thus achieved by different mechanical parts of the apparatus and cannot be equated with just one of those components. If the film's skin were reducible to a single aspect of cinematic technology, then to touch the film would be to touch only a part of it, not to become intertwined with it in the kind of tactile embrace that, following Merleau-Ponty, I have described. The film's skin is a complex amalgam of perceptive and expressive parts—including technical, stylistic, and thematic elements—coming together to present a specific and tactile mode of being in the world.

Beyond screen and celluloid, then, the film's skin includes all the parts of the apparatus and the cinematic experience that engage in the skin's activities—this simultaneous expression and perception, this revelation and concealment—and constitute its texture. The film perceives the world, but that act of perception is concealed, invisible to and untouchable by the viewer. The film also expresses the world and reveals it, in a way that the viewer can see and feel. The revealing and concealing functions are enacted with every touch of my skin upon the film's skin and vice versa. In the moment that my skin and the film's skin press against or envelop one another, the film becomes accessible and transparent to me. At the same moment, though, it is also partially inaccessible and opaque, because I may touch the film's surface, but I cannot touch either the entire process of its making or the pro-filmic world of which it is a trace. This is because, as Merleau-Ponty wrote, "I am always on the same side of my body."[15] While there is contact and intertwining, there is never a collapse or dissolution of the boundary between us. Thus, this touch is a teasing one. The viewer's skin and film's skin allow a fleeting, incomplete kind of access to the other, which is pleasurable in its impermanence and incompletion. Their role at and as the surface of a body, as texture that both reveals and conceals, marks the fundamental affinity between the human skin and the film's skin.

The average viewer's body will not need to be convinced that the film's various textures actually press against, caress, wrap around, or come into direct contact with the spectator in any real way. In case the mind hasn't come around to the idea, I offer an example from elementary physics. Though the emission and reception of light are usually considered to be a phenomenon of vision, they are actually a matter of light falling on and reflecting off or being absorbed by an object before it ever becomes visible. If that object happens to be a retina, then we can call that vision. But what if the object happens to be an ear, a shoulder, or a knee? Light falling on any other part of the body still falls like light; it is still reflected or absorbed and has an impact. This description of light's physical impact has its roots in Classical philosophy. The atomists, whose ranks included Leucippus, Democritus, Epicurus, and Lucretius, held "that all sensation is caused by direct contact with the organ of sense and therefore that a material effluence must be conveyed from the visible object to the eye."[16]

Light has been described by physicists either as a particle or a wave, terms that aptly describe light's touch upon the skin. It is described as hitting the skin, where it bounces off or sticks like a speck of dust, or it is thought to wash over the surfaces of the body like a wave of water, thick and tangible. If light didn't make contact with the skin so directly, how would we know the welcome warmth of a bright winter sun or the coolness under a shady tree? The substance of cinema touches us in the same way, coming at us like particles or washing over us like a wave, and it leaves a trace on our skins, warming them, scratching them or drawing forth a shiver. As Gilberto Perez states in *The Material Ghost*, "If Einstein taught us that light falls like any other body, Bazin taught us that light leaves a track like any other body, an imprint the camera makes into an image."[17] Perez refers here to the imprint of the pro-filmic world on the negative, which is rendered into an image. But the same thing is true of the light of the screen, falling on the eye of the spectator and on the sensitive emulsion that is the spectator's skin. The light of a film must also leave an imprint, which the spectator feels as warmth, chill, smoothness or roughness, or simply pressure, for example. Roland Barthes describes the impact of the photographic image upon the viewing body in similar terms: "The photograph is literally an emanation of the referent. From a real body, which was there, proceed radiations which ultimately touch me, who am here; the duration of the transmission is insignificant; the photograph of the missing, as Sontag says, will touch me like the delayed rays of a star."[18] The contact between the film and viewer is a literal, tangible, physical contact between two bodies. We and the film are adjacent to one another, pressed against each other, in contact.

This contact is not "merely" material, but also meaningful at a number of levels; in fact, its emotional, social, historical significance is inseparable from the particular tactile forms it takes. Barthes, for example, writes of photography's ability to "touch" its viewer in physical and emotional senses of the word. He describes two elements of the image: the *studium* and *punctum*. He defines the *studium* as that element which evokes a denotative, intellectual reference to a body of cultural knowledge, whereas the *punctum* is that element which disturbs the *studium,* a detail that "attracts or distresses me."[19] Though he identifies the *punctum* as an element of the image proper, its ability to attract, distress, or awaken a certain type of response in him suggests that it is not merely a quality of the image but also of the subjective experience of the image. This expanded significance of the term entails a kind of mutually subjective/objective relation between viewer and the image and is demonstrated by Barthes's subsequent analyses of his own experience of photographs, such as the one he discovers of his late mother as a child. The *studium* and the *punctum* evoke modes of experience, ways in which the viewer addresses the photograph. The former is a "polite" intellectual interest in the photograph, the latter something altogether more striking, an interest that is more personal, passionate, poignant, and unmistakably physical: "It is not I who seek it out (as I invest the field of the *studium* with my sovereign consciousness), it is this element which rises from the scene, shoots out of it like an arrow, and pierces me. A Latin word exists to designate this wound, this prick, this mark made by a pointed instrument. . . . *Punctum* is . . . sting, speck, cut, little hole—and also a cast of the dice. A photograph's *punctum* is that accident which pricks me (but also bruises me, is poignant to me)."[20] That the *punctum* is described in such physical terms, rising from the scene and "pricking" the beholder, contributes to the sense that the intellectual and emotional "content" of the viewer's experience are provoked and, indeed, shaped by the tactility of the encounter. The photography literally and figuratively leaves an impression, makes a mark.

If Barthes's *Camera Lucida* demonstrates the tactility of photography, other scholars have explored the role of touch in the experience of painting. "By custom," Richard Shiff writes, "art criticism allows visuality to infect the material realm of touch; but we can just as well allow the relationship of touch to transform what is usually understood as visual."[21] Of course, the tactility of the film experience differs greatly from that of a photograph or painting, at the very least because it involves time and movement of the "object" itself, not just its viewer. Several scholars have begun to consider the embodied materiality of the film experience, including that which manifests itself in the skin, as a key component in cinematic affect.[22]

In the relationship between film and viewer, the distinction between touching and touched is always blurred. Spectator and film might settle onto each other like mist, glance off one another like pelting rain drops, or slip and fold around one another in an embrace. As the discussion of the film's body in the previous chapter pointed out, following Vivian Sobchack, the film and viewer perform similar modes of perceptive and expressive behavior in different ways that are determined by the specifics of their enabling bodies. So, the viewer caresses the film and the film caresses the viewer or the pro-filmic world, for example, but each uses different embodied means to enact that touch. The viewer caresses by moving the eyes along an image softly and fondly, without a particular destination, but the film might perform the same caressing touch through a smoothly tracking camera movement, slow-motion, soft-focus cinematography, or an editing style dominated by lap dissolves, for example. The film and viewer each respond in their own uniquely embodied ways to one another's style of touch. Antonia Lant provides a lovely example of the accidental, playful, and imaginative forms the spectator's touch upon the film can take. Citing a prose passage from Virginia Woolf, Lant says that Woolf "fuses (or confuses) fluff caught in the projection gate with the representation of a tadpole, and that with novel evocation of emotional states, and she describes her attention wandering . . . moving across the surface of the screen, but also probing into depth, selecting for interest the gardener mowing the lawn beyond (or above) Anna Karenina and her lover."[23]

The Latin word for touch—*contingere*—is the root of such words as "contact" and "contiguity," which aptly describe the relationship of film and viewer in the film experience. Significantly, though, *contingere* is also the root of "contingency," which refers not only to the notion of chance and coincidence but also (though more obscurely) to a natural affinity between two things.[24] The connection between contact and contingency (in both its meanings) is worth mentioning because quite often, the touch of film and viewer across one another's skins has a quality of the accidental. That piece of fluff dancing across the projector's gate in much the same way that Woolf's distracted gaze skips across the screen, stopping here and there just for a moment before moving on, is a good example of the aimlessness and serendipity that sometimes characterize the tactile contact between film and viewer, as well as the deeper affinity that can exist between film and viewer as each responds in kind to the other's unique styles of touching. A spectator's tendency to be distracted by the slippery, peripheral, and perhaps even accidental aspects of the cinematic image may create what Christian Keathley calls "the cinephiliac moment," which, he notes, "is not just a visual experience, but also a more broadly sensuous one; it is an experience that has been linked in critical writing to the haptic, the tactile, and the bodily."[25]

In *Atlas of Emotion,* Giuliana Bruno notes the reversibility that is a defining feature of the skin but also takes things a step further, to remind us that skin doesn't just reside at the fingertips:

> The haptic, as its etymological root suggests, allows us to come into contact with people and the surface of things. Thus, while the basis of touch is a reaching out—for an object, a place, or a person (including oneself)—it also implies the reverse: that is, being touched in return. This reciprocal condition can be extended to a representational object as well; indeed, it invests the very process of film reception, for we are moved by the moving image. Furthermore, we should consider that, as a receptive function of skin, touch is not solely a prerogative of the hand. It covers the entire body, including the eye itself, and the feet, which establish our contact with the ground.[26]

In answer to the question of how a viewer can touch the cinema without ever laying hands (or feet, for that matter) on the film or the screen, I offer an intriguing argument by Elena del Río, who writes that "affective investment . . . projects both image and body outside their visible limits. Touched by the surface of the image and transformed itself into a surface, the body by no means becomes absent. Instead, . . . the body is always outside its visible form."[27] Thus the viewer's skin extends beyond his or her own body; it reaches toward the film as the film reaches toward it. In a passage concerning a scene in *Speaking Parts* (Atom Egoyan, 1989), in which two lovers watch each other through a video-phone screen as they perform a mutual erotic display, del Río describes a kind of shared contact that could just as well characterize the connection between viewer and film. In this moment, tactility makes difficult the notion of a separate, mutually distinct self and other. She criticizes "the hypothetical separation between the realm of vision and the site of corporeality, . . . [as well as] positivist notions of the body as a self-contained monad with fixed and stable boundaries. As the image becomes translated into a bodily response, body and image no longer function as discrete units, but as surfaces in contact, engaged in a constant activity of reciprocal alignment and inflection."[28]

Del Río's words reiterate the mutuality inherent in the film experience, bringing to mind a new version of a familiar riddle: if a film is projected in an empty theater, does it still make a sound and throw out an image? That there be someone there to catch and reflect that light and sound back to the film is a necessary expression of cinematic perception, the other half of the communicative cinematic act. Del Río insists, and I agree, that "the notion of human and electronic bodies as surfaces in contact is not in keeping with rigid binary demarcations of externality and interiority."[29] This notion of viewers' and films' bodies as surfaces in contact also problematizes the strict division between subject and object in the cinematic experience, suggesting instead a more mutual experience of engagement.

EROTICISM

In the palpable tactility of the contact between film's skin and viewer's skin, and in the extent to which that contact challenges traditional notions of film and viewer as distant and distinct from one another, the tactile relationship between the film and the viewer is fundamentally erotic. Film and viewer come together in a mutual exchange between two bodies who communicate their desire, not only for the other but for themselves, in the act of touching. Alphonso Lingis describes eroticism as an experience in which "the other is structured as . . . the exterior relief of one's own inward feeling, not by a move of a mind to posit an object before itself, but in a move of one's body to depose itself before the other, not in a laying out of objectivities . . . but in an exposure of oneself to contact, not in a sovereign appropriation, but in denuding and dispossession."[30]

In the mutual contact of one another's skins, each recognizes the other as a perceptive, expressive, and desiring subject. Not only do we perceive the other, as we make contact with it, as a "real" and tangible subject, but we also perceive ourselves more tangibly as well. The touch between our skin and another's brings our own perceptive and expressive act into greater relief. In pressing ourselves against the other, we can feel ourselves touching. We and the other render each other real, sensible, palpable, through mutual exposure. In some sense, the touch of our skin upon the world and that of the world on our skin is what brings us into being (a particularly dramatic example being the slap on the rear end we receive at birth: that contact is what gets us breathing and ushers us into the human world).

But, as Lingis makes clear, in eroticism there is no mastery of the other, nor is there submission to the other; there is only the mutual "denuding and dispossession" of two bodies existing toward one another.[31] The erotic touch is not about ownership or complete knowledge of the other, but is truly intersubjective. Just as, in the exchange of glances with an other, we can see ourselves seeing, in the contact of our skin with another's, we can feel ourselves feeling. We feel ourselves as if for the first time in that moment, and as if from an external "point of touch." In the moment of coming into contact with another, we come to know what we must feel like from the outside.

The remainder of the chapter dwells on a style of touching in the film experience that Laura Marks refers to as "haptic visuality," and it has a great deal to do with eroticism. Marks defines haptic visuality as a kind of looking that lingers on the surface of the image rather than delving into depth and is more concerned with texture than with deep space. She argues that "haptic images are erotic in that they construct an intersubjective relationship between beholder and image. The viewer is called upon to . . . engage with the traces the image leaves."[32] Much more will be said about the specifics and the history of haptic visuality very shortly, but here I'd like to begin by considering its significance as an erotic form of communication between film and viewer.

The defining characteristic of Marks's term is the reciprocity it implies between film and viewer. "A film or video (or painting or photograph) may offer haptic *images*," Marks writes, "while the term haptic *visuality* emphasizes the viewer's inclination to perceive them."[33] This intersubjectivity is what makes haptic visuality erotic: it operates through an intimate relationship between two bodies—the viewer and the work of art—coming into contact with one another in an act of "denuding and dispossession" such as Lingis described.

I can think of no more elegant description of the effect of the touch that occurs between film and viewer than this one: "By engaging with an object in a haptic way," Marks writes, "I come to the surface of myself."[34] In letting our gaze wander over the surface of the image, we *do* come to the surface of ourselves, feeling ourselves more keenly in the touch of our skin against the film's skin, a touch in which we and the film constitute one another and bring each other into being.

When Marks argues that "the ideal relationship between viewer and image in haptic visuality is one of mutuality, in which the viewer is more likely to lose herself in the image,"[35] she uses terms evocative of an erotic embrace, in which we sometimes cannot tell where one body ends and the other begins. However, the idea that one "loses oneself" in the image deserves careful consideration. I appreciate the distinction noted by Marks in an earlier essay, where she describes the erotic encounter between film and viewer as one "in which union does not obliterate the self so much as fray its boundaries."[36] For in the caress between our skin and the film's, we "come to the surface of ourselves," denude and dispossess ourselves to the other, but we don't quite "lose ourselves" in the image. If anything, it could be said that we are both "here"—at the surface of our own body—and "there"—at the surface of the film's body—in the same moment. When the film's and viewer's skins caress one another, there is *fusion* without *confusion*. We are up against each other, entangled in a single caress, but we do not elide the boundaries altogether between our body and the film's body; rather, we exist for a moment *just on both sides* of that boundary, as if feeling ourselves from the outside and the inside in the same moment. We come to the surface of ourselves but *remain* there, at and *as* the boundary between bodies. Put simply, the act of "denuding and dispossession" goes both ways. We don't "master," possess, or know the other (the film) completely in that touch, nor do we lose ourselves or give ourselves over completely to it.

However, I agree with Marks's claim that, "by interacting up close with an image, close enough that figure and ground commingle, the viewer relinquishes her own sense of separateness from the image—not to know it, but to give herself up to her desire for it."[37] Desire puts us in touch with one another but doesn't take us completely outside our own bodies, for even when we give ourselves up to our desire, we're still living in our own skins, even as we reach toward and against another that we desire. The erotic relationship is one in which we're constantly feeling our skin *from the inside and out,* feeling ourselves being touched in the act of touching. This is a matter of feeling ourselves pressed against the film's skin, not being absorbed or erased by it. We lose the sense of our separateness from the film, but we don't lose our sense of our*selves.*

This general discussion of the tactile, reversible, and erotic relationship between film and viewer necessitates a move to a description of the specific ways in which viewer and film touch one another's skin. This calls for a return to haptics, which will enable a more precise definition and tangible examples of how the erotic relationship between film and viewer reveals itself in the touch of one against the other, our surfaces skittering, sliding, and pressing against one another in ways that foreground the shared sensitivity and expressivity of our skins.

Cinema entails a whole range of possibilities of touch against our skin: films can pierce, pummel, push, palpate, and strike us; they also slide, puff, flutter, flay, and cascade along our skin. And, as Lant's description of Woolf's alternately wandering and probing gaze at the film screen suggests, the viewer's touch upon the film varies as well. We might touch the film gently, with a placid and undemanding gaze, but we can also touch the film aggressively, with a searching look and keen ear that palpate and investigate the film. This palpating touch may be affectionate, as we linger appreciatively over details of the film, or challenging, in the sense that a viewer's attention examines the film for weak spots, errors, and implausibilities. As viewers, we can also attempt to pin down the film by our manner of watching. In films where the film obscures its object with distant camera position, a rough film grain, low light levels, etc., I find myself squinting at the image, trying forcibly to squeeze or twist it into something familiar. (Viewers at home exert a similar force on the image by manipulating the controls on their VCR or DVD player to slow, pause, or fast-forward a film's images.) If our attention upon the film is a kind of attentive pressure, our boredom with a film is an absence of pressure or friction. Images skirt past us without being touched, and our attention never gets caught on their surface. We may be able to re-focus our attention and "watch the scratches," as filmmaker Norman McLaren liked to do, but if the film lacks even the slightest bit of texture, we say it is "dull," and we mean it both literally and figuratively.

The particular type of touch this chapter addresses is that which moves along the surface of the film's and viewer's skin, a touch that has much to do with what some art and film historians and theorists have described as "haptic" imagery. In its simplest sense, "haptic" means "relating to or based on the sense of touch," from the Greek term *haptein*, to fasten.[38] The term "haptic" has often been used interchangeably with "tactile," but in its most general sense, the haptic includes tactile, kinaesthetic, and proprioceptive modes of touch. (This book addresses those three modes of touch in separate chapters, linking them with the skin, musculature, and viscera, respectively.) However, certain writers have used the term more narrowly to designate a horizontal look along a flat surface, and it is this sense of the term that interests me.

Many who have written on haptics explicitly, in the study of art history and film history, have founds its origins in a specific time period and in relation to a particular genre. In his study of the period of transition between antiquity and early Christianity, art historian Alois Riegl noted the tendency of Egyptian textiles to privilege surface texture over depth, which he characterized as the pivotal moment in the transition "from the tactile 'near vision' in the case of the Egyptian pyramid to the purely optical 'distant vision' of the Roman Pantheon."[39] Film scholars Noel Burch and Antonia Lant have employed "haptics" to describe the distinctive qualities of early cinema. Their uses of the term differ greatly, however: Burch takes haptic space to mean a graspable, inhabitable, three-dimensional space that develops in the early decades of the twentieth century in cinema, whereas Lant defines it as a perplexing fluctuation of far and near, flat and deep, emergence and recession, most clearly displayed in films that employ an Egyptian motif.[40]

Marks weaves a particularly detailed discussion of the history and characteristics of haptics together with her own more specific and descriptive term, "haptic visuality," which she defines as a way of looking that "tends to move over the surface of its object rather than to plunge into illusionistic depth, not to distinguish form so much as to discern texture. It is more inclined to move than to focus, more inclined to graze than to gaze." Marks turns to intercultural experimental film and video productions for a wealth of examples of this "look that moves on the surface plane of the screen for some time before the viewer realizes what she or he is beholding."[41] She disagrees with Riegl's point that haptic art disappeared with the fall of the Roman Empire, arguing instead that haptic art and haptic visuality have been sublimated, but not erased, by Western culture. She treats contemporary examples of haptic visuality as based in cultural experience; female artists and Third World artists, for example, have developed (or retained) a more sensuous and specifically haptic way of looking than Western artists and male artists have done.

This kind of tactile perception of the world manifests itself in art that emphasizes texture and materiality—the grain of video imagery, for example—and encourages the viewer's gaze to move horizontally over the image, like fingertips caressing a particularly lush fabric or the dry grain of a sandy beach. Haptic art abounds with "intimate, detailed images that invite a small, caressing gaze."[42] The reciprocity between the film's mode of revealing itself and the viewer's mode of perceiving it suggests that in the erotic encounter between film and viewer, each "other" is indeed "structured as . . . the exterior relief of one's own inward feeling"—the film's skin moves according to the viewer's desire, and vice versa. Marks's focus on the "caressing gaze" redresses what she finds to be an overemphasis on masochism and abjection in Steven Shaviro's theory of cinematic tactility, which describes the touch of film upon viewer primarily as an assault.[43] "A tactile visuality may be shattering," she writes, "but it is not necessarily so."[44]

In what follows, I'm interested in a category of touch that is distinctly haptic—in that it moves horizontally along the surface of the (film's and viewer's) skin rather than into depth—and always erotic, but which is neither always shattering nor always delicate. Haptic touches—including the caress, the scrape, and the smear, for example—involve an opening of one body onto another that is erotic, but they may express a panoply of possible attitudes. The category of "haptic" as I employ it includes styles of touch that may be placid and gentle or aggressive and cruel, comforting or uncomfortable. The analyses that follow reflect this variety by addressing film experiences whose erotic, haptic styles of touch are either pleasurable, horrible, or a complex combination of the two. Indeed, the analysis of *Hiroshima mon amour* at the chapter's end makes clear what is implied in the analyses that precede it: that the pleasures and horrors evoked by haptic tactility are anything but mutually exclusive. Furthermore, these material pleasures and horrors are necessarily enmeshed with memory and history for, as Tarja Laine writes, "haptic perception is . . . a mode of bodily consciousness in which consciousness is present to the world *through* the senses, and the world has meaning to the consciousness with the body as a centre of reference."[45]

PLEASURE

When we want to express the fondness that we share with someone else, we say, "we're close." When we feel an inexplicable pleasure in being close to someone, we call it "attraction," and indeed, love and friendship are usually expressed by a need for and pleasure in proximity: we want to feel the other against us, so we kiss the other's cheek, sit near one another, and embrace one another. There is a fundamental human need for and pleasure in the touch of another body, well documented by social biologist Ashley Montagu in his seminal book, *Touching*, where he writes that "almost every kind of cutaneous stimulation that is not intended to be injurious is characterized by an erotic component."[46] As Lingis's description of eroticism as an mutual unveiling of oneself to the other suggested, this erotic, tactile relationship between two bodies may be, but isn't necessarily, expressive of adult sexuality. In an essay on the "eros of parenthood," Noelle Oxenhandler describes eroticism as encompassing a whole range of relationships, only one of which is sexual: "If we are honest, we can acknowledge that in the pleasure of giving a baby a bath—in the slippery softness of warm, soapy skin, the exchange of glances, the coos, the giggles—we find ourselves at one end of a continuum of human sensation and emotion that reaches to the place inhabited by adult lovers."[47]

The erotic relationship described by both these writers seems closely linked to what Didier Anzieu, in *The Skin Ego*, calls the "attachment drive," which leads us to seek simple contact with another body. Anzieu describes the desire for contact as a need for pleasurable qualities such as "gentle-ness, softness, furriness, hairiness."[48] In the relationship between film and viewer, haptic images and, more important, haptic visuality satisfy this need for contact, inviting the viewer into what Marks calls "a desiring and often pleasurable relationship to the image."[49]

More than that, haptic visuality can substantially reconfigure our rela-tionship not only to the film with which we're brought into contact but also, more broadly and profoundly, to objects and other subjects in the material world in which we are mutually caught up. In his essay on mate-riality and child's play Bill Brown writes, "one must imagine that within the child's 'tactile tryst' the substantiality of things emerges for the first time, and that this is the condition for reshaping the material world we inhabit."[50] That "tactile tryst" is not only the subject but also the mode of Satyajit Ray's *Pather Panchali* (1955), which immerses itself and its view-ers in the erotic sensuality of a child's relation to the world and to others.

While *Fuses* is resolutely erotic in both senses of the word, *Pather Panchali* offers an example of the sensual, but not particularly sexual, eroticism of childhood. Indeed, if eroticism is partly defined by the mutual exposure (but not possession) of two bodies to one another, what is more erotic than the child's relation to the world, a relationship in which the pre-dominant attitude is one of discovery rather than mastery of one's sur-roundings and of oneself in the process? This film invites the viewer to make contact with the film's skin in the spirit of wonder, joy, and sadness, in the same way we might take pleasure in a cool rain on our shoulders or the touch of something that once belonged to a loved one. Though not hand-touched in the literal sense that *Fuses* is, Ray's film luxuriates in the textures and surfaces of daily life and everyday objects.

The film's tactility surfaces both in the relation between film and viewer and within the narrative itself. The children take a particularly tactile pleas-ure in their surroundings, and their relation to one another and to those around them is articulated through touch. They run and play in the forest around their home, rolling in mud, climbing in trees, and enjoying a cool summer rainstorm. Their one argument comes when Apu takes a piece of tin foil from his sister's prized box of personal treasures, odds and ends picked up here and there. The close-up of Apu pressing the tin into a mus-tache on his face emphasizes the distinctly tactile, material quality of their play, and Durga's fury at his having stolen from her box of bits and pieces makes clear the value these little textured objects hold for them.

Durga's particularly close relationship with her old aunt is expressed by a shared delight in the textures of food and landscape. The first time we see

Durga is in a close-up, as she peeks from behind a banana leaf nearly as big as her small face; she is stealing bananas from another aunt's orchard. The first appearance of her aunt is a close-up of her hands, mashing the banana that Durga has brought her. Later, when Durga is accused of stealing a much-admired shiny string of beads from her cousin, Durga's mother overturns her little toy box, looking for the beads. Afterwards, the old aunt carefully picks up every last trinket and replaces it gently and respectfully into the box, which is Durga's prized possession. Earlier, the mother had accused the old aunt of stealing and threatens to look for the evidence in the aunt's own box, suggesting that both she and Durga have a similar box of simple treasures. Not only are Durga and her aunt similarly associated throughout the film with textures of objects and food, but they have the same relationship to them as well: sensual, playful, and yet respectful of the stuff of the world.

Though the children and old aunt are most explicitly associated with pleasure in textures of nature, the entire family exhibits a tactile relationship to the world and to each other, though in more subtle forms. Although the mother seems too beleaguered to take such childish pleasure in things, it should be noted that she has her own box of tactile treasures: a woven basket contains dishes that are part of her dowry, and she takes great care with it, lingering over each object as she cleans and replaces it in the box, and fondling these things wistfully as she prepares to sell them for money with which to feed her desperate family. And in one sequence, as evening draws near, each member of the family retires to his or her respective tasks, all of which are rendered as particularly tactile in nature. These activities are a blend of work and pleasure: father and son write and do lessons, respectively, and we hear the boy's pen scratching across the surface of his paper; the mother brushes her daughter's hair; and the old aunt mends a piece of tattered fabric. Darkness and quiet descend on this intimate scene, each person intently focused on the movements of their fingers across the material at hand.

As with *Fuses,* the erotic tactility of *Pather Panchali* is expressed and lived not only by its characters and objects, but also by the film itself. It displays (and elicits from viewers) a tactile joy not only in scenes in which children romp in falling rain and delight in a crinkled square of tin foil discovered amid a treasure chest of found objects, but also through transitional shots in which no children are present, but the camera itself stares for long moments at water bugs skittering along water's surface, for example, or rain pelting the shiny surface of banana leaves. This focus on tactile pleasure begins with the credit sequence, in which extraordinarily delicate lettering, rendered in calligraphic pen and ink on porous paper, emerges at the right side of the screen and slowly scratches its way across to the left. This sequence inscribes the film's theme of childlike tactile wonder in ordinary surfaces; these quick, skittering scratches along a dry surface appeal to us tactilely, visually, and aurally, and they will find their echoes later in the images of rustling leaves, dancing water bugs, and raindrops splashing on lily pads. For audiences who may be unfamiliar with Ray's native Bengali, the writing's indecipherability contributes even more so to its status as pure texture.

This film caresses and palpates its subjects, and invites us to do the same to the surface of the film itself. In many cases, the image is held long enough to transcend its narrative meaning and become significant solely as texture upon our skins. Figure and ground mingle continuously in this film with the help of cinematic effects that flatten the image into pure surface and texture. As the father nervously awaits the birth of his son, for example, his face is lit in high contrast and shot with a telephoto lens, so that he becomes nearly indistinguishable from the craggy, mud-packed walls of his home, past which he paces nervously. His features are sculpted in light and become a surface over which to run our fingers, their very roughness a tactile expression of his anxiety. He blends into his surroundings, and the effect is not only sensual but thematically powerful, for this character speaks lovingly of the spiritual connection he has with this place, his home and homeland. The face of the old aunt is likewise treated as expressive, meaningful texture: as she tells the children a bedtime story, for example, all three characters' candlelit faces are dwarfed by the profiled shadow of the aunt's face, which stretches across and becomes inseparable from the knobby wall behind them. A daytime shot of the aunt walking slowly along a row of rugs being hung to dry has a similar effect, this time achieved with camera placement: the frame is filled half with her face in close-up and half with the textiles past which she moves. In the juxtaposition we are invited to compare the intricate, sun-warmed weave of the rugs to the dry, papery softness of her creased face, as well as to consider the intimate relationship between this family and the material thread that binds them to one another and their daily lives to their ancestral past.

Camera placement and lighting combine in a great many long shots of the children in the forest to reduce them to tiny figures amidst a vast landscape of leaves and branches. They nearly get lost in these images, and it is hard to tell whether what we see moving across the screen is the fluttering of leaves in the wind or a child running through the trees. The film's style literally "horizontalizes" figure and ground, making everything resolve into a single,

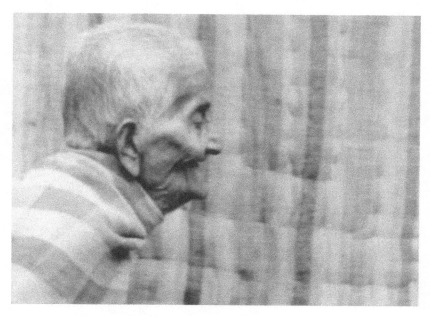

2. *Pather Panchali* (Satyajit Ray, India, 1955)

horizontal plane that I hesitate to call "flat" because of its richly textured surface. This horizontalization of figure and ground evokes the film's theme, which suggests the degree to which this family is one with its surroundings, finding joy, sorrow, and dignity in an organic, rural existence.

Certain textures hold a special appeal for this film. It exhibits and encourages in its viewer a tactile fascination with water, in particular, which comes to express a full range of emotions, including joy, longing, fear, and grief. Watery surfaces are sometimes whimsical, as in the shot of the children racing after the man who sells candy to the villagers, in which they appear as a string of silhouettes reflected on the surface of the pond near their home. A close-up of the mother reading good news from her husband, who has gone in search of work, dissolves to a shot of rippling water, then to several shots of lily pads and dragonflies flitting about on the surface of the pond for long moments. Then the monsoons come, and at first the rains incite Durga's joyful frolicking in the downpour, as Apu looks on, charmed by her delighted abandon. But the rains quickly turn deadly, beating at the doors of the house where Durga lies gravely ill, having caught her death of cold. Finally, Apu stands at the edge of the pond, shocked by his sister's death and staring silently at the water, now still and dour.

This film speaks through texture, making meaning at the surface of our fingertips. Its tactility is not a stylistic idiosyncrasy but is deeply embedded in and expressive of its theme. Its story of death, memory, and the loss of childhood innocence is expressed in the tactile register as strongly as in the narrative. The children's experience of life is immediate, not goal-oriented, but tactile and happenstance. Things happen, and they stop to see or touch. They get waylaid and distracted by the textures of the world, and so does this film, stopping all narrative just to linger on the surface of the water, where water bugs skitter playfully or rippling waves lap at the edge of a pond. Death, too, is experienced as accidental, unexpected, and a peculiarly tactile event. The deaths of both the old aunt and young Durga register as a tactile loss. Mourning the old woman's death, Durga sits on the porch where her aunt took up residence, and as she sits, she slowly rubs her mouth across her sleeve, evoking the textures of both skin and fabric, which were repeatedly emphasized in the scenes involving the aunt. Later, when Durga herself has passed away from sudden illness, the mother is unable to tell the girl's father upon his return. When he blithely presents a shawl he has purchased for his daughter on his travels, the touch of the new fabric against the mother's face is her emotional undoing.

Pather Panchali touches and is touched by its figures in a particularly tactile manner, experiencing and expressing them as surface and texture, and allows us to do the same. In fact, it may be said that the film indulges our own tactile tendencies and desires, stopping to touch when and where we're inclined to do so. This style of touching is mutual; the film responds to our tactility, and invites it, and recruits it into its story. If we feel *for* the children in this tale, it is in part because we feel *with* them, experiencing the film with the same tactile fascination that they have toward their world. We sympathize with their feelings, in the sensual and emotional meanings of the word. If Ray's story is poignant, it is so in more than one sense, for "poignant" means emotionally touching, but it derives from the French *poindre* and the Latin *pungere:* to touch or to prick. This film pricks us, tickles us, cascades over us: its emotional power is conveyed in the meeting of its skin with ours. It encourages, through its every surface, a sensuous engagement that dissolves the binary opposition between subject and object. For viewers of the film, as for Durga and Apu, "our very capacity to accumulate things around us stands in inverse proportion to our capacity to experience them as things."[51]

Lest one think that only experimental and art films touch us so meaningfully, I offer the example of a Hollywood blockbuster whose critical success owes much to the human need for touch and texture. *Toy Story* (John

Lasseter, 1995) earned praise for its winning appeal to both demographics within its audience: children presumably love the story and the characters and are drawn to the cartoon form, while adults chuckle at the witty double entendres and cultural references (many of them nostalgic) that children are unlikely to appreciate. But this assumption about the film's dual address misses something crucial about the film, which is that both its nostalgic charm and its kid-appeal are inseparable from its tactile allure. *Toy Story* calls up its adult viewers' nostalgic impulses by appealing to the sensual childhood memories that reside at the surface of their skins. American audiences of a certain age will remember the feel of those little plastic green soldiers—the smooth flatness of the platforms to which their feet are fused and the intricate detail of their guns and helmets, for example, and the sharp edges they get when they've been chewed by the family dog. We laugh knowingly with this film, not only because we remember being a child, but more specifically because we may remember what it feels like to dip our fingers into the box of yellow plastic facial features and stick just the right ones into the smooth, rotund face of Mr. Potato Head, or to shake the piggy bank in hopes of feeling the rolling, tumbling weight of a few coins in its hollow belly. And as with *Fuses* and *Pather Panchali*, the film's tactility is not merely a matter of subject matter, but also a matter of *matter*, of the film's own material form. *Toy Story*'s slick computer-generated imagery not only accentuates the surface of its objects but creates for the film itself a skin that is without imperfection, at times hard and at times soft, but always as cool and smooth as a Fisher-Price toy. This film entices us to run our fingertips over it, and its tactility invites a childish kind of tactile enjoyment in its viewers, both young and old.

Both *Toy Story* and *Pather Panchali* encourage us to indulge our delight in textures and surfaces in the way we did as small children, when we played happily for hours with the stuff of life: pots and pans, wooden spoons, stuffed animals, rubbery plastic toys, clay, water, and finger paints, for example. However, even though both films tease out our inner child by inviting us to let our fingers play over their surfaces, each has an entirely different feel. *Pather Panchali*'s images are organic, evoking the feel of sand, dirt, water, and the elements, of child's play in nature and among simple things. *Toy Story* recalls sensual memories of a particularly urban, consumer culture. Its texture is completely manufactured and processed, and even if we didn't know that this film was the first feature in history to consist entirely of computer-generated imagery, we would *feel* it. This film's skin has no grain to it, no roughness, no messiness: it is as smooth as a plastic Magic

Eight ball. Its giddy Play-Doh colors are manufactured, so rich and bright that they could hardly exist outside toy stores and candy counters: every red is a smooth candy-apple red, and every pink is a squishy bubble-gum pink. The tactile memories this film evokes are historically and culturally specific: though its setting is contemporary, it recalls America of the 1950s, the era of Formica, Frigidaire, and the Radio Flyer wagon, of smooth textures and bold colors designed to soothe and brighten the American landscape after a rough and dismal few years at war.[52] Despite a frequent complaint that computer-generated imagery is somehow cold, inhuman, and not as sensual as images shot on film, Toy Story's digital imagery is, indeed, digit-ally appealing: it beckons our fingers and thumbs as avidly as films like Fuses and Pather Panchali do, even though its tactility derives from binary code and video monitors rather than celluloid and screen. My inclusion of Toy Story is meant to suggest that digital media are not without tactility, though the forms of their tactility may be different from those of film.[53] There is no scratching or painting of the celluloid (or even celluloid at all) in Toy Story, but it does have a skin, which it offers up to our touch both haptically and erotically, and in such a way as to remind us of the degree to which emotion, memory, and history emerge in and are shaped by tactile engagement between film and viewer.

Toy Story was preceded by Pixar Studios' short film Tin Toy (John Lasseter, 1989), which likewise indulges the viewer's pleasure in the touch of smooth, bright Fisher-Price–like images. This film is shot from a toy's perspective, following the trials and tribulations of a tin toy, a doe-eyed mechanical drummer boy who attracts the attention of his drooling, infant owner. The toy evades the baby's sticky grasp and finds safety under the sofa where, he realizes, the baby's other toys are in hiding too, quivering in fear of being discovered. When the baby bursts into tears at the loss of his new plaything, the tin toy is deeply affected, and he bravely, if reluctantly, emerges from under the sofa and sacrifices himself to his overjoyed owner. This film is even more explicit about the nature of the viewer's pleasure, in that its baby expresses our own desires for tactile pleasure. Like the little tin toy who offers himself up to the baby's grasp and his sticky fate, this film exists solely for our tactile enjoyment. But, even as Tin Toy encourages us to take pleasure in the textures of its images, it also invites disgust. The baby drools copiously over every toy it touches, and as it toddles toward its prey, its body is a hulking monstrosity of baby fat and flesh, smooth and soft but also wet, soggy, and gooey in a most unpleasant way. No wonder the toys are terrified. I am reminded of Steven Shaviro's claim that there's a "panic in the face of excesses of the flesh."[54] This panic is what those little toys must feel, huddled under the sofa as the monstrous baby blubbers and slobbers a few feet away, and we may feel it too, as those smooth, cool images become slightly grotesque. Seeing this in a theater, I have heard audiences giggling fondly, but there's a hint of "ewww" in their laughter. *Tin Toy* reminds us that, not only within the image but at its surface, what is pleasantly smooth and slick is only a hair's breadth from being slimy and disgusting.

HORROR

If Laura Marks dwells on the pleasurable aspects of the erotic, haptic contact between film and viewer, Shaviro is mostly concerned with those other, painful and dangerous, aspects of that contact. Indeed, the flip side of the attachment drive, whereby we receive pleasure in the touch of our bodies against another's, is the loathing and disgust that the touch of another's skin against our own may inspire. William Ian Miller sees contact as the defining characteristic of disgust. He writes that "the disgusting is what's strange and estranged but threatens to make contact."[55] This contact is not just any contact, but specifically a tactile one, for, as Walter Benjamin reminds us, "All disgust is originally disgust at touching."[56]

Shaviro characterizes disgust at touching and being touched as a matter of contagion. If proximity and contact with another body can bring us warmth and comfort, they can also bring moisture, clamminess, germs, and disease. Shaviro's thoughts on George Romero's *Living Dead* trilogy (1968, 1978, and 1985) are worth quoting at length in this respect:

> The rising of the dead is frequently described as a plague: it takes the form of a mass contagion, without any discernible point of origin. The zombies proliferate by contiguity, attraction, and imitation, and agglomerate into large groups. The uncanny power of Romero's films comes from the fact that these intradiegetic processes of mimetic participation are the same ones that, on another level, serve to bind viewers to the events unfolding on the screen. The "living dead" trilogy achieves an overwhelming affective ambivalence by displacing, exceeding, and intensifying the conventional mechanisms of spectatorial identification, inflecting them in the direction of a dangerous, tactile, mimetic participation. Perception itself becomes infected, and is transformed into a kind of magical, contagious contact.[57]

"Contagious contact" is the predominant theme in Roman Polanski's *Repulsion* (1965), and in that film, as in the Romero films, "repulsion" not only describes character relations within the film but also, more profoundly, defines the relationship between film and viewer. The film draws us in with a caress, but that caress quickly becomes a repulsive smear. *Repulsion* insidiously invites us to get close and to take pleasure in the placidity of its images, only to horrify us when those images begin to slither, creep, and erupt with things we'd rather keep at a distance. The title of the film refers to the heroine's pathological disgust at anything relating to the body, but in the end it tells us just as much about our own relationship with the film as it does about her relationship with the world around her.

The film tells the tale of Carol, a young woman strangely withdrawn from her surroundings. We gradually become aware that Carol is repulsed by all things sexual and, more generally, corporeal. She recoils from a suitor's kiss, shudders at the sounds of her sister's lovemaking in the next room, and is horrified to find a male guest's toothbrush and soiled t-shirt in her bathroom. Left alone by her sister for a weekend, Carol moves through their apartment in a daze, disturbed by everything she sees and touches. Ordinary objects and sounds—dripping water faucets, cracked plaster ceilings, the skinned rabbit her sister had planned to cook for dinner—take on menacing qualities. Carol's retreat from the world culminates in her stabbing of a sweaty, lecherous landlord and bludgeoning murder of her own amorous boyfriend, followed by her eventual removal from the scene when her sister returns to find her in a catatonic state, into which she has escaped from the surface of the world.

The disturbance Carol feels in the film and that viewers might experience while watching it are equal parts repulsion and fascination. She gazes raptly at the ordinary, flat surfaces in and around her apartment: her own shiny reflection on the side of a toaster, a man's razor blade. What horrifies her (and the viewer) is that these smooth, flat surfaces give way to disgusting and disturbing textures: plaster walls metamorphose into slimy, groping hands; a sidewalk crack seems to spread ominously like a fungus; cracks in the plaster burst violently across the walls of Carol's apartment; grotesque eyes grow on the skin of a potato; and flies and mold gather on the skinned rabbit. The film is full of eruptions and oozings of the horrific upon slick, clean surfaces. Even the soundtrack exhibits this unsettling tendency to crack and ooze: discordant crescendos of bass tones, for example, unexpectedly erupt amid the calm flute music that plays throughout.

For its viewer, *Repulsion*'s repulsiveness lies in its exposure of the grime and seediness lurking, growing, or decaying beneath seamless surfaces. The emphasis is on the touch of disgusting things (and images and people) upon the skin, both in the narrative and in the film's tactile engagement with the viewer. Again, this is a matter not just of skins and surfaces within the film, but of the film's and viewer's skins as well. The skin of *Repulsion* appears at first glance to be smooth, clear, and unblemished, and for a while our eyes move over the crisply elegant black-and-white images without a hitch. But just as we settle into the caress between our skin and the film's skin, the film startles and disgusts us with the violent eruption or unsettling smear of materiality in places and images where it seems not to belong. Things creep, slither and ooze everywhere we touch, smooth surfaces dissolving into disgusting, dark, viscous imagery. Catherine Deneuve's own face is one of the beautiful surfaces that erupts into something terrifying as she descends into madness. She appears placidly beautiful in the beginning, but gradually she is transformed: by the end of the film she is disheveled, sweaty, distraught, and distorted, her face appearing not so much coolly detached as stricken with horror. She fascinates and repulses at the same time.

In general, humans experience the skin as a limit and a container: it is the thing that brings us into contact with the world, but always also that which separates us from everyone and everything else. What is so upsetting about *Repulsion* (for viewers and for Carol) is the violation of the skin as container, as smooth and clean surface that should conceal the oozing stuff inside and protect us from what's outside but fails do that here. In this film, things, animals, and people constantly get cut, are sliced open, ooze, sweat, drip, and slither. A rabbit looks horrifically unfamiliar in its raw and skinless state, for example, and smooth plaster walls crack and transform themselves, reaching out to attack the main character in her own home instead of keeping her safe from the outside world. Even early on, at the salon where Carol works, beauty shows its ugly side, as Carol palpates her client's face so aggressively that its fleshiness becomes unnerving, and when filing the woman's nails, Carol cuts her and stares, as we do, at the blood that seeps from the wound. Perhaps the most horrifying image in the film, though, is the reflection of an unidentified attacker (a figment of Carol's memory or imagination, presumably) that appears only for a second in the mirror on a wardrobe door. As Carol closes the wardrobe, the man's reflection skitters across the screen and across the viewer's skin like a sudden, chilling breeze along the back of one's neck or the faint tickle of a spider's legs across one's skin in the night. The intruder himself does not move, but thanks to the swinging of the mirrored wardrobe door, his image glances across the screen and our skin. That he appears in the glass surface of a mirror resonates with the overall tactic of this film, which is to disturb our perception of glassy, smooth surfaces with the touch of something sordid or putrescent, something that reminds our skins of their own vulnerability to violence and decay. That something sordid need not even touch our skins at all to have a tactile and emotional effect: its nearness is enough, for as Sara Ahmed writes, "fear responds to what is approaching rather than already here. It is the futurity of fear which makes it possible that the object of fear, rather than arriving, might pass us by."[58]

This emergence of the material in unsettling ways along the smooth surface of the skin is not only stylistic, but also thematically and politically significant. The film exposes the sordid underbelly of what on the surface seems to be a picture-perfect childhood. During the landlord's visit to Carol, he and the camera peer closely at a framed family portrait that depicts what appears to be a happy family gathering. In the film's final shot, however, the camera moves slowly toward that photograph, finally getting so close that what had appeared to be a smooth black-and-white image becomes grainy and murky. There, in extreme close-up, we see in young Carol's fearful, hateful glance toward a nearby male figure a painful history of abuse. Though the camera moves toward the photo, closer and closer, the shot ultimately is less about penetrating into depth than it is about lingering at the surface: the image of her eye gradually disintegrates into pure texture, until there is no further to go, and our eyes can only move over it horizontally. In this moment, we feel the family's dirty secret *as* something dirty, soft and porous to the touch. Here as in the rest of the film, horror derives from the exposure of smooth surfaces—sidewalks, countertops, skins, photographs, family histories—as the sordid, festering things they really are. As under a microscope, clean surfaces are everywhere revealed to be diseased and repulsive.

While it would be interesting to analyze the film by focusing on its visual metaphors, only an approach that considers the "feel" of the film can grasp its more radically horrific meanings. While a visually oriented psychoanalytic reading, for example, might argue that the disgusting textures of sex and corporeality are linked to Carol and are washed away with her removal at the film's end, a textural analysis would have to admit that something sordid taints the entire film, even after the visual and narrative layers ostensibly "clean up" after the materiality that permeates the film. *Repulsion* makes us face our own fears and neuroses as it exposes the cool, smooth surface reality being smeared and soiled with the "stuff" of horror and illicit, cruel desire.

While this sort of textural analysis provides an alternative approach to *Repulsion*, one that reveals what may be missed by a more traditional reading, *Eraserhead* (David Lynch, 1977) is, simply put, incomprehensible without it. There can be no "traditional" reading of this film that doesn't take into account its texture: it doesn't make sense any other way. At the narrative level, one might get the idea that there's something strange going on, but it is impossible to put one's finger on it. Only in the tactile register does the hero's poignant malaise make sense; only there does this film's surreal enigma resolve into a touching tale of a young man trapped in the strange, baffling world of first-time fatherhood and industrial America.

The world of *Eraserhead* is quite a different one from that of *Repulsion*, its horror rendered much differently. If Polanski's film seeks to reveal gradually the seamy underbelly creeping out from what appears on the surface to be smooth and calm, *Eraserhead* negates even the illusion of clarity and cleanliness to begin with. If *Repulsion* hints obliquely at disgusting things we can't see directly, *Eraserhead*, like many of David Lynch's other films, puts them on display, as if—to borrow an image from *Blue Velvet* (1985)—a well-manicured lawn has been turned inside out, and we slither among the unseemly roots of the soil's underside. *Eraserhead* is a film that sticks, scratches, slithers, and smears itself along the viewer. It is a murky, malevolent swamp in which vision gets stuck. It tells its story of a young man's descent into urban alienation and nightmarish domesticity in tactile terms: we and the main character, Henry, are horrified by the very textures of his life.

This film, from its first shot to its last, makes vision difficult. People and things are obscured through low light and heavy shadow, dirty windows, and oblique angles. Henry's girlfriend, Mary, for example, is first seen in a tattered, torn photograph held in his hands and, in a clever visual joke, is similarly obscured by the dirty window in which her face appears in the succeeding shot. Primordial muck and ooze and gnarled textures populate every layer of the film. Following the surrealist tradition, the film takes objects out of context so that they're completely foreign and unrecognizable, compelling in their strangeness. Even something that should be an emblem of antiseptic cleanliness becomes tainted: a pot of boiling water, in extreme close-up and juxtaposed with the hideous boils on Henry's screaming infant, looks suspect. The link created between the boiling water and the baby's skin also casts doubt upon the child's humanity: this ontological question (which bothers Henry as well, judging by the look on his face) arises from our fingertips, because human skin simply isn't supposed to feel like that.

The oppressive nature of Henry's life reverberates throughout the soundtrack as well, which also dissolves into pure texture. Sounds are made strange by a refusal to identify their material sources or to attach to them any narrative meaning. Like the image track, the soundtrack seems coated with a layer of audible grime that sticks to the skin of the viewer who comes into contact with it: urban industrial noises that permeate every scene; the awful wailing of his infant; the raucous suckling of dogs that seems to go

unnoticed by Mary and her mother, though it makes conversation impossible and destroys any illusion of domestic normalcy. The muffled quality of
the soundtrack, the inconsistent sound levels, and the constant presence of
ambient noise that drowns out dialogue all function, as do the murky low
lighting and grainy image, to make it difficult to identify what we see. The
only way to experience this film is to feel our way through it.

Like *Repulsion, Eraserhead* plays with and violates the notion of skin as
a boundary between inside and outside, as well as between human and nonhuman. Images and sounds of skins and the stuff they're supposed to conceal frequently bleed together in this film, juxtapositions that draw their
power to disgust from our own keenly tactile familiarity with what bodies
feel like. When Mary rubs aggressively at her itchy eye, the gesture is
accompanied by an exaggerated gritty, squeaking noise, giving the viewer a
palpable sense of the "stuff" inside her eye that shouldn't be there and that
we certainly shouldn't be feeling. Snakes get squashed quite audibly as
they are thrown against the walls of Henry's apartment and, later, stomped
by the woman in his fantasies set inside the radiator, and the film makes
much of the sound and image of their viscous insides splattering on walls
and floors. In the last radiator-fantasy sequence, a pile of what looks like
dirt on a theater stage oozes blood.

In one remarkable image, Henry's lover sinks below the surface of what I
can only describe as a milk-jacuzzi that has turned up in Henry's bed, and her
long black hair rises in a tangled mass to the smooth surface of the milk-white
liquid. The image is at once fascinating and disgusting because of the unexpected union of two disparate images—hair and milk—one belonging on the
surface of the body and one emanating from the inside, and both intensely
corporeal. The images are highly connotative, of course. The hair suggests sex,
and the milk suggests motherhood, so that the image refers to the
Madonna/whore complex and the cultural taboos that arise from it. But in
this instance, the horrifying nature of these textures' commingling registers
first to our fingertips, perhaps even to our tongues. It is the contact between
film's and viewer's skin that enables and encourages the notion that these two
things—sexuality and motherhood—are somehow "wrong" together. In his
study of the various categories of things that humans find disgusting, William
Ian Miller discusses the many-layered significance of hair and skin, and he
relates an interesting anecdote, in which his own infant discovers a human
hair in his mouth.[59] The look of sheer disgust on his baby's face made it clear
to Miller that, before the child could learn to be disgusted by such a thing, he
felt intuitively that food belongs in the mouth and hair does not: hair is supposed to stay on the *outside* of the body. Perhaps that boundary—inside

versus outside—is prereflective and only later reinforced by learned social behavior. This moment in *Eraserhead* reminds us that tactile experience and specific cultural attitudes are intimately and complexly related.

Eraserhead reveals just how flimsy the skin is, as both container and shield. The skin is supposed to mark the limits of the self, but it offers Henry very little in the way of protection from other people and things. In one of the most disturbing images, his future mother-in-law attacks him in the corner of the living room, groping him and covering his face and neck with wet, noisy, open-mouthed kisses, whose overwhelming tactility is expressed by the sound of smacking lips and tongue as much as by the image of their grappling bodies. Henry is bewildered by the sudden explosion of carnal lust that presses her body far too close to his for comfort and violates every social boundary he knows.

Ironically, naked lust is what got Henry here in the first place: his impending marriage to Mary is a "shotgun wedding." The child that results from this marriage is a slimy, writhing, fleshy reminder of what horrors may be borne of the contact between skins, the exchange of fluids, and the transgression of boundaries. The baby's behavior is childlike and may even elicit sympathy—it cries desperately for attention and seems to want only to be held, after all, like any infant does. But on the surface and in close-up, the child is not recognizably human. Its skin is horribly wet, gooey, bilious, bubbly, and utterly uninviting to the touch. We and Henry recoil in horror at the sight of that child because it provides tangible evidence of the flimsiness of skin. This baby is the outward manifestation of something inside Henry, after all; it is his flesh and blood. The skin not only fails to keep others away from Henry, it also fails to keep Henry to himself.

What offends Henry so deeply is the transgression of the boundaries between the sexual and the maternal and between himself and others, both of which occur in the figures of his pregnant fiancée, lustful mother-in-law, and the women in his dreams. These dangerous transgressions are expressed and perceived not in the narrative but on the surface of the film and the body (both Henry's and the viewer's). It is in the tactile, surface contact between the film's skin and our own that we grasp the theme of Henry's ambivalence about marriage, fatherhood, and the social rules and taboos of the bourgeois life into which he has stumbled.

Two scenes in particular from *Repulsion* and *Eraserhead* express in no uncertain terms the terrifying fragility of the skin. In Polanski's film, Carol arrives home to her flat shortly after her sister's departure. She stands in the kitchen, her face blank, and slowly, haltingly, peels off the glove that

3. *Repulsion* (Roman Polanski, U.K., 1965)

she's still wearing. The camera lingers in extreme close-up on the glove being pulled away from her fingers, and at the edge of the frame, Carol's body visibly jerks at the snapping sound it makes as it comes off. She then opens the refrigerator to find the rabbit that had been skinned for dinner lying atop a plate. As she stares at its lifeless, skinned body, the similarity between skinned animal and Carol's "skinned" forearm is unavoidable. In a scene with only a slightly less creepy and more ironic tone, *Eraserhead*'s Henry arrives home after trudging through the muddy streets of his urban hell. He sits on his bed, lifts his foot across his knee, and slowly peels off his sock, staring with a look of fascination that resembles Carol's expression. He hesitates, as if puzzled or baffled. The paleness of his skin against his dark trousers and amidst the dark tones of the bedroom make it appear that he is tugging at his own skin, just as Carol had seemed to do. Like Carol's glove, Henry's sock sticks to his leg like a second skin, coming off only with effort, and slowly.

These two scenes recall a bit of Walter Benjamin's essay, "One-Way Street," that bears the appropriate but never directly invoked subtitle "Gloves": "In an aversion to animals the predominant feeling is fear of being recognized by them through contact. The horror that stirs deep in man is an obscure awareness that in him something lives so akin to the

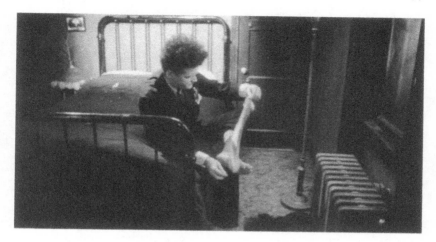

4. *Eraserhead* (David Lynch, U.S.A., 1977)

animal that it might be recognized. All disgust is originally disgust at touching."[60]

Benjamin's words reveal the tactile underpinnings of the sometimes horrifying and uncanny nature of our flesh. Both pleasure and horror arise from the skin's function as boundary—as something that keeps the carnality within us concealed and the carnality of the world at bay—but also as something that brings us into contact with the things in us and around us at the same time. The skin, then, puts us in an ambivalent place on the border of self and other, inside and outside, and proper and improper. Julia Kristeva's definition of "abjection" hinges on this ambivalence and the "border anxiety" it produces.[61] Iris Marion Young, paraphrasing Kristeva, writes that, "as distinct from the object, . . . [the abject] is other than the subject, but is only just the other side of the border . . . next to it, too close for comfort."[62] The glove and the muddy sock that Carol and Henry peel from their skins are the tangible figures of this border, or skin, that thinly separates them from the animalistic and carnal stuff of the world and of themselves.

Interestingly, Merleau-Ponty has also made reference to gloves, in his description of the reversibility within the flesh. The finger of a glove that is turned inside out is an image of the flesh or chiasm, he says, where "in reality there is neither me nor the other as positive, positive subjectivities. There are two caverns, two opennesses . . . which both belong to the same world. . . . The end of the finger of the glove is nothingness—but a nothingness one can turn over, and where then one sees *things*. . . . There is not identity, nor non-identity, or non-coincidence, there is inside and outside turning about one another."[63]

In the two scenes mentioned above, *Repulsion* and *Eraserhead* make palpable the horrifying aspect of such intimate proximity to the other. In peeling off the glove and the sock, Carol and Henry reveal the ontological ambiguity that is the theme of both films. Carol feels that her skin is at once too corporeal, like a piece of meat, and too thin, unable to protect her from the disgusting germs and fluids of the world around her. The film expresses her feelings of vulnerability in tactile terms such that, by the time it shows us the photo that tells the story of her past victimization, we have already sensed, quite literally, the reasons behind her fear and psychosis. Henry is constantly horrified, or at least befuddled, to discover the earthly, animalistic roots of his own humanity: he is taken aback by the noisily suckling dogs in Mary's apartment, for example, and balks at the task of carving up the comically creepy Cornish hens served up at the family's dinner table. (His horror in this regard bears some resemblance to Carol's repulsed fascination with the skinned rabbit planned for dinner.) He is appalled by the disconcerting animalistic appearance of his infant son, who bears a strange resemblance to both the dogs and the fowl, but who is a product of Henry's very own body. He is unsettled, too, by the social transgressions in which he is caught up and which are expressed in tactile terms throughout the film. In both films, Carol's and Henry's heightened awareness of the sliminess, prickliness, scratchiness, and stickiness of things and bodies elicits the profoundly troubling, even disgusting, realization of their own carnal connection and vulnerability to the world around them. More than this, they have felt the extraordinary fragility of the skin, which is unable to keep both the exterior of the world and the interior of their own bodies at a safe distance.

As Carol and Henry discover their own carnality and the inability of their skins to protect them from it, others, and themselves, the viewer discovers in the experience of these films the carnality of vision and may be horrified (and thrilled, quite possibly) by the ease with which the film's skin can touch our own, contaminate us, and give us the creeps. Our skins are fragile coverings that offer intimate contact with, and little protection against, the textures of the film, which smear and slither and sweat against us.

HISTORY *MON AMOUR*

As *Repulsion* and *Eraserhead* have shown, the skin conceals and reveals, protects and exposes not only our innards but also our emotional states and our personal histories. It is the surface through which we experience and express feelings, of both physical and emotional varieties. Thus, when we're too easily insulted or hurt, we're said to be "thin-skinned," and when nothing affects us at all, we're called "callous." When the world has touched us too cruelly, we are said to be "scarred" for life. It is the mingling of corporeality, emotion, and human history on the surface of the skin that concerns Alain Resnais's *Hiroshima mon amour* (1959). In this film, history, memory, and loss manifest themselves visibly and sensuously in the press of skin against skin, both within the film and between film and viewer. This film ruminates with philosophical seriousness on memory and experience in the context of the bombing of Hiroshima and the French Occupation. It considers history to be something inescapable and yet elusive at the same time. How can one grasp the significance of distant history, and how can one embrace the past and go on living at the same time? These questions are posed and answered through a brief encounter between a Japanese architect and a French actress who spend two nights and a day in Hiroshima together, making love and meaningful conversation about love and loss.

In the struggle of these two lovers to come to terms with their desire for one another and with their own pasts and that of their native countries, the film suggests that art cannot represent the deepest truth of human events unless it is a fully sensual experience, and an erotic one, in the sense of two subjects being in contact with one another, in the mutual denuding and dispossession that Lingis described. The architect and actress open onto one another—as do the film and the viewer, as do the past and the present—in a mutual act of concealing and revealing.

The film begins as she tells him what she has seen in her tour of Hiroshima and swears she now understands Hiroshima. He argues that she has seen nothing. The entire film takes up this debate, ultimately suggesting that it is only through touch that the lovers can experience the truth of themselves, each other, and the past. For there is an erotic contact as well between the past and the present: pressed up against one another, they mingle, never quite confused but so close that they cannot help but affect one another. This touch of the past upon the present is rendered metaphorically, literally, and sensually in the touch between two lovers. Furthermore, it is only through a haptic relationship between viewer and film that this treatise on history is made sensible to us.

The first extended narrative sequence of the film seems to propose two different ways of experiencing the past and the present, one haptical and one optical. Throughout the film, we and the female character are somewhat torn between these two forms of experience, but the film ultimately comes down on the side of haptic visuality as a means of true comprehension of the relationship between self and other and between past and present. I will begin by discussing the series of optical images in the first sequence following the credits, as it brings the haptical images into greater relief by comparison.

As the female character describes to her lover, in voice-over, the things she's seen in Hiroshima during her tour of the city, we see the images she describes: images of victims' bodies and landscapes tragically devastated by the bomb. In the shots set in the museum that she has visited, the camera tracks slowly, horizontally, past glass cases that hold evidence of what happened at Hiroshima—a twisted bicycle, mannequins wearing the singed clothes of victims, an unrecognizable lump of steel. (In two cases, the camera tilts slowly upwards along the surface of a still photograph depicting a victim's burned skin, but these types of camera movements are rare in comparison to the tracking shots.) Documentary footage from the day of the bombing is presented in a similar fashion, with the camera tracking slowly, horizontally, past the multitudes of suffering victims and devastated buildings, and the camera in the hospital footage operates the same way, moving slowly along a row of bedridden patients who return its gaze impassively.

The images are shocking and appalling, but they are only the visible surface of the past disaster, kept at a distance from the female character and from us by the glass that surrounds them, by the distance of the cameras from the bodies they film, and by the stillness of the bodies depicted in photographs. To look at them is emotionally moving, certainly, but to see them this way is not to touch or be touched by them as intimately as one must in order to understand. As powerfully affecting as these images are, I believe they are examples of what Laura Marks calls "optical visuality, which sees things from enough distance to perceive them as distinct forms in deep space."[64] Their salient characteristic is that, like all optical images, they "[depend] on a separation between the viewing subject and the object."[65] The distance is quite literal in some cases: the documentary footage of survivors, for example, is shot at such a distance that they appear as entire bodies, not as surfaces close enough to feel or too close to identify clearly. In other cases, the separation between image and viewer is a matter of stillness: the few shots that do get close enough to victims' bodies that they become momentarily unidentifiable are the still photographs, in which the only movement is that of the camera, tilting up along the photographs to inspect the evidence in a way that's somehow too clinical to be described as a haptic touch.

These shots are pensive, allowing us to reflect upon the magnitude of those events and that suffering. The act of reflection requires distance from immediate experience, which these shots give us. The slowly tracking

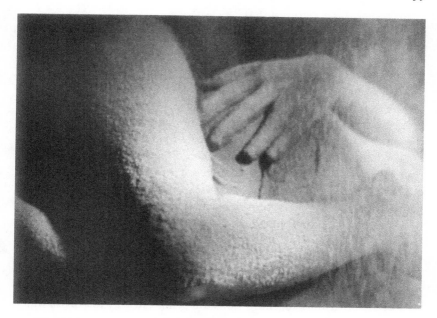

5. *Hiroshima mon amour* (Alain Resnais, France, 1959)

camera allows an event to unfold over time that originally occurred with horrible suddenness, and the reflective glass cases and distant cameras keep us from coming face-to-face and skin-to-skin with the traces of that disaster. Unlike haptic images, these optical images put literal time and space between us and those events, temporal and physical distance that translates into emotional distance.

The distance—temporal, physical, and emotional—between viewer and image in these documentary examples explains to some degree her lover's claims that the woman has seen nothing. Though he does not put it in precisely these terms, she has not gotten close enough to see the real suffering and the real significance of Hiroshima. This is not to say the images are not powerfully moving or that she and we are not touched by them. On the contrary, they turn our stomachs and make us cringe, and as she says, "what else can viewers do but weep" at images like this? My point is that they are not touching in the close, skin-to-skin way that haptic images are.[66] For an example of haptic visuality that will prove my point, we must look backward, to the first image of the film that follows the credit sequence.

The opening shots of the film are a crucial and profound instance of haptic visuality. These images of the lovers' caresses are famed for their enigmatic beauty. Separate bodies glide along and over one another's surfaces to become layers of each other. These are some of the few shots in the film that are haptic in the strict sense that Marks defines: they keep the viewer's eye at the surface of the image by making the objects they present indecipherable to us.[67] We cannot tell exactly at what or whom we're looking; we can only see skin in contact with more skin. These bodies do not yet register as characters or as historical figures, only as bodies; they take up the entire screen and there are no depth cues to locate them in space. These images compromise vision (and visual identification), forcing us to experience them as skin and to *become* skin in order to make sense of them. The only way to understand them is to caress them, letting the eyes wander gently over their surface with no particular destination.

The haptic quality of the images is heightened also by the way the surfaces of these bodies are covered with various textures: in successive shots the bodies are coated with layers of what may be perspiration or rain, then snow or mud or ash. These textures are incomprehensible as narrative fact (is it snow or is it ash?) but exquisitely sensible as texture. It is interesting to note also that these opening shots are demarcated by dissolves, which themselves are a kind of cinematic caress: a dissolve moves us from shot to shot by allowing the surface of one image to press against the other as they merge slowly, *dissolving* into one another. The two images are in contact all along their surfaces, not merely adjacent at their edges as are two images in a straight cut, but overlapping, each one infusing and infecting the other with its heat, its texture, and its meaningfulness. The film expresses the haptic qualities of this sequence with every part of its body, through cinematography, mise-en-scène, and editing.

Marks writes that "while optical perception privileges the representative power of the image, haptic perception privileges the material presence of the image. . . . Haptic visuality involves the body more than is the case with optical visuality."[68] This distinction aptly describes the difference between these first shots of the lovers' bodies and the ensuing documentary images of Hiroshima victims. The contrast between them continues even after this opening shot: as the woman's voice-over continues to describe the images of Hiroshima that she has seen, the film cuts back repeatedly to this scene of lovemaking, to close-ups of hands upon skin. Not until the very end of this sequence, and the end of the recitation of images that she has seen, does the film present the two lovers from enough distance that we might see their faces. Prior to that moment, we experience them only as skin. The recurring images of the lovers' bodies invite us into an erotic relationship with the film that will continue to be available, though perhaps less explicitly, throughout the film. In other words, these shots (privileged by their place at the very beginning of the film) establish the mode of viewing that will be most revealing and meaningful for its viewers. They encourage us to look at the rest of the film in the way we have looked at these images.

Optical and haptic visuality are a matter of degree, as Marks makes clear; this fact is borne out by the remainder of the film. The two modes of viewing are contrasted throughout the film but never again presented in quite the extremes that they are in this first sequence. Rather, the rest of the film proceeds by a complex arrangement of images that are haptical or optical to varying degrees. We and the actress are continually exposed to and engaged in both ways of seeing and experiencing the relationship of the past to the present. By the end of the film, though, she and we will have learned the value of haptic visuality, because it alone reveals to us the profound connections between past and present.

As an example of the subtlety with which haptic visuality is contrasted with optical visuality elsewhere in the film, consider the camera's treatment of modern Hiroshima and wartime Nevers, the woman's hometown. Both are filmed repeatedly with tracking camera movements. However, the shots of Hiroshima are of modern buildings (a result of the city's devastation and regrowth, of course) from which the camera is always at some distance, passing by skyscrapers and office buildings as we would in a moving car. In one dramatic sequence of many similar shots cut together, the camera races forward through city streets, buildings speeding past left and right in a veritable visual essay on Quattrocentro perspective. If the images in the museum had suggested a clinical gaze, these shots evoke a touristic one, surveying but never getting very close. The shots of Nevers, however, feel closer and more intimate, as if made by someone who lives there. The camera passes old French mansions and houses, whose ancient brick and stone appear more "touchable" than the glass and steel of Hiroshima's modern architecture, an effect due not just to differences in building materials but largely to camera placement: the camera simply gets closer to its subjects in Nevers than it does in Hiroshima. Furthermore, and perhaps most important, even when their subjects are equally distant, the Nevers images evoke texture in a way that the Hiroshima shots do not. The distance between camera and subject is undisturbed in Hiroshima, but in Nevers, things get in the way. For example, in the many shots in which the camera tracks to follow our young heroine as she rides her bicycle through the town, the thickness of the forest intercedes, obscuring the town behind it, brushing up against the camera and tickling our skin with every branch.

The contrast between optical and haptic visuality in the opening sequence and, more subtly, throughout the film underscores the film's theme, which is that what is merely seen is less enlightening than what is seen and also touched. Indeed, it is our haptic relationship with the film that yields understanding. Marks's own description of the political and philosophical value of haptic visuality is worth keeping in mind; it does in fact hew very closely to the project of *Hiroshima mon amour*:

> Haptic visuality frees the viewer from the illusion that cinema is capable of representing the profilmic event—what Stanley Cavell calls the "inherent obscenity" of cinema. The image indicates figures and then backs away from representing them fully—or, often, moves so close to them that they are no longer visible. Rather than making the object fully available to view, haptic cinema puts the object into question, calling upon the viewer to engage in its imaginative construction and to be aware of her or his self-involvement in that process. Where eroticism is based more upon interaction than voyeurism, haptic visuality is erotic.[69]

It is the main character's initially voyeuristic approach to the horrible history of Hiroshima to which her lover objects, reminding her that she has seen nothing and understood nothing this way. She believes she has "mastered" the history lesson she came for, but he suggests that she hasn't learned anything at all. The museum images are horrifying and disturbing, but to see them under glass while walking past them (as a tourist might do her sightseeing or window-shopping) is not to engage with them intimately enough to grasp their full meaning. To do that, she must get too close for comfort. It is only through her erotic relationship with the Japanese architect, who leads her to recollect her own first love and tragic loss, that she comes to understand. "Tactile epistemology involves thinking with your skin," Marks says plainly, "or giving as much significance to the physical presence of an other as to the mental operations of symbolization."[70] This is the lesson that we and Resnais's heroine eventually learn, that tactile experience has its own truth to tell. It fleshes out whatever objective information she and we may learn from the museum images and documentary footage. When she first arrives in Hiroshima, history is something the actress respects but holds at some remove from herself. But through her own tactile experience and tactile memories, history is brought to bear directly on her own body.

The same can be said for us: it is through the tactile experience of the film that we come to understand. Through the skin, we gain a clearer picture of ourselves in relation to others and to history, and we come to recognize that relationship as one of mutual permeability. As Ahmed writes,

It is through the intensification of pain sensations that bodies and worlds materialise and take shape, or that the effect of boundary, surface, and fixity is produced. To say that feelings are crucial to the forming of surfaces and borders is to suggest that what "makes" those borders also unmakes them. In other words, what separates us from others also connects us to others. This paradox is clear if we think of the skin surface itself, as that which appears to contain us, but as where others *impress* upon us. This contradictory function of skin begins to make sense if we unlearn the assumption that the skin is simply already there, and begin to think of the skin as a surface that is felt only in the event of being 'impressed upon' in the encounters we have with others.[71]

The erotic tactile contact between actress and architect is a perpetual process of concealing and revealing through and across their skins. In this film, the skin is a container not just of blood and bone but also of memory and history. In one of the film's most erotic images, the architect stands before the actress on the set of the film she's making, and he reaches for her. But rather than touch her face, as he does so often, he reaches for the head scarf that she had donned earlier as part of her costume. He places his hand atop the scarf and very slowly pushes it away, so that her hair is revealed. She dips her head, shyly averting her gaze (something we don't see her do anywhere else in the film—it is that intimate a gesture), and her hair falls in front of her face. Much later, she tells him (and we see) that her hair had been cropped in Nevers as a punishment for her desire, of which it is apparently an outward sign. And even later, its regrowth is the thing that gives her hope amidst the misery of her imprisonment and delirium, tangible evidence that she will survive. As she tells him this in a later scene, we see her younger self lying in bed, fondling the newly grown length of hair at the back of her head. As the film cuts back from that past moment to the present one, she runs her fingers through her hair as she remembers. Hair and skin are, in this film, tangible expressions of both past and present, horror and pleasure, pain and desire, and the experience of touching them is the medium of understanding.

By touching the body of the Japanese architect, and by feeling herself touching and being touched in the process, the actress eventually comes to understand Hiroshima and her own past. It is these lovers' touch upon one another's skin that urges her to reveal her personal history: each touch of the architect's hands against her face and her body elicits another bit of her story. By recalling her own tragic past, which she experienced intimately and directly upon her skin, the actress comes to feel and understand the tragedy and pain of Hiroshima's past, which she did not witness herself.

The woman's memories are themselves tactile. "The hands," she says, "always the hands"—this is how she remembers her first love. She recounts her history not as a linear narrative but as a series of fragmentary moments defined and cued by touch. In her narration and in the accompanying flashback images, she shivers with cold in the cellar to which she is banished after her affair with a German soldier is revealed. Fighting madness and struggling to remember, she scrapes her hands along the cellar wall and licks the blood from them, feeling the pain on her fingers and tongue in such a way that makes the German's death real for her. Touching her hair as it grows back is how she understands that she will survive her ordeal. She knows that winter has ended and she will soon be free because of a child's marble that drops into the cellar; rubbing it against her lips is what finally brings her back from the depths of her despair.

Once her own tactile history of love and loss has been brought again to the surface, and has been recalled by her own skin, the actress has a better understanding of Hiroshima. In the opening sequence, she had described the images of bombing victims accurately but impersonally: "human skin, hanging free, still writhing, in its first agony. . . . Anonymous hair." But later in the film, it is her own skin that hangs free, after she's scraped it along the cellar wall, and the hair is hers, being cropped and later returning with her health, no longer anonymous but a tangible sign of her own pain and hope.

If touch is revealing for her, it is for him, too. The architect realizes, as she does not, initially, that beauty and horror appear on the surface of the skin, but that it is not enough merely to see them. Beauty and horror alike must be touched to be believed, understood, appreciated, and survived. As an architect, he finds (and creates) beauty in what lies underneath the surface: foundations, the past. This is why he hounds her to tell her story of Nevers, which he thinks holds the truth of the woman she is now. Her past is the scaffolding of her self. To know her past, he must touch her. And he does, constantly, not only in the act of lovemaking but, perhaps more significant, in the acts of talking and listening. He presses his hands to her face as if to feel its architecture: her skin conceals her blood and bones but reveals them at the same time, in the shape of her jaw and the blush of anger, shame, or desire. As she speaks to him for the first time of Nevers, he presses his hand against her throat: he is not just hearing but *feeling* her words and her story. He verifies the truth by touching her speech, which by itself (as in the disembodied voice-over we and he hear in the beginning) isn't enough. Touch is the guarantor of truth, the only way to discover the secrets of history and desire that are concealed by the skin.

Touch is the thing that moves her and him and the viewer from past to present, as well. Just as tactile sensations evoke her memories, the architect's touch upon her skin often brings her back to the present. The film emphasizes cinematically this role of touch as the liminal space between past and present: it is almost always a close-up image of flesh that serves as a segue between then and now. In one particularly memorable transition that occurs early in the film, the woman stares at the architect's hand, which twitches slightly as he sleeps. That image gives way to a brief image of her long-ago lover's hand, twitching in the moment of death (as we discover much later). Here as elsewhere, the painful past appears as an eruption upon the smooth, calm image of the present, and it touches us as it does her, physically as well as emotionally. Quite often, the connection between past and present is made by an image of the lovers' hands touching, to which the film cuts forward from a documentary image of the hand of a disfigured bombing victim, for example, or from which it cuts backward to a close-up of the hand of the actress as a younger woman. The film also occasionally cuts from an intimate close-up of a face from the past to an equally close shot of one from the present, or, in one case, from an embrace between the lovers to a past embrace between a daughter and mother. Always, though, the movement between present to past is expressed visually by touch, just as it is cued narratively and emotionally by the touch of the lovers' skins against one another.

The erotic relationship is one of mutual unveiling through contact: fusion without confusion. The actress comes to know herself better through her erotic denuding and dispossession (of her body and, more important, of her past) to the architect. The line between fusion and confusion, however, is a slippery one. In her recounting of the past, for example, there is a play of pronouns that seems to elide the difference between her two lovers. Asking about the German, the architect refers to him as "I" or "me," and she speaks of the soldier as "you" rather than "he." This confusion of her lovers, however, does not imply that the actress is herself confused with an other, for regardless of the pronoun used for her lovers, she is always herself in both the erotic encounter she describes and the one she's living. The question in these moments is merely whether she is the "I" she was then or the "I" she is now.

It may also seem that past and present get confused in the mixing of the pronouns, but the confusion only exists linguistically, not cinematically, for we can always tell which images are past and which are present. The visual transitions make clear the proximity of past and present—they are pressed up against one another by dissolves and cuts—but they are never confused. Not only does the actress look unique in each temporal setting (in the past images her hair is very short or very long but in the present images it is somewhere in between), but Nevers and Hiroshima are completely different in appearance: the former a softly sketched (and more softly focused) rural dreamscape of forest and field, the latter a sharply drawn metropolis of straight lines and angles.

In one crucial moment, however, erotic contact does threaten to become confusion and the actress's own sense of self is nearly lost. Her German lover died in her arms, but the exact moment of his death escaped her because, she says, "I couldn't feel the slightest difference between his body and mine. All I could feel was how alike we were. How terrifyingly alike we were!" She is overwrought by this confusion and screams in anguish in the telling of it. The architect slaps her twice, hard, which jolts her out of her state of confusion. His slap reminds her of where she is in time and space, of who she is, and of who he is. Moments later, after she's finished her story, they embrace and she exclaims how wonderful it is to be with someone: she's relieved to be here, with him, in this moment, but also to have remembered a part of herself previously repressed. The touch of their bodies—both gentle and violent—has brought her back to herself.

In this scene as in many others, style and subject mirror one another. Here, a "whip pan" lives up to its name, whipping against our skins in much the same way that the architect's hand strikes his lover's face in that violent slap. As she recounts the details of her lover's death for the first time, the film cuts from an image of her younger self running to meet the German soldier to an image of his body, lying in the street. Suddenly, a whip pan brings us to a view of a house overlooking the alley where he has fallen, from which, she explains, the shot was fired that killed him. We had seen fragmented images of this moment before—his body, this house—but had not seen or heard the event as a whole. This is the culmination of her long story; all roads have led here. We have become mesmerized by and wrapped up in her story, as past and present embrace us as a single entity. This whip pan has the effect of both drawing us into and pulling us out of the death scene: its violence expresses the violence of that gunshot and, even more so, of her shock at discovering his body, but it also startles us out of the pastness of this recollection, in which we verge on getting lost. The whip pan moves as fast as a gunshot, but also faster than she does at that moment: she is paralyzed by the scene, and her lover lies still in the street. It is doubtful that, at the time, she had realized so quickly that the shot came from the building above, but in retrospect she already knows it, and so the fact is revealed to us suddenly, startlingly. The whip pan reassures us at once of the reality of the past (and of that scene), but also of its pastness, in the way that the architect's slap underscores the violence of the scene that she's remembering even as it rescues her from the past and returns her safely to the present. The whip pan exists *between* us and the film, *between* past and present; in this sense, it functions as skin, as the thin layer through which film and viewer (and past and present) are in contact with each other but also separated from each other. There is fusion, but not confusion.

This film uses the erotic encounter between the actress and architect to eroticize and make palpable the relationship between past and present. Past and present are fused, pressed and intertwined like the limbs of the two lovers in the openings shots. The nonlinear narrative structure expresses this erotic relationship, pressing past against present, mingling them, rendering them in tactile form (through, for example, "whip pans," gently tracking cameras that stroll through the halls of memory, and superimposed images of sweat, rain, and nuclear ash falling upon the bodies in the first shots). At moments it really is hard to tell which is which, but ultimately past and present do not become the other. Rather, we understand them better in the contact between them.

Hiroshima mon amour suggests that human history is rife with pain and suffused with pleasure, and that both are spoken most eloquently and understood most deeply through the touch of skin upon skin. Touch is not only the source of pain (contagion, disease, heat, nuclear blast) but also the source of salvation and redemption from pain (the caress, the kiss, and even the slap that brings one back from the edge of despair). The path of human history, the film suggests, is to embrace both of these. The architect says, after the actress has finished her story, that he will remember her, "when stories like this come up again, as they are bound to do." History repeats itself, and the path of cruelty will be taken again. But, the architect and the film suggest, the path of gentleness and loving touch will be there as well, and it will bring us back from that place of cruelty and forgetfulness.

Like any two bodies involved in an erotic relationship, we and the film are structured as the exterior relief of the other's inward feeling, in Lingis's words. Our reciprocal gestures—caresses, shivers, slaps, and pricks—are the results of shared attitudes. The way any embodied subject touches the world is an expression of its projects and attitudes toward objects and others in the world (desire or repulsion, for example). Films both inspire us to join in their attitudes towards the world and respond to our own. Our attitudes and the tactile behavior that expresses them are thus commutable, exchangeable, or (in keeping with the theme of the chapter) contagious.

We and the film are mutually contagious, contracting each other's desires, fears, repulsions, sorrows, and styles of touch through direct skin contact. Thus the caress that moves between our skin and the film's skin is borne of a mutual desire of the film and viewer for the object filmed, and when our skin creeps and crawls, it is because of a shared sense of disgust and horror.

The film's and viewer's forms of touch differ necessarily, but they express shared feelings and desires. So, *Fuses* seeks to arouse and describe viewers' original pleasure in touching, and in doing so it becomes aroused by the touch of textures on its own surface. In *Pather Panchali,* our gaze wanders over the screen while the film lingers with long takes upon miniscule things and textures unrelated to the narrative *per se* but integral to the natural surroundings that shape the children's, the film's, and our own understanding of events. The film experiences and expresses joy, wonder, and nostalgia in the surface of things, and we are invited to respond in kind. In the cases of *Repulsion* and *Eraserhead,* we and the film both experience and express horror: we may gasp or cringe or squirm in our seats, whereas the film expresses its horror through bursts or oozings of texture and sound. These things are expressions both of the horrible itself, meant to disgust us, and of the film's own squeamishness, which we mimic. *Hiroshima mon amour* invites our pleasure by taking its own pleasure in the form of sensuous dissolves, for example, and invites our horror by being horrified, which it expresses with a startling whip pan. In each of these examples, and generally in the relationship between a film and a viewer, the film's style (its external structure) appears as the "exterior relief" of our own feelings, just as our responses to the film appear as the "exterior relief" of its feelings. Film and viewer co-constitute one another in the act of touching, skin to skin.

The fleshy contact that occurs between film and viewer is only one form of their sensuous correlation. As Marks writes, "Touch is a sense located on the surface of the body: thinking of cinema as haptic is only a step toward considering the ways in which cinema appeals to the body as a whole."[72] The following two chapters take up her implicit call to investigate film's appeal to the entire, sensuously embodied viewer. They will continue the focus on the correlation and reciprocity of the film's body and the viewer's body as perceptive and expressive of certain attitudes and desires, but they will do so by describing a kind of touch that exists and operates not only at the surface of the body but also in its depths: in the musculature and the viscera.

2. Musculature

> It is really a kind of automatism that makes us laugh, an automatism . . . closely akin to absentmindedness.
> HENRI BERGSON

> Without cliffs and without gravity I don't know where I would be.
> CHUCK JONES

THROUGH A GLASS DEFTLY

If the film has a body, it must also have body language. The film's and viewer's relationship to each other is experienced and expressed not only on the surface of their skins but also through movement, comportment, and gesture, in the way they carry themselves through the world. To say that the film "mirrors" the viewer in muscular ways, though, would be at once correct and overly simple, for reasons made clear by the following two scenes. They are mirror images of one another in many respects, but with one key difference that encourages a more precise understanding of the reversibility and delicate balance between similarity and difference that marks the mutual engagement between film and viewer.

In *Duck Soup*'s famous mirror scene (Leo McCarey, 1933), Groucho Marx is at first taken in by what appears to be his reflection in a hotel room mirror. Of course, we and he both quickly realize that it is not his image in the mirror and that, in fact, it is not a mirror at all. It is Harpo on the "other side" of the empty space where a mirror ought to be, mimicking Groucho's every move. I say that Groucho is at first "taken in" by the false mirror image, but questions of the illusion's credibility and Groucho's gullibility are of scant interest, deemphasized to the point of irrelevance: he exhibits clear signs of skepticism within seconds of glimpsing his apparent "mirror reflection," and the scene's editing is not organized so as to make Harpo's joke a surprise to the viewer. The scene continues for long moments after the illusion is debunked, during which Groucho skips, crouches, bunny-hops, twirls, and prances ever more elaborately while Harpo keeps up his (pointedly, playfully inaccurate) mime act. The scene and its players seem interested neither in staging a seamless deception nor in exposing the illusion for what it is, but in feeling out the precise nature of the relationship between body and image.

The physical performance of the scene is taken up not just by the human figures but by the film itself, which performs its "act" by means of structure, composition, and editing. All the finesse belongs to the Marx brothers, though: the scene is remarkably abrupt, even jarring, in its drastic but seemingly unnecessary reframings and cuts between long and medium shots.[1] The editing does not "suture" us *into* the cinematic space: we are "in on the joke" but only intellectually, not bodily "inside" it. While we may be able to piece it together logically, the space created by these awkward changes in camera position is uninhabitable, because every embodied behavior of the film works to keep viewers *out*. Groucho is "taken in" by the illusion, bodily incorporated into it, but we are not. In a scene that is explicitly concerned with the nature of mimicry and the relation between viewer and viewed, both the actors' and the film's performances place a significant emphasis on physical distance and difference.

This scene finds its reverse image in the scene in which Buster Keaton's suave detective, Sherlock, Jr., likewise encounters what appears to be, but isn't, his mirror image (*Sherlock, Jr.*, 1924). If the humor of *Duck Soup's* mirror scene lay in the unmasked difference between the body and "image," the source of Keaton's joke is the semblance of semblance. Keaton stands primping and posing before the mirror. The camera is situated roughly 45 degrees to the left of the mirror, so that viewers can see the mirror and Keaton standing directly in front of it but cannot see Keaton's image *in* the mirror. From his actions and attitude, we assume he's gazing at his own reflection, but when he steps toward and then, to our surprise, *through* the mirror, we realize that Keaton's well-appointed room has the same design flaw that Groucho's did: there is no mirror where one should be.

If *Duck Soup's* uneven editing kept viewers from inhabiting that scene, Keaton's mirror scene firmly seats us inside it, but in a quite limited viewing position. It unfolds entirely without editing until the joke is over, so that our viewing bodies occupy and cannot move beyond our designated spot in the room. The joke is definitely on us, for Keaton's detective (as he does so often) sees something we can't see from where we're sitting.

This moment of his stepping *through* that empty space is both a contradiction in terms and a picture-perfect image of the relationship between film and viewer, for it is a moment of pronounced *difference* and *sameness* at the same time. The image we had been led to imagine in that space is simultaneously *not him* (i.e., it is not the reflection of him we'd expected to see) and *profoundly him* (where the image of Keaton should be, Keaton

6. *Sherlock, Jr.* (Buster Keaton, U.S.A., 1924)

himself now is). Like so many of the funniest flourishes in Keaton's oeuvre, this is an artful "quick change": illusion transmogrifies into material presence, and "image" becomes the "real thing." In that moment, Keaton goes from being presumably *like* the image to *being* the image.

That empty space through which he steps and where the mirror should be is the threshold between body and image, between viewer and viewed, and between touch and vision. This threshold is precisely what interests me, but if the previous chapter considered that threshold in terms of skin and surfaces, here it becomes a physical, inhabitable space that we and the film negotiate with muscular movements and behaviors.

Whereas *Duck Soup* scene has the feeling of a clever but somewhat bloodless conceptual exercise, Keaton's version strikes the funny bone precisely because it invites the entire body "into" the joke. Keaton's illusion catches not just our minds but also our muscular bodies off guard by incorporating us bodily, ambivalently, and ironically into the cinematic space.

Sherlock, Jr. itself takes pains to draw our attention to that threshold, but until it "gets in our way," we might scarcely take notice. In this scene, it is literally, visibly marked by (and as) a wooden beam, which one might reasonably assume to be lower edge of the mirror's frame, until of course one realizes that the mirror is nonexistent. After that, it serves no purpose at all; it is just a dangerously tall beam running across the middle of the apartment floor for no apparent reason. It is important to note that Buster Keaton isn't the only one who navigates this threshold: immediately after he steps across it and disappears from the scene, his assistant (played by his father, Joe Keaton) sets one foot over the beam and straddles it for several seconds before the film cuts to Keaton preparing in the next room to leave for a hard day's detective work. In this chapter, I will suggest that our muscular engagement with the cinema allows us to take up a similar position, wherein we straddle that threshold between "here and there," body and image. In the cinematic experience, we inhabit both places at once, with varying degrees of success.

The previous chapter argued that we share with the film certain behaviors and structures of the skin, through which we perceive the world and express our relationship to it. This chapter argues that we and the film are in a *muscular* relationship as well, a form of mutual engagement that dates back at least to the fabled panicking spectators of early cinema described in decades' worth of historical accounts of the Lumière Brothers' *Arrival of a Train at a Station* (1895) but already being satirized in films like *The Big Swallow* (James Williamson, 1901) and *Uncle Josh at the Picture Show* (Edwin S. Porter, 1902). Contemporary action-adventure films are often referred to as "thrill rides" and "roller-coasters," and, indeed, many viewers *do* respond to films and roller coasters in similar ways: they sway, swerve, and grip the armrests of their seats during frenetic chase scenes, for example, and even the most blasé of filmgoers has jumped with surprise during one suspense film or another. I will argue here that viewer and film are two differently constructed but equally muscular bodies, acting perhaps in tandem or perhaps at odds with each other, but always in relation to each other. Viewers are not passive participants in this engagement: we may be drawn to the film and also (perhaps even simultaneously) pushed away by it, but at the same time, we might move closer to the film or pull back and resist its invitation.

This chapter is organized around a pair of muscular "encounters"—the handshake and the chase—that occur not only within films but also, more profoundly, between films and the viewer. In each of these encounters, two bodies' muscular movements or gestures, which are mimetic to some degree, together create an entity that is larger than the individual movements of either one alone. We cannot shake hands by ourselves, and it takes at least two to make a chase scene. The mirroring of the film's and viewer's gestures in these encounters makes it difficult, as it was for Groucho Marx, to tell who leads and who follows.

Though the chapter begins by identifying and describing the muscular relationship between film and viewer, it cannot end there, for it is important to see how this empathy between film and viewer is meaningful for film analysis and, moreover, how our understanding and perception of muscular empathy can arise *from* film analysis. Thus, the first part of the chapter seeks to describe the muscular engagement between films and viewers and to discover what provokes it and how it is expressed, and the second part of the chapter deals with the meaningfulness of this muscular reciprocity. The empathy we experience with films shapes the way we understand them; and in turn, by focusing our critical attention on this empathy and the specific forms it takes, we gain a better critical understanding of the films themselves, whose meanings are conveyed not only through cognition and emotion but also through motion and physicality. Toward this end, the latter half of the chapter discusses the handshake and the chase as they are integrated thematically and made meaningful within individual genres and films, namely, the silent comedies of Buster Keaton and several chase-heavy action films.

EMPATHY

Viewers empathize with the body of the film to such a degree that we can experience and "grasp," in our muscles and tendons as much as in our minds, the exhilaration of a "close call" or the intimacy of a close-up, for example. In any cinematic experience, we and the film have a muscular empathy for one another, which is derived from similarities in the ways the human body and the film's body express their relation to the world through bodily comportment, and similarities in attitudes and projects that both film and viewer have in the world. The viewer's empathy with the film's body should not be confused with or reduced to identification with characters.

Linda Williams's essay "Film Bodies: Gender, Genre, and Excess"[2] touches on the idea of mimicry in the film experience. Williams considers viewers' responses to horror, pornography, and the maternal melodrama—in the form of screams, arousal, and tears, respectively—as a kind of mimicry, wherein the viewer empathizes with and imitates the behaviors, whether actual or implied, of on-screen characters. Williams problematizes this initial hypothesis by taking into account gender-specific cultural attitudes embedded in those responses, and ultimately she argues that viewer responses to these films are not a case of a simple one-to-one mimicry of characters, because the nature of identification is more complicated. The dynamics of character-identification, she warns, are too complex to be a simple case of mimicry.

This empathy with on-screen characters is precisely the criterion that Williams sets out for what she calls "body genres." She excludes from that category the comedy and the musical, for example, because we don't mimic specific characters in our bodily responses to those genres. But perhaps that's a good reason to expand, rather than limit, the category of "body genres" to include all films whose forms we mimic (and that mimic us). Laugh-out-loud comedies and toe-tapping musicals could be body genres in this larger sense. Indeed, every film, regardless of genre, evokes some kind of bodily response, even those films we find dull and uninspiring (the ones that "bore us to tears"). Viewers' responses to films are necessarily physical, full-bodied responses, because our vision is always fully embodied, intimately connected to our fingertips, our funny bones, and our feet, for example.

By stretching Williams's concepts of mimicry and empathy somewhat, we might take the discussion in a different direction. Beyond thinking of spectators' identification with characters as being too complex to be called mimicry, we could argue instead that mimicry is too complex to be only character-centered. That is, viewers' bodily responses to films might be mimicry in another sense: not mimicry of characters, but of the film itself. Perhaps viewers respond to whole cinematic structures—textural, spatial, or temporal structures, for example—that somehow resonate with their own textural, spatial, and temporal structures.

It may be possible to reframe this reversible relationship between the viewer's body and the film's body in terms of mimesis, which Laura Marks describes as "a form of representation based on a particular, material contact at a particular moment, such as that between a child at play and an airplane . . . , a moth and the bark of a tree . . . , or a Songhay sorcerer and a spirit. . . . Mimesis, in which one calls up the presence of the other materially, is an indexical, rather than iconic, relation of similarity."[3] Marks refers here to Frankfurt School philosopher Walter Benjamin, who described the mimetic faculty as an innate ability in humans to perceive and invent correspondences or similarities with objects.[4] His concept, Miriam Hansen writes, "envisions a relationship with nature that is alternative to the dominant forms of mastery and exploitation, one that would dissolve the contours of the subject/object dichotomy into reciprocity and the possibility of reconciliation."[5]

The mimetic faculty parallels in many ways the perpetual and reversible activity of perception and expression, for mimesis is an activity whereby a subject perceives an object and represents (or expresses) that object back to itself. Michael Taussig, in his reading of Benjamin's "On the Mimetic Faculty" essay, insists that that "what is crucial in the resurgence of the mimetic faculty" is precisely the "palpable, sensuous, connection between the very body of the perceiver and the perceived."[6] For me, what is crucial is the slipperiness of that very contact, for as Jennifer Deger claims in her own creative revision of the concept, "to try to pin mimesis down to a definitive definition is to miss the point—and the utility—of the concept."[7] All these descriptions of mimesis underpin my argument in this chapter that the film and viewer are in a relation of muscular empathy that is an oscillation between difference and similarity, proximity and distance. I want to spend this chapter exploring that odd but palpable sensation in the cinematic experience of feeling "there" with (and within) the film and "here," where I am.

This empathy between film and viewer isn't simply a matter of the viewer sharing a character's physical location by means of point-of-view shots and first-person narration, for example. It is instead a kind of empathy between our own body and the film's body that happens even in a non-narrative film or one without actors, for example. Our bodies orient and dispose themselves toward the body of the film itself, because we and the film make sense of space by moving through it muscularly in similar ways and with similar attitudes.

Our bodies' muscular empathy with the film's body emerges partly from experience. When the film swivels suddenly with a whip pan, or moves slowly with a long take or a tracking shot, or stretches itself out in widescreen to take in a vast landscape, we feel those movements in our muscles because our bodies have made similar movements: we have whipped our heads from side to side, moved slowly and stealthily, and stretched out our bodies in ways that are distinctly human but inspired by attitudes like those that inspire the film's movements. When the film "ducks" or "swerves" or "races" or "stalks" its subjects or "crashes" into something, we can relate, having performed many of these basic gestures ourselves, in our own way. Our responses to the film's body are a case of kinaesthetic memory, akin to the one described by Robert Frost, recalling a day at the ballpark:

> Americans would rather watch a game than play a game. Statement true or false? Why, as to these thousands here today to watch the game and not play it, probably not one man-jack but has himself played the game in his athletic years and got himself so full of bodily memories of the experience (what we farmers used to call kinesthetic images) that

he can hardly sit still. We didn't burst into cheers immediately, but an exclamation swept the crowd as if we felt it all over in our muscles when Boyer at third made the two impossible catches . . . that may have saved the day for the National League. We all winced with fellow feeling when Berra got the foul tip on the ungloved fingers of his throwing hand.[8]

The moviegoer, too, experiences a "fellow feeling" with the film's body, which moves in ways that our own bodies can recall. But an explanation of this empathy cannot rest here. There are at least two complications to consider. The first is that we do not perform our bodily movements the same way the film performs its own, for the obvious reason that our bodies are very differently built. Empathizing with the sting of Yogi Berra's fingers requires that we have fingers of our own that we can imagine being likewise stung. How does muscular empathy occur between two bodies as vastly different as the film's and the viewer's? The second complication is that we haven't always experienced the movements or activities that a film has, and yet we feel them anyway. How is it, for example, that we viewers can feel in our muscles the sensation of velocity while watching contemporary films whose computer-generated effects produce movements so much faster than our bodies have ever experienced?

The first complication can be addressed with a phenomenological definition of musculature. As with the previous chapter's definition of skin, the musculature isn't reducible to biology or mechanics; this chapter is not out to discover what constitutes a film's "biceps," for example. Rather, a body's musculature is defined by its expressive and perceptive functions. The musculature isn't a set of body parts that we have, but something through which we live and experience the world. In part, the musculature constitutes the "ecstatic" body, which in a happy coincidence conjures up a body leaping and flinging itself exuberantly into space, but which denotes, more modestly, any aspect of the body that we can employ consciously to do our bidding, to carry us toward the world and into our particular projects in that world.[9] The ecstatic body is the part of the body we can control consciously. It is no more expressive or perceptive than the recessive body, which comprises those parts of the body we *don't* control, and which is the topic of the next chapter, but the recessive and ecstatic aspects of the body are expressive and perceptive in very distinct ways. We can "perform" a gesture—a friendly wave or a nod of the head—in a way that we can't purposely "perform" goose bumps or a heart palpitation, for example. However, we may not always be conscious of our muscular movements and how others might perceive them. (We may send a very clear message by slouching, for example, and not even know it.) The musculature enables bodily comportment, and it gives us the means to express ourselves through our movements and the arrangement of our body in space. Swaggering, skulking, cowering, reaching, flinching, swaying, swerving, leaning, or simply standing upright, for example, all send messages about our place in and attitude toward the world and toward one another.

The film's and viewer's muscular bodies both function this way. But just as the viewer's and film's skins are constructed differently, from different materials and in different configurations, so the film's musculature differs from ours in fundamental, obvious ways. We comport ourselves by means of arms, legs, muscles, and tendons, whereas the film does so with dollies, camera tracks, zoom lenses, aspect ratios, and editing patterns, for example. We mark our position in relation to space by such things as shoulders and hips, whereas the film's "frame" is marked off by the edges of the celluloid strip, viewfinder, screen, and theater. Still, despite the differences, we and the film both present ourselves to the world by moving through it, carrying ourselves and arranging our bodies a certain way in relation to space and things.

What the previous chapter demonstrated holds here as well, that the film's body and spectator's body exist in a relationship of analogy and reciprocity. Though neither identical nor completely divergent, the film's body and the viewer's body are irrevocably related to one another. The film's body models itself on human styles of bodily comportment, and the viewer's body in turn might mirror the muscular behavior of the film's body. They are counterparts, their muscular behaviors inspired, imitated, and sometimes resisted by one another. Again, this similarity isn't one of physical make-up, for clearly my legs are not "like" a dolly any more than my eyes are "like" a camera lens. Rather, we exhibit likenesses in behavior and comportment and in the way we use the muscular body as a means of expression.

Sensuous empathy between an artwork and a spectator is not exclusive to the film experience. Long before the advent of cinema, Enlightenment thinkers posed that formal arrangements in art elicit emotional and muscular reactions. Nineteenth-century German art critic Robert Vischer described this phenomenon as *Einfühlung*, an empathy that goes both ways, from art object to viewer and vice versa.[10] One's body may swell when entering a large room, for example, and sway when it sees a tree being blown and bent by the wind.[11] These notions bear resemblance to Mikel Dufrenne's phenomenological description of the ways art objects and perceivers resonate with one another.[12] They also recall Eugène Minkowski's concept of "reverberation":

If, having fixed the original form in our mind's eye, we ask ourselves how that form comes alive and fills with life, we discover a new dynamic and vital category, a new property of the universe: reverberation (*reten-tir*). It is as though a well-spring existed in a sealed vase and its waves, repeatedly echoing against the sides of this vase, filled it with their sonority. Or again, it is as though the sound of a hunting horn, rever-berating everywhere through its echo, made the tiniest leaf, the tiniest wisp of moss shudder in a common movement and transformed the whole forest, filling it to its limits, into a vibrating, sonorous world.[13]

I begin from the assumption that this empathy exists also between film and viewer and manifests itself in the muscular movements and comport-ment and gestures of each.

In order to talk in more specific terms about cinematic and human mus-culature, we might think of film's and human's muscularity as they are focused in, and communicated through, gestures. Gestures are a muscular form of speech, for both humans and films. A gesture is an expressive bodily movement that is "intentional," in that it is directed toward a world, but not always "intended," in the sense of being consciously chosen and performed. In other words, a gesture may be a consciously enacted signal but need not always be. A conspiratorial wink constitutes a deliber-ate signal, for example, whereas a straightening of the shoulders (in the presence of an authority figure, say) may be expressive but not con-sciously so. Furthermore, gestures are never vague, although they may be ambiguous or ambivalent. They take specific forms and have specific meanings depending on their context. Their meaning depends upon situ-ation and style, that is, upon the "situation" in space and personal style of the body that makes them. Not only is my smile different from someone else's, but my wry smirk is also quite different from my smile of genuine, surprised pleasure, and even that smile may look different depending on my audience or my mood.

Films make gestures, too. A film expresses itself to the world through its muscular gestures, which take the form of specific cinematic devices or techniques, individually or in combinations. The film's gestures are a means of communication, the "words" and "phrases" of its body language. And like our own, its gestures are contextual, so that any given type of camera movement or cut does not always mean the same thing. The elab-orate, circular tracking shot in *Le crime de M. Lange*'s courtyard shooting scene (Jean Renoir, 1935) expresses something different from the one at the end of Michelangelo Antonioni's *The Passenger* (1975), for example. For a tactile film analysis to grasp the subtleties in a film's complex meaning, it must take into account the specific and contextual significance of its unique body language and gestures.

Every part of a film's muscular body can contribute to its expressive behavior and comportment. A film might plod along pensively with a slow tracking shot or long take; turn its back on something by cutting away from it; lean forward curiously with a forward-moving tracking shot; or proudly puff out its chest with the use of CinemaScope. A Steadicam shot sweeps along gracefully and confidently or lurks stealthily and with menace, whereas a scene shot by a wobbling hand-held camera might approach each corner trepidatiously, with palpable fear. Editing patterns work muscularly and expressively, too. Elsewhere I have pointed out a moment in Antonioni's *Chung Kuo China* (1972) in which the film is "taken aback" by a man's aggressive approach toward the camera.[14] The film moves back like a person whose personal space has been violated, a gesture that is in this case performed by a cut from a medium shot to an extreme long shot. It is important to note that these muscular acts of curiosity, stealth, and dismay aren't attributable to or performed by human characters in the movies; they are enacted by and expressive of the films themselves.

A film displays not only an attitude toward the world, but also toward its spectator. What Dufrenne writes of the aesthetic object in general is true of the film, that it "first manifests itself to the body, immediately inviting the body to join forces with it."[15] The film might beckon or embrace us, keep us at a distance, or push us away. It might push me forward when I dread to see what might be there, or it might hold me back when I'm desperately curious. John Ford's Westerns, for example, make both intimate, inclusive gestures using close, circular compositions that gather us into a community or a family, and expansive gestures using monumental wide-angle vistas that are like someone throwing their arms open to take in the whole scene, making us feel small and yet exhilarated amidst the vastness of the American landscape.

Smile, and the world smiles with you, it is said, but frown, and you frown alone. That's not entirely true, of course: a frown is a gesture enacted toward and perceived by a world. It exists in the meeting place between subject and object, an expression we throw out to the world for the world to "catch" and return to us in some form. Whether we frown purposefully or not, others see it, feel it, and respond to it (purposefully or not) with frowns of their own. Soon, everyone's frowning and no one knows why. Likewise, the film's gestures provoke a response from its viewers, who reflect and react to them with gestures of our own. Stealthy tracking shots at the beginning of a suspense film, for example, subtly encourage our own feelings of unease, long before the suspense story gives us a reason for feeling uneasy. We in turn express that unease with our own gestures: perhaps we tense our bodies, cross our arms protectively over our chests, or warily sink lower into our seats.

The response evoked by a filmic gesture is not a matter of "identification" in the way film theory has traditionally described it, as character-centered or camera-centered. There is room for many kinds of empathy within the film's and viewer's exchange of gestures. Stanley Kubrick's *The Shining* (1981), for example, contains a number of complicated gestures to which we might respond with equally complex gestures of our own. As Shelley Duvall's character searches for her husband in the vast and empty room he has taken for his writing studio, for example, the camera tracks very slowly alongside her. It gives the impression of searching, and as it passes behind structural posts and partial walls, we may lean to see around those things as we, too, search for something. A moment later, as the wife stands alone at her husband's abandoned desk and reads what he has produced, the camera again tracks very slowly behind the same posts and walls. This time, though, the gesture is menacing, because it has been divorced from her body and her intentions. As the camera lurks behind her, we may slouch nervously into our chairs, anticipating something horrible. Perhaps by cowering this way we are "identifying" with a character being stalked by the camera, but as we lean and crane our necks in order to "see" around the things behind which the camera lurks, we may also be "identifying" with the film itself in its act of stalking, for this act has not been attributed to any character. My point here is that the film's gesture—a repeated, slow-moving, surreptitious camera movement—demands a reply of some kind from the attentive spectator's body. It evokes a corresponding, but not predetermined, gesture from our bodies.

Gestures, it should be noted, are not always repaid in kind. Some people might see a frown and respond with a smile, in hopes of changing the other person's attitude. Viewers, too, can resist the pull of the film by means of specific gestures. A frenetic action film may move so fast as to throw us off, and we might respond by hanging on tightly to the edge of our seat, refusing to let go. The film might refuse to take us where we want to go, and so we may respond by leaning closer to the screen the way one prods a stubborn horse by inching oneself forward in the saddle. Such a moment occurs elsewhere in *The Shining*, when the couple's young son turns a corner and is startled by two ghostly murder victims standing eerily still at the end of a long hallway. The boy is paralyzed with shock, and so is the film, apparently.

In the shots immediately preceding this one, the camera had raced along with the boy as he rides his low-slung "Big Wheel" through the hallways, but now the camera refuses to move any closer to the vision at the end of the hallway. We can barely see these creepy girls, and we may find ourselves inching closer and closer, squinting hard at the screen, courageously trying to go where the film won't take us. The editing patterns during the remainder of the film continue this refusal of the film to look too closely: many of the characters' horrifying visions flicker by much too quickly for us to *get hold* of them and see what we need to see.[16]

Often, a film encourages a muscular gesture in the viewer and then expresses its empathy with us by performing the same gesture itself. This happens whenever a sound occurs off screen, cueing us to look (or, to want to look) in the appropriate direction of the image, only to have the film cut to a shot of the source of the sound. In a more elaborate example from *Touch of Evil* (Orson Welles, 1958), the aftermath of Janet Leigh's kidnapping is revealed to us in an extreme close-up of her face, but she appears upside-down. For a moment we may be tempted to twist our necks so as to identify her, and we might even do so. After a brief hesitation, the camera itself responds to that muscular inclination, slowly spinning and righting itself, as if on our behalf.[17]

The mimetic, empathetic relationship between film and viewer goes both ways. Psychologist and early film theorist Hugo Münsterberg argued that film's structures are based on human structures of perception, attention, memory, and imagination.[18] The close-up, for example, evolved as a result of viewers' need for a closer view, aesthetically and narratively speaking. What he didn't say explicitly is that our mental structures are embodied, borne out and at the same time inflected by our bodily behaviors (which are themselves embedded in culture and history). We want to see more closely, so we lean in, step forward, or crane our necks; it is those muscular movements that inspire the close-up, the zoom, and the crane shot, for example. Film and viewer share certain deep-seated muscular habits, beginning with the very tendency to move through the world in an upright position. We and the film are both inclined that way, as we are inclined to move and look forward, to face things directly. We are both disoriented when we're positioned otherwise, as evidenced by the tendency to rectify the situation with a gesture, such as the twisting of the neck and camera in the example from *Touch of Evil*. Likewise, it is our habit of turning our heads from speaker to speaker while following a conversation, for example, that gives impetus to the shot/reverse-shot editing pattern so often used in the filming of conversations. The film adopts our proprioception, the sense we have of our bodies in space; it may confirm it or thwart it by its own movements, but always it is indebted to it.

These similarities in comportment and inclination are both historical and immediate. In other words, humans' tendency to get a close look by moving physically closer inspired the historical development of the close-up, and also, in a more immediate sense, the viewer's desire for a better look at a particular face or object in a particular film inspires *that* film's cut to a close-up. Of course, the film inspires in us the very desire to see more closely, piquing our interest perhaps with a long shot that doesn't allow us to see something the film makes us want to see. But this is the nature of the reversibility that characterizes the subject/object and self/other relationship as described by Merleau-Ponty: in the touch of one body against the other, it becomes difficult to say who's touching, provoking, moving, and inspiring whom first.

The similarities between our movements and the film's are not necessarily a conscious effort on our part or on the film's part to mimic what we see and feel. Rather, this is an everyday experience, one described by phenomenologists as a normal part of our approach to the world. Hubert Dreyfus writes, for example, that "according to Merleau-Ponty, in everyday, absorbed, skillful coping, acting is experienced as a steady flow of skillful activity in response to one's sense of the situation. . . . One does not need a goal or intention to act. One's body is simply solicited by the situation to get into equilibrium with it."[19] The cinematic experience, when we're not thinking about it at some remove, can bear a striking resemblance to "everyday, absorbed, skillful coping." It solicits our bodily engagement and our responsive behavior, and we respond.

HERE AND THERE

Siegfried Kracauer described the immersive physicality of the film experience this way: "Film not only records physical reality but reveals otherwise hidden provinces of it, including such spatial and temporal configurations as may be derived from the given data with the aid of cinematic techniques and devices. The salient point here is that these discoveries . . . mean an increased demand on the spectator's physiological make-up. The unknown shapes he encounters involve not so much his power of reasoning as his visceral faculties. Arousing his innate curiosity, they lure him into dimensions where sense impressions are all-important."[20]

Beyond the notion that the film experience involves the senses at least as much as the intellect, I am interested here in the "lure" Kracauer describes, which I argue is not only visceral but also haptic and muscular. This "lure" is an invitation not only to press ourselves haptically against the film images but also to *inhabit* them. Film not only reveals "hidden provinces" of physical reality but also actually incorporates the viewer's body into these configurations (in some cases, only to eject us again).

We are invited and encouraged to commit ourselves to the film's space as well as our own, caught up "there" and "here" at the same time. We hitch ourselves to the film's body because we can, because it seems so easy, because the film's body moves in ways similar to ours. The empathy between the film's and viewer's bodies goes so deeply that we can feel the film's body, live vicariously through it, and experience its movements to such an extent that we ourselves become momentarily as graceful or powerful as the film's body, and we leave the theater feeling invigorated or exhausted, though we ourselves have hardly moved a muscle.

Alexander Sesonske, writing about cinematic space, aptly describes this phenomenon. "While seated in the theater we can at the same time be taken (visually) into the space of the film, see the action as from inside the space, move through it at great or little speed, be rejected or excluded from it. Some of our most vivid experiences of film occur in scenes where we seem to be deep inside the action-space and wholly immersed within the events of the film."[21]

Although for Sesonske, cinema space is a purely visual construct, it is not only visually but also tactilely "vivid." We don't entirely "lose ourselves" in the film space, of course: even as we are caught up in the encounter with the film's body, we never quite leave our own bodies behind and, in fact, could hardly relinquish our bodies' hold on the real world while watching movies, even if we wanted to. We are always still sitting in a movie theater, perhaps fidgeting in an uncomfortable seat, slightly aware of the smear of popcorn butter on our fingers, distracted by late-arriving patrons or the air-conditioned chill. These things remind us that we're always in our own body, after all, regardless of where the film and our attention to it—both mental and physical—might lead us.

However, tactile reminders of our place in the theater are not enough in themselves to keep us anchored in that single spot. Bodily sensations can be ambivalent and are subject to transportation and commutation. One's tactile sensations aren't necessarily bound by the physical limits of the body: they can be provoked by one's own bodily situation *and* that of the film's body. The feeling of my posterior in my theater seat exists alongside and in competition with such tactile sensations as the tumult my body feels during *Vertigo*'s vertiginous camera movement through the mission staircase in its climactic scene (Alfred Hitchcock, 1958), for example.[22] This is not to say that we aren't situated at all and are floating anchorless, but that we are *doubly* situated. We have the distinct feeling of being in two places at once, even if we never literally leave our seats.

Indeed, one could argue that our body *must* be caught up by and alongside the film's body, in order to "get" the film at all. If, as Merleau-Ponty attests, I comprehend space not objectively and theoretically, but by living in it, then if I am to comprehend filmic space at all, I must live quite literally in two places while watching a movie: my own and the film's.[23] We might return to the notion of the "ecstatic" body for a moment, for the etymology of "ecstatic" is revealing and relevant here: it is "the state of being 'beside oneself,' thrown into a frenzy or a stupor, with anxiety, astonishment, fear or passion."[24] Passionately invested in the spectacle of the film and in its muscular projects, we *are* "beside ourselves," existing in two places at once.

The phenomenon of feeling, if not being, physically in two places at once is a hallmark of the cinematic experience. Sesonske argues that as moviegoers, "we are very susceptible to becoming wholly absorbed in the object of our attention. . . . The slightest invitation will persuade us to abandon our ordinary lives and live wholly within the world of the film. Cinema space presents that invitation."[25]

The film experience is predicated upon a kind of "ambidexterity" of the body's self-perception. Take, for example, two seemingly contradictory, but in fact intertwined, phenomena. When I'm concentrating on something outside myself, like a film, I occasionally forget where I "left" my arm or my hand or my foot. Just looking down at it doesn't convince me that I've "found" it: I must wriggle my fingers to assure myself that what I'm looking at is really my own arm, for example. On the other hand, when a film surprises me with the sudden appearance of a villain in the frame, I jump back, even though there's nothing "here," in the theater, where I am, from which to jump back. The film experience rests on the viewer's simultaneous ability to *not feel where I am*, and to *feel where I am not*.

But the question remains, how is it that our experience of the film's bodily movements and the space in which it moves is so powerful, so *moving*? Why isn't the film experience just like passively watching somebody else do something? Why does it feel like we're doing it ourselves? If all the while I'm sitting safely in my theater seat, how is it that I actually jump when startled, lean closer during intimate scenes, tighten my shoulders during a close call, and cringe during brutal fight scenes? Merleau-Ponty gives us an answer in very simple terms when he writes that "my body is wherever there is something to be done."[26] This pertains to his description of spatial perception, but it applies to the cinematic experience as well. The film's and viewer's muscular gestures are responses to projects they have in the world; when we and the film are taken up in the same projects, we enact similar muscular movements, although they may differ in degree as well as form. In other words, we can enter the situation carved out by the film and lived by the film's body because that situation asks of us certain behaviors of which we're capable. "The body is no more than an element in the system of the subject and his world, and the task to be performed elicits the necessary movements from him by a sort of remote attraction."[27]

In everyday life, and in the film experience, we are able enter a situation even though we're at a physical remove from it, an ability Merleau-Ponty describes this way: "The normal person *reckons with* the possible, which thus, without shifting from its position as a possibility, acquires a sort of actuality."[28] The filmgoer "reckons with the possible" every time she sits in a movie theater and invests herself in the film, moving comfortably in and between the actual (her seat in the theater) and the possible (the space of the film). During the film experience, the spectator's body lives in two places at once, because she directs herself through her body toward her own space and the film's space at the same time.

This ability to commit our body to a situation at some remove from our own has everything to do with intentionality, that much is clear. If we can "identify" with muscular gestures of the film, and if we can mimic them or respond to them with our bodies, this is because the muscular movements of both viewer and film express a particular interest in and attitude toward the world. We empathize with the film's body not merely because we and the film are both muscular, expressive bodies, but also because we are invested in its projects, whether by inclination—by its very nature, for example, a film is engaged in the act of looking, and as filmgoers, we are hard pressed not to share the film's desire to look—or invitation—the film involves us narratively in specific projects, such as catching the criminal, winning the race, and getting the girl. When viewers and films share certain attitudes, tasks, or situations, they will move in similar ways. We and the film may approach the world curiously, aggressively, aimlessly, lazily, or fearfully, for example, and these attitudes will be expressed through the way we carry ourselves and through specific gestures.[29]

Merleau-Ponty describes a rendezvous between one's body and the world wherein "my actual body is at one with the virtual body required by the spectacle, and the actual spectacle with the setting which my body throws round it."[30] He refers here to a scientific experiment involving a kind of funhouse mirror that sends one's "right-side-up" surroundings into topsy-turvy oblique angles, but that spectacle bears a distinct resemblance to the film experience. In the experiment he describes, a subject is seated before a mirror image that reflects the room in which the subject sits. The mirror image is canted at 45 degrees, so that an object dropped to the floor seems to fall at a strange angle and a man walking through the room seems to lean to one side as he moves. At first, the experimental subject does not relate to the room reflected on the mirror. He is not "at home" in it, because its oblique orientation doesn't correspond to that of his own body. However, "after a few minutes, provided that he does not strengthen his initial anchorage by glancing away from the mirror, the reflected room miraculously calls up a subject capable of living in it. This virtual body ousts the real one to such an extent that the subject no longer has the feeling of being in the world where he actually is, and that instead of his real legs and arms, he feels that he has the legs and arms he would need to walk and act in the reflected room: he inhabits the spectacle."[31]

In this experiment, Merleau-Ponty writes, "I am borne wholly into the new spectacle and, so to speak, transfer my centre of gravity into it."[32] That delightful description suits the film experience perfectly. As the mirrored room rights itself to its viewer's eyes and body, so does cinematic space appear plausible and inhabitable because we live in it and because we orient our body toward it, because we assume its field and forces of gravity.

Indeed, the film experience is even more fully sensual than this experiment, thanks to the culminating effects of, for example, camera movements that sweep us up, editing that moves us, narrative that involves us, and sound that surrounds us. Hugo Münsterberg described the sensual and muscular component of cinematic spectatorship in similar terms, saying, "We feel that our body adjusts itself to the perception. . . . We hold all our muscles in tension in order to receive the fullest possible impression with our sense organs."[33]

The idea that the viewing subject might destroy the illusion by "strengthening his anchorage" in the room he physically occupies explains the need felt by some viewers to turn their heads away from a scene that threatens to overwhelm the senses, as a means of denying the film's ability to catch them up and sweep them into its space. This demonstrates the imbrication of vision and touch: it is the combination of our gaze at the movie screen and our muscular body's commitment to the film space that allows for our feeling of being there, and it is by looking away from it that we break the connection, because by looking away, we have disrupted our fully embodied relationship with the film. Interestingly, the crowd with whom we watch a film can be another "anchor" for our bodies away from the space of the film. When we all jump back in our seats or gasp aloud as a group, our attention is diverted from the screen to the theater, and we are each reminded of our situation *here*, with *these* people, in *this* room.

Another situation that sheds light on the film experience is that of psychic blindness, also described in detail by Merleau-Ponty. A psychically blind person is one who can't "just" perform a simple, abstract movement out of context. Psychically blind patients can only perform a movement by throwing their whole bodies into it, because the entire body is involved in every movement, and because any given movement is only significant, and only possible, as part of an intentional task. So, to cite examples from Merleau-Ponty, for a psychically blind person to mime "hair-combing," he would have to mime all parts of that task, including the holding of a mirror in the other hand. A psychically blind person couldn't simply mime a "salute" by raising a hand to one's forehead, but also must stand rigidly at attention while making the hand motion.[34] These examples, though pathological, do demonstrate one aspect of the normal state of being, which is that space isn't known to us except as it is lived and embodied. We inhabit space, and if we are able to map it, that mapping is possible only by understanding the way it is lived by us. Space is not experienced as a collection of abstract points in "objective" space, but as "a collection of possible points upon which this bodily action may operate."[35] In other words, the thing we call "space" is, like a certain credit card, "everywhere you want to be."

To a certain extent, the psychically blind person might appear to be like the filmgoer, who forgets herself momentarily and gives her body over to the film completely. But this is not to say that the average filmgoer is pathological. There's a crucial difference between the psychically blind patient and the "normal" person, which is that "the normal subject can immediately 'come to grips' with his body."[36] Whereas the psychically blind person can only experience the body as part of concrete set of actions (e.g., can only perform a "hair-combing" movement within the context of the actual act of hair-combing), the normal person can function in the abstract, can enjoy and control her body outside the context of literal and concrete actions. That is, the normal person never completely loses track of her body; she is able to maneuver and understand her body *both* in the context of its actual, daily activities *and* in imaginary, abstract contexts. The normal person moves comfortably in and between the actual and the possible. "In the case of the normal person, the body is available not only in real situations into which it is drawn. It can turn aside from the world, apply its activity to stimuli which affect its sensory surfaces, lend itself to experimentation, and generally speaking *take its place in the realm of the potential.*"[37] We viewers take our place in "the realm of the potential" in the act of going to the movies.

There are moments, however, when our own self-consciousness disrupts our graceful coexistence in the film's space (the "potential") and our own (the "actual"). Sesonske describes such disruptions as a painful surprise: "In a decent theater and with a good print, I think that our usual sense of our relation to the events of a film is that we see them from within the film's action-space. Usually a somewhat unpleasant shock occurs if we are thrust back into an awareness of our place in the normal place in the theater."[38] When we're startled by the surprise appearance of a villain, for example, we jump back in our seats as if we had been in the space we're watching on screen. But the actual gesture we make—the jumping back in our seats with surprise—may not be disruptive in and of itself. What *is* disruptive is the moment that immediately follows it: often, we laugh at ourselves, embarrassed at our own "gullibility," at having thrown ourselves into the film to such a degree. (Again, the crowd comes into play: it is having been seen by others in our moment of gullibility that embarrasses us.) In this moment, we are rendered inept, like the psychically blind person of whom Merleau-Ponty writes, "If his performance is interrupted, and he has the experimental situation recalled to him, all his dexterity disappears."[39] In the embarrassed filmgoer's case, our self-consciousness robs us of our own "dexterity." Up *until* the moment of that self-conscious "realization," we are confidently and comfortably "reckoning with the possible." But *at* the moment of realization, we are suddenly reminded of the common logic that says we can't be in two places at once. It is as if we have been caught playing a child's game of pretend, when we as adults know what's real and what's not, and that the two things are mutually exclusive. Our bodies believe—know, even—that it is normal to be in two places at once while watching a film, but received ideas interrupt that fluency and make us "slip up," and we admonish ourselves for having believed in our own fluency and fluidity in the first place. This recalls Merleau-Ponty's point about synaesthesia, which is that the act of reflection convinces us that the senses are separate, though direct experience tells us differently.

Nowhere has the film viewer's disorienting moment of self-consciousness been represented more aptly, and more comically, than in the figure of Wile E. Coyote, whose perpetual pursuit of Road Runner in the memorable Warner Bros. cartoons closely resembles the relationship between the viewer and the film. Coyote leaps and thrusts himself into "impossible"

7. *Fast and Furry-ous* (Charles M. Jones, U.S.A., 1949)

spaces and, miraculously, it works. He *does* defy gravity, but only for an instant before he realizes that he's entirely out of place, doing the impossible. It is that moment of realization that sends him plummeting to the ground with a crash, and it is the moment that lies precisely between delusion and realization that makes us laugh for, as Henri Bergson explains, "a comic character is generally comic in proportion to his ignorance of himself."[40] Bergson's theory of what's funny poses that the comic is a function of "rigidity of momentum," "mechanical inelasticity," and "absentmindedness," all of which come together to make a fool of the character whose wild enthusiasm for the object of his attention (which is elsewhere) sends him slipping on a banana peel or plummeting off the edge of a cliff.

Critic Richard Thompson calls Coyote's dilemma a function of the "intuitive/rational dynamic."[41] As long as Coyote's rational mind does not register that his body has stepped off the edge of a cliff, he can remain successfully suspended in mid-air. It is only when he stops to think about his (bodily) situation that he falls. "The Coyote is rigorously required . . . to become aware of his doom, to recognize and understand his fate, before it can occur."[42] His body is foiled by his mind, convinced only after the fact of the ridiculousness of its "situation." "He thinks, thus he loses," Thompson writes, "doomed by his own intellectuality."[43]

In Coyote's self-conscious look back at the camera just before he falls, we can see him thinking, "Damn. I've done it again." And he has our sympathy, for when we chuckle nervously after being startled by a suspense film, aren't we thinking the same thing? Coyote's predicament is very like the viewer's, characterized by the conflict between received ideas and lived experience. The viewer's bodily feeling of being simultaneously in the film's "potential" space and one's own "actual" space flies in the face of logic, which tells us we can only be in one place at any given time. Like Coyote, who has become so caught up in his desire to get the bird that he has flung himself into spaces where only Road Runner is "at home," we viewers invest ourselves so strongly in the projects, desires, and goals we have in the film's world (and that the film invites us to share) that we launch ourselves into it, only to be pulled out of the film space entirely by our self-conscious realization that "it's just a movie." We, too, are "doomed by our own intellectuality."

And yet, neither we nor Coyote can keep from launching ourselves into that "realm of the potential." As the film's body encourages our inclination to follow and move with it, so does Road Runner lure the eager Coyote to follow his lead. The attraction of Coyote for Road Runner is unswerving, despite the fact that Road Runner moves at unfathomable speeds and can defy gravity, momentum, two-dimensionality, and all the laws of physics, as Coyote cannot. Road Runner wildly surpasses the limitations of Coyote's body, as the film's body surpasses our muscular limitations, and yet we and Coyote never stop trying to catch up, to hang on, to go along for the ride.

Coyote and Road Runner's relationship is like ours with cinema also in the sense that it is a constant dialectic of attraction and repulsion, likeness and similarity. They are bound to one another despite (indeed because of) their differences. They seem to have established a romance, a contract, or a game, in which they both willingly participate. Every chase begins with the teasing lure by Road Runner, that impertinent "beep-beep" that Coyote is powerless to resist, though his attempts to catch the bird always fail. Like the film and the viewer, these two are inescapably tethered to one another, though they never quite come to terms.

That same inescapable connection exists between the film and viewer, and it is likewise characterized by a dialectic between invitation and rejection, or between envelopment and estrangement.[44] This dialectic includes moments where we and the film are in perfect harmony, inhabiting a shared space as comfortably as winning contestants in a three-legged sack race. Other times, there is resistance. The film might drag us along while we try to pull away during scenes that are "too much," emotionally or sensually. Conversely, harrowing chase scenes see the film pushing us away, flinging us out of its spaces while we try desperately to hang on and to pull ourselves back into the space of the film. Critics and producers describe exactly this phenomenon when they lure us to summer blockbusters with promises of "the ride of your life" or an "action-packed jump-out-of-your-seat thrill ride."[45]

The muscular envelopment and estrangement of film and viewer can take any number of forms—consensual, forced, tentative, playful, erotic, hostile. In any case, this reciprocal relationship is always lived out by means of specific gestures. What follows is a study of two particular gestures that occur between the film and the viewer: the handshake and the chase. (The chase, of course, consists of many separate gestures, which will be discussed, but it is treated here as a meaningful gesture in itself.) The choice of these two gestures is driven first by the fact that they are by nature reciprocal. Each involves two bodies that mimic one another's muscular behavior, and each gesture is at once an expression and a perception, in the sense that a handshake is an acceptance of and response to another's overture, just as to chase someone is to respond to their movements with similar movements of one's own. In both cases, too, the movements of one body or the other are meaningful not in themselves but together, as part of a larger whole. Second, these gestures are both reflective of the dialectic of envelopment and estrangement that characterizes the film experience as a whole, in ways that will be explained further on.

So far, our muscular empathy with the film has been discussed in very general terms (the movie experience as a whole) and very specific terms (examples of particular gestures). But we must not lose sight of the forest for the trees, or vice versa. The point to all of this is to appreciate the thematic, narrative, and emotional significance of the muscular empathy between film and viewer and to understand its usefulness for film analysis. After all, we don't empathize with cinema just in theory but in the experience of individual films. In what follows, the handshake and the chase will each be discussed within the context of a specific body of films. For the handshake, I've chosen certain Buster Keaton silent comedies, and for the chase, I've chosen several contemporary action films in which the chase scene is a central focus. Both Keaton films and chase films explicitly emphasize the muscular aspect of performance and spectatorship alike, and both tend to evoke feelings of invitation and expulsion, luring and letting go,

though the dynamics are different for each body of films. Keaton's comedies seem to emphasize gestures of connection and agreement, whereas the
chase films delight in throwing us off, but both exhibit a balance between
gestures of both types.

Scholars and critics have approached Keaton's comedies and contemporary action films from any number of directions, but this chapter emphasizes the importance of a sensual understanding of the themes and attitudes
of these films. Their themes come across visually and intellectually of
course, but I'd like to offer an approach that not only addresses the visual,
aural, and narrative aspects of the film experience but also embraces the
sensual, wholly embodied relationship between these films and their spectators. We *feel for* Keaton's earnest characters and the frantic heroes of
chase films precisely because we *feel with* them. Our emotional sympathy
for them derives from our muscular empathy with them, and so to take a
sensual approach to the analysis of these films is to grasp their meanings
and their significance more fully than a strictly aesthetic, narrative, thematic, psychological, or historical approach might do, for example.

This is not to say that an analysis that foregrounds the sensual aspects
of the experience of these films is one that dismisses such concerns as narrative, theme, psychology, and history. Rather, this approach should simply
remind us that those aspects of a film cannot be separated from—indeed,
are conveyed and understood through—our sensual, muscular experience
of the films. An historical comparison of Keaton's chase films and contemporary chase films, for example, might make the point that both bodies of
films respond to a particular notion of "modern life." Keaton has trouble
keeping up and is constantly bewildered by the rules and laws of the world
around him; in the face of a hostile, mechanistic world that would seem to
leave no room for him, he succeeds just barely, and only by perseverance
and luck. The contemporary chase film, with its emphasis on fast machines
and faster digital effects, exacerbates its audience's feeling of being out-
paced by a world in which instant messaging and fast food are *de rigueur*,
even as it gives us the means, however illusory and temporary, of keeping
up. I hope to show that an historical study of Keaton's comedies and chase
films, for example, would benefit from an understanding of exactly how we
experience such phenomena as velocity and gravity, which are so much a
part of the way the films make sense to us.

My analysis of several Keaton comedies and contemporary chase films
is meant to demonstrate the extent to which the films' themes are
expressed and perceived in sensual, muscular terms. To "get" these films is
to "grasp" them, literally as well as intellectually. Keaton's successes in

"fitting in" are made all the more poignant and funny because we feel his close calls muscularly: our body tenses up and then releases once he's safe and the film has reached equilibrium. This empathy is not just character-based: his films make and nearly miss connections just as he does, and we empathize with the films themselves. Chase films, too, are thrilling precisely because of the muscular invitation they extend to us. They lure us in and take us along for the ride at first, before threatening to shake us off. Chase films (particularly those of the digital era) are like Road Runner himself, "beep-beeping" their cheeky contempt of our plodding, all-too-human slowness. Like Coyote, we persevere, perversely keen on the abuses and humiliations we must suffer as we try to hang on and catch up to a film we know will outrun us. We understand these films, as we do all films, sensually and muscularly as well as emotionally and intellectually. And though all films are muscular in the way they express themselves, these films are especially so.

A TENUOUS GRASP

The handshake is a gesture of agreement, or of attempt at agreement. It is a muscular gesture of two bodies coming to terms with another, terms that might be legal, financial, sportsmanlike, or purely moral. Through the handshake, we display our mutual recognition of one another's subjectivity and the similarities between us. Even if we are members of opposite teams, for example, by shaking hands, we agree to overlook our differences in the service of a larger goal. In this way, the handshake at its most basic is a gesture of reciprocity.

Jean-Paul Sartre described the meeting of one's gaze with another's as a hostile and threatening experience. In the act of being seen, one's own subjectivity is pitted against another's. In Sartre's world, we are victims of the look.[46] Merleau-Ponty, however, was more interested in the notion of "co-being," which includes the possibilities of the hostility and alienation described by Sartre but also the possibilities of love and mutual respect.[47] His philosophy of the gaze suggested that when two subjects look at one another, they alternate between the roles of seer and seen. Indeed, if we combine Merleau-Ponty's view of the intersubjectivity inherent in the act of looking with his metaphor of one hand touching the other, we arrive at the handshake. To overcome the feeling of alterity with a stranger whose gaze meets ours, we might shake hands upon meeting, as if by grasping another's hand we recognize the other person and try to establish some basic agreement: "you and I are both in and of this world." The handshake is a gesture of co-being, of complicity, of agreement and acceptance, of "fitting in."

The handshake isn't always successful, of course. Occasionally it is awkward or overmatched or insincere. The "cold fish" handshake expresses a lack of conviction in the shared similarities between two people, perhaps because one has disdain for the other. A handshake in which one hand threatens to crush the other may reveal a misunderstanding of the shared similarities—one person might not "know his own strength"—or a lack of conviction in the agreement entered into, which one or both persons try to disguise as enthusiasm. A handshake can even be completely false, as in the trick of extending one's hand to another but pulling it back at the last moment. That fake handshake is a gesture of complete alienation, a parody of agreement and connection.

Moreover, and more simply, the handshake is a gesture of mimicry, each body moving toward another in roughly the same way, extending a hand in a matched, if reversed, gesture that meets in the middle. Each participant mirrors the movements of the other, and each individual movement is meaningless except as a part of the whole, unified gesture, the handshake as performed by two bodies moving similarly but in opposite directions.

Our empathy with the film's body can be considered a kind of handshake. We extend our bodies to the film, and it extends its body to us simultaneously, and in doing so, we agree on certain terms. We commit ourselves to the film's world without ever abandoning our own world, for the limits of our bodies are never forgotten or confused in the handshake. We know where "we" end and the other begins. Again, the film and the viewer "extend a hand" in decidedly different ways. The act can be performed in a variety of different ways by the film, such as through inclusive blocking and inclusive camera movements, close-ups, match-cuts—in short, nearly any cinematic device that makes it easy for us to move *with* the film's body. For the viewer's part, we may perform this gesture by leaning close, by relaxing our shoulders, or by stretching or straightening in response to a vast landscape shot or expansive camera movement, for example. Regardless of the mechanical or biological form the movement takes, when the film and the viewer "shake hands," it is a mutual gesture of reciprocity, mimicry, and some degree or style of agreement. The handshake between film and viewer can, of course, be as tenuous, superficial, insincere, or incommensurate as human handshakes can be.

The desire to connect, fit in, and come to an agreement with the other and with the world finds its perfect representation in Buster Keaton. "If he seems the loneliest of all comedians, it is because he's the one to whom companionship matters the most," writes Gilberto Perez in an especially thoughtful essay on the man he calls "the bewildered equilibrist." "If all comedians are outsiders, Keaton is the outsider who will not give up the attempt to join in, to connect with others," Perez writes. "Buster is unique in earnestly seeking a genuine togetherness."[48] Perez describes Keaton's comedy as stemming from his heartfelt desire to fit into the world and its systems—spatial, physical, logical, geometric, and gravitational, as well as cultural, social, emotional, and even historical. Keaton is invested in the world he tries to fit into because he has a project there: to win the war, solve the mystery, get the footage, steer the ship. Almost always, these projects are subsumed under a larger goal: to get the girl. It is the girl who defines, explicitly or not, the challenges that Buster must meet if he is to win her affections and a place in the world she represents.

Keaton's earnest attempts to fit in are precisely what make him stand out. Perez describes the comedian's unique brand of brilliant conformism by referring to Robert Bresson's statement that originality is the failed attempt to do the same as everybody else.[49] Keaton's strokes of genius are usually undertaken in a humble attempt simply to get the job done and to do what's expected of him. He can't seem to do things according to convention, and so he must take unusual measures just to keep up and fit in. For reasons unfathomable to him, for example, his character in *The General* (1925) is prohibited from joining the Southern army as his girlfriend wishes him to do, and so he must stretch his imagination to prove his heroism. He employs his ingenuity not for show, but to survive and save face.

Keaton's triumphs are never resounding celebrations of his wit and prowess; they are always uneasy. He may win his sweetheart with cleverness and courage, or by sheer coincidence; either way, his success is fragile. He barely makes every deadline, fits into awkward spaces with not an inch to spare, and relies an awful lot on luck. We sympathize with his desires, admire his perseverance, and cheer his every triumph, but all the while we know he could just as easily fail. In this respect, while Keaton does succeed in holding fast to the world around him, his films emphasize the tenuousness of the agreement between himself and the world around him.

The opening scene of *The General* articulates this pervasive theme of "fitting in" and "measuring up," which is attributed here not to Keaton himself but to two young admirers. The boys, who are enthralled with the idea of being a train engineer like the one Keaton plays, tap Keaton on the shoulder. He turns, and they each extend a hand for him to shake, which he does. He then turns away again and crouches to inspect something on the train, and the boys crouch right alongside him. A moment later, Keaton stands and waves to the crowd of disembarking passengers, and the boys do exactly the same. Once finished with his duties, Keaton walks through town toward his sweetheart's house, and the boys follow close behind him, doffing their hats as he does to passersby. As these boys mimic Keaton, so Keaton does his best to look and act like everyone else and to play the role expected of him. Another handshake in *Steamboat Bill, Jr.* (1928), this time between Keaton's college boy and his estranged father, is a less successful and more awkward gesture than that between Keaton and the two boys, but it is no less earnest. Father and son don't agree on anything, as quickly becomes clear, but in that first meeting, Keaton gamely extends his hand, a display of his genuine attempt to fit in, to be "family" and familiar. In *College* (1927), Keaton meets the rowing crew of which he has just been named the captain, much to the sailors' dismay. He extends his hand gamely across the table around which the antagonistic athletes sit and is promptly dragged across its surface every which way by their mocking, too-vigorous handshakes. He winds up lying prostrate like a torch singer on a grand piano; from this position, he meekly offers his hand to the disgusted coach.

The "handshake" in Keaton's films is rarely a matter of literal handshakes between Keaton and another character, however. More often, the "handshake" takes place more generally between Keaton and the world around him and is performed with his entire body. As Keaton fits his body into and against his surroundings, his "comedy of kinetics" draws a muscular response from his audience.[50] Like a human version of Felix the Cat, Keaton expertly adapts his body to his strange surroundings and vice versa. Sometimes this adaptability is a matter of genius, as when, in *One Week* (1922), he perfectly matches his rubbery, acrobatic body to the idiosyncratic angles and unpredictable behavior of the house he's struggling to build. More often, though, his success is a matter of luck, as when a cyclone-blown house façade falls over an unsuspecting Keaton in *Steamboat Bill, Jr.*, only to leave him standing squarely in the tiny space left by an open window. Watching these scenes, the viewer is at once tensed with the apprehension and graced with the dexterity that Keaton's body expresses in his efforts. We feel and express a muscular empathy with him in all kinds of situations: as the house falls over him, we may find ourselves hunching our shoulders, drawing our bodies inward as if to make ourselves a little smaller; as he races around the house leaping onto mismatched balconies and stairways, we may jump and swerve empathetically, however slightly, in our seats; and his narrow escapes and successes leave us feeling relieved and perhaps a bit nimbler than before. His agility and amazing good fortune seem to rub off on us, and as Peter Parshall writes, "the suppleness of his movement creates a sense of kinesthetic freedom in the audience."[51]

We feel for Buster Keaton a deep empathy, not just because he's the underdog, but also because even before we identify with his character, our bodies identify with his body's attempts to "fit in." As filmgoers, we seek what he seeks, to fit into the world (the film world, in this case) as a geographical, physical, geometrical, and muscular space. We fit ourselves into the space the film carves out for itself and for us, and when Keaton performs his amazing acrobatic feats and manages to catch hold and cling fast to the world around him, we are exhilarated by his success in doing what we would like to do ourselves.

"Whether it is a question of another's body or my own, I have no means of knowing the human body other than that of living it, which means taking up on my own account the drama which is being played out in it, and losing myself in it."[52] Merleau-Ponty's words refer to the way we know the human body, but could as easily refer to the way we know the film's body. We have no way of knowing the film's body except by living it and losing ourselves in it, and that's just what Keaton does in *Sherlock, Jr.*, a film that concerns itself explicitly with the tenuous grasp in which the film and the spectator hold one another. Keaton's situation, as the projectionist who falls asleep and dreams himself onto the screen and into the role of consummate detective and romantic hero Sherlock, Jr., is fanciful enough to be the stuff of great comedy but is actually very close to what we spectators go through in every moviegoing experience. As projectionist, spectator, star, and director at the same time, Keaton expresses the filmgoer's desire to "fit" with the film, to make ourselves commensurate with it, and he succeeds on our behalf.

In other films, he's trying to fit into a social or physical world, but in *Sherlock, Jr.*, Keaton attempts to fit into the *film's* world, specifically and explicitly. As the awkward and unsophisticated projectionist, Keaton reads up on "How to Be a Detective" in hopes of impressing the girl who has jilted him due to a misunderstanding. When he falls asleep in the projectionist's booth, his dream-self attempts to make his way into the film that he had been screening before he fell asleep, a detective film and romance titled *Hearts and Pearls*. He is literally in two places at once, his body doubled as one Keaton remains asleep beside the projector and the other Keaton wanders toward and into the film-within-the-film. In this dual-situation of his body, Keaton stands in for us: he is our stunt-double. Once he is firmly ensconced in the film-within-a-film, he lives not only in his own body but also *in the body of that film,* and in cheering his efforts, we celebrate our own ability as filmgoers to live in two places at once.

After the dejected projectionist falls asleep, a specter rises from him: it is Keaton himself in superimposition. This specter leaves the projection booth and takes a seat in the theater to watch the film that's playing. That he appears first in superimposition makes sense both logically and phenomenologically: at that moment he hasn't found his way into the film, hasn't committed himself to it with his whole physical being, and so he's not entirely embodied. Only later, when he enters the physical space of the film and meets it on its own terms, does he appear as flesh, blood, bone, and muscle.

In this early scene, which recalls *Uncle Josh at the Picture Show,* Keaton takes offense at the treatment of the female heroine of *Hearts and Pearls* and launches himself bodily into the film several times to defend her honor. His efforts are met with varying degrees of failure and success. His first attempts are presented in a long shot from the rear of the theater, with the screen as proscenium in the upper center of the frame and the audience and organist visible below. Keaton, seated toward the front of the theater in his recognizable porkpie hat, jumps up to the stage above which the screen hangs and leaps into the action, only to be tossed on his ear by the man in the "film." (This conflation of "stage" and "screen" is accomplished by a neat and still impressive trick of mise-en-scène that makes a single plane of action appear to be two.) Keaton has no more success than Uncle Josh does, and the scene's presentation as a proscenium set accentuates his *difference* from the film: it is large and he is small, his distance from it marked clearly as a matter of planes.

Of course, Keaton perseveres. He leaps again into the frame and this time manages to stay there, on screen. But his balance in that space is a fragile one, because the film attempts to "shake him off" by changing scenes every few seconds, forcing Keaton to adjust his body to the new locations provided by each scene. The steps leading up to the house of the woman he plans to rescue are transformed in a single cut to a small stool in a garden. As he begins to sit, the scene changes and he finds himself dodging traffic in a busy street. As he turns to walk down the sidewalk, it becomes a mountain cliff, and he catches himself just before stepping to his death. With another edit, Keaton is surrounded by lions; yet another cut finds him in a desert, nearly run down by a speeding train. As he sits on an earthen mound to ponder his predicament, another edit renders the mound an island over which a huge ocean wave crashes. Diving into the water, he finds himself upended in a snow bank; a moment later, leaning against a tree in this wintry scene, he is returned to the garden and the small stool. The stool is too short for leaning against, and Keaton falls again. It is a virtuoso demonstration of the match-on-action, and Keaton deals with the rapid location changes with characteristic aplomb. He is successful, but only barely, in his attempts to stay in the film, to adjust his bodily movements to changing scenery that threatens to dislocate him, quite literally. His balance and his footing are never really confident because he doesn't truly belong in this space. His out-of-placeness is underscored throughout this sequence by the persistence of the proscenium stage setting, which sets the screen apart from the "real world," the theater where Keaton belongs. The screen itself is a foreign land, as are the locales it depicts, and Keaton is not "at home" there, in any sense of the word. In this scene, he becomes what Andrew Horton calls a "victim of film language."[53]

As the film goes on, however, Keaton overcomes this threat of dislocation and makes himself comfortable inside the world of the film. This change is marked by the fade to black at the end of the scenery-jumping scene. When the image fades up again, the proscenium setting is gone and we and Keaton are actually *in* the film. The frame of the film screen is no longer set off from the "real" world of the theater and stage in which we and he had belonged before. Now, the film-within-a-film has expanded to become *the* film; its frame has become the whole frame. Our vision and the film's vision are now neatly matched: our field of vision is the same as the frame for the duration of this film-within-a-film.

The first shot of Keaton following this transformation is a close-up of his gloved hand reaching for the doorbell to the very same house from which he had been violently ejected in the previous scene. This shot recalls a familiar image from serial adventure films: the hero has just fallen over the cliff during a fierce battle and the audience sits in breathless astonishment, unable to believe he's really gone. Then, in a close-up of the cliff's edge, the hero's hand appears from the edge of the screen, reaching and clawing desperately for a firm hold with which to pull himself up. The audience breathes a collective sigh of relief and applauds the hero's temerity. A close call, indeed.

Keaton's hand reaching for the doorbell functions the same way. Although the changing scenery threatened to dislodge him from the film altogether, he appears to have scrabbled his way into the film's world at last. And his hold is fast: Keaton stays "in" this new film—the detective film *Hearts and Pearls*—until the final scene of *Sherlock, Jr.* He now dresses the part and walks the walk that allows him to be welcomed into the scene as the detective who will solve the case that baffles everyone else.

Keaton heroically pulls off this act of "fitting in" and plays the part of the detective with grace and dexterity. Whereas in the scenery-jumping sequence, he had barely managed to escape the dangers into which the film had thrown him with each successive cut, this time around, as Sherlock, Jr., he deftly avoids every trap laid for him by the villains.

Whereas Keaton the projectionist (an amateur detective himself) had utterly failed to trail the rival who framed him for theft (and who "de-framed" him by throwing him "off screen" and into the audience during Keaton's first attempt to get himself into the film), in this new guise of detective and with his new comfort level in the film's world, he steadfastly follows his man. In one scene that displays an astonishing combination of acrobatic skill and precision engineering typical of Keaton's best stunts, he walks to the edge of a rooftop on which he has been stranded by his arch-enemy and grabs a railroad crossing gate that stands upright near the side of the building, reaching up to the roof. As the gate drops into place on the track, it neatly deposits Keaton into the backseat of the oblivious villain's getaway car. If Keaton the projectionist had exhibited a tone of desperation in his scenery-jumping sequence, Keaton the detective executes this move with the utmost cool. Safely ensconced in the getaway car, he puts his feet up on the seat and relaxes. He makes it look easy.

For Keaton's projectionist, as for us, the experience of the film is a fully embodied one. He launches himself into the film and feels not only the weight of it on his shoulders and under his feet but also the weightlessness of it in his graceful leaps through space and time. He doesn't just watch the film, he lives it, enters into it, and "shakes hands" with it. Keaton's suave sophistication and confidence inside *Hearts and Pearls* registers not only in his body language but also in the film's body language: it seems to feel as comfortable with him as he does with it. Once Keaton enters it fully, the film-within-the-film mimics cinematically the newfound mobility and gracefulness of Keaton's cinema-savvy alter ego. Peter Parshall accurately notes that whereas the framing film about the bumbling projectionist consists largely of static shots punctuated by straight cuts, *Hearts and Pearls* is characterized by smooth and competent tracking shots, for example.[54] Indeed, the swiftness and surety of *Hearts and Pearls*, like that of its detective hero, is palpable.

In a particularly memorable sequence, Keaton as Sherlock, Jr. finds himself on the handlebars of a driverless motorbike on which he races madly through a vast array of settings, blithely and narrowly escaping disaster at every turn. This wild ride begins in a residential neighborhood, then passes through a busy downtown area, past a ditch being dug, through a wooded picnic area where he interrupts a game of tug-o'-war, over an unfinished bridge, through a rail yard, and ends finally in the remote cabin where the damsel in distress has been hidden away. The sequence cuts from location to location as did the scenery-jumping sequence early on, but here, Sherlock, Jr. and the film itself transcend the limits of space gracefully. (Notably, too, this sequence is part of the narrative, rather than a sequence that doesn't "fit in" to the rest of the film-within-a-film; the sequence is integrated more smoothly than was the scenery-jumping scene.) Not only does he manage to hang on, but he's absolutely nonplussed by these events, as the projectionist hadn't been in the scenery-jumping sequence. He's positively masterful in his ability to mimic and move *with* the film's body now, no longer tossed around by it willy-nilly. Interestingly, though, Keaton's confidence wavers when he realizes the driver is missing. At that moment, he loses his composure and very nearly his balance, too. Once again, his experience evokes that of the filmgoer, for like Keaton and Wile E. Coyote, we spectators lose our dexterity when we become self-conscious about the experience of being in two places at once.

Whereas, in his first attempts to get inside the film, the projectionist's body is flummoxed by the cinematic configuration of time and space, Sherlock, Jr. dives into purely cinematic spaces and doesn't come up for air; he *lives* there, in the cinema, for the most part unself-consciously. Two sequences in particular demonstrate his ability to hitch himself, as viewers do, to the film's body. In the first, Keaton infiltrates the villains' hideout in disguise, confronts them, and yet escapes unnoticed. He does this first by setting a large round box containing a woman's dress in the window of the villain's cabin. He then allows himself to be dragged by the villain's henchmen into the hideout, where he learns the details of the villain's kidnapping plot. As he enters the hideout, the long shot of the building itself (in which only the window and external wall of the hideout are visible) dissolves into the same set-up, but now the external wall has been cut away, making visible the interior, the window, and the exterior. This full view seems momentarily awkward, until Keaton launches a dramatic escape by somersaulting through the window, the box, and the woman's dress in a single motion and in a single shot. He emerges on the other side, now disguised as a woman, and saunters away, unrecognized by the henchmen who scramble in confusion.

The dissolve from partial view to full view of the building preserves the whole space and the integrity of the stunt in such a way that allows us to appreciate the fluidity of Keaton's athletic performance. What's interesting here is that Keaton's agility is marked by a special effect (the dissolve to the cutaway set) that seeks to show everything and hide nothing. The trickery is in Keaton's athleticism and the blocking and choreography of the event, not in the film technology per se. Indeed, the editing and mise-en-scène of this scene are designed to downplay cinematic illusion, to preserve the space of the action; this stunt would be equally impressive on a vaudeville stage. Keaton is one with the film's mise-en-scène in this moment, and it is perfectly matched to and illustrative of his acrobatic skill, which, indeed, he developed on the vaudeville stage.

However, Keaton also shows himself to be equally at home *inside* cinematic illusion, in the world created by lightning-quick editing and *trompe l'oeil* set pieces. Whereas the previous stunt shows his amazing finesse in "real," three-dimensional space, a later stunt displays his muscular affinity for the film medium proper. In this scene, which finds Keaton being pursued by the henchmen, his faithful assistant provides an escape route so bizarre that even Keaton is disbelieving at first. The assistant, who is dressed as a woman, carries around his neck a display case of men's ties; he points to the case and suggests by pantomime that Keaton jump inside. As Keaton's pursuers round the corner, the assistant backs against a fence and Keaton charges towards him, dives into the case, and disappears. The assistant then steps forward and the henchmen are left scratching their heads. This scene is jaw-dropping not solely because of Keaton's physical prowess, but because of the invisibility of the edit that makes the illusion possible. In this stunt, Keaton's body jumps not just through space, as he had done in the previous sequence, but also through time. His movements are as nimble as those of the editing and projection.

And don't we do the same thing, when we follow seamlessly a film's progression from cut to cut without wavering or losing our balance? Haven't we also learned to keep up and fit in? The difference between the projectionist's flailing ineptitude when he jumps into the film and Sherlock, Jr.'s astonishing agility and confidence seems to correspond to the historical development of the viewer's own muscular relationship with cinematic time and space. During the scenery-jumping scene early in the film, Keaton is not quite fluent and can just barely keep up. So it was with early cinema audiences, who had yet to learn the ways of the cinema and to adjust their bodies to the film's body.

It is not by coincidence, I think, that the early scene in the theater recalls *Uncle Josh at the Picture Show*, for in many ways Keaton's projectionist resembles the widely held impression (but not necessarily historical fact) of early cinema's "naïve spectator." The film does not explicitly invoke this historical time difference, but in the cross-cutting between real life and dream life in this film, the projectionist is associated with naïve presexual adolescence (witness his charmingly innocent awkwardness with the girl) and early cinema (certain details of the mise-en-scène in the theater scenes, including the curtains and the seats, suggest that this may be a former vaudeville theater that's been converted into a cinema). Sherlock, Jr., on the other hand, is associated with suave, sexual adulthood and the narrative feature film. He is so familiar with genre conventions that he dresses the part and doesn't need a primer on "how to be a detective" like the one the young projectionist is reading on the job in his first appearance on screen. Over the course of *Sherlock, Jr.* the projectionist seems to grow up a bit and he begins to get his feet under him, both emotionally and cinematically.

Of course, film scholars have reconsidered—as myth, legend, cultural bias, and/or historical misperception—accounts of early cinema spectatorship that characterize (and caricature) early filmgoers as gullible, incompetent, panicked and overly credulous. As early as 1902, after all, *Uncle Josh at the Picture Show* addressed a viewer sophisticated enough to "get the joke" about naïveté in the face of cinematic illusion and to laugh at themselves—or, more likely, to laugh at "other" viewers, those of a different class and cultural status who ostensibly lacked such sophistication.[55]

The final scene demonstrates the projectionist's tenuous dual position in both the film-within-the-film and in his own space, so similar to the dual position we occupy as spectators. When the projectionist's girlfriend arrives at the theater to make amends with him, Keaton moves to kiss her, but he looks to the film screen for inspiration. From his projection booth, Keaton gazes straight ahead at the screen, emulating the hero of *that* film, who holds his lover in a suave and artful embrace. Framed in the perfect square of his projection booth, though, Keaton looks out at us, too, from his place as the hero of *this* film. He is doubly situated, framed in a square within a rectangle, in his own space and in the film's space at the same time.

There exists a crucial difference between Keaton's projectionist and the spectator, however. We do indeed experience film with a physical immediacy akin to what the projectionist feels during his dream. Like him, we inhabit the film in a very real sense, although his experiences are exaggerated. But our physical inhabitation of the film's space doesn't require sleep or fantasy, nor do we ever completely forget or lose our hold on our bodies as one does in a dream-state. Instead, our transportation into the film's world while firmly rooted in our own is, as I have stated, a matter of being in two places at once. Rather than a dream-state or fantasy, which implies fallacy, confusion, illusion, and incompetence, our situation is one of actual co-habitation, competence, dexterity, a natural state of being, and a "genuine" experience that only seems false once we stop to think about it. In a dream/fantasy, we *mistakenly* believe we can occupy "that space there." But in the experience of film, we *can* and *do*, because "that space there" is a fully embodied, inhabitable possibility.

In an essay that explores the ontological questions raised by *Sherlock, Jr.,* Garrett Stewart addresses the notion of distance and proximity between spectator and screen. "What I think we feel about the impossibility of stepping through the screen frame into the movie," he writes,

> is not so much that the screen would stop us, as that once through it there would be nothing there to inhabit or accost but unbodied illuminations. And so the viewing imagination is gripped by perhaps the ultimate illusory myth of cinematic manifestation: that screen people are closer to sculptures in light than to a veneer of reflection. We know we cannot touch them, yet when Buster does so it causes more of a rent in our aesthetic common sense than a tear in the white sheet of screen, which is not intuited by us in the midst of our voyeurism as an opaque scrim so much as a bordering and a threshold.[56]

Stewart's argument turns on that phrase, "we know we cannot touch them." We do *know* the impossibility of stepping into the movie and touching the figures inside it, but I would argue that we don't *feel* that impossibility as we're watching the film; we realize it only after the fact. The disbelief on our part is a function of reflection. If we really felt this way, movies wouldn't move us. We may think this way in our self-conscious moments, but the actual experience of a movie isn't always self-conscious and reflective, which is something Stewart himself attests earlier in the essay. The viewing imagination is "gripped," as he says, but it is important to note, as Stewart does not, that when the film grips us, it is a sensual experience, not solely a reflective, cognitive one. His argument suggests that our disbelief is suspended over the edge of common sense. "Common sense" usually refers to those things we all would know if we stopped to think, but there's another kind of "common sense" at play here, which is our bodies' prereflective sense that we belong up there, in the film, because it beckons us with its movements and contours and projects. It is this more literal "common sense" that allows us to be moved by the movies, and this "common sense" is embodied and intuitive, not reflective and objective. We don't experience the flat screen as flat unless and until we think about it, and when we're watching movies, we're not always thinking about it. What we *feel* about the (im)possibility of stepping into the movie is that it is not impossible at all: we *can* do it.

Keaton experiences two moments of shock that make him stop and think and thus lose his balance: one as Sherlock, Jr., when he realizes that there's no driver of the motorcycle on which he thought himself just a passenger, and one as the projectionist, when he falls off his chair at the end of the dream. In both these cases, he loses his cinematic dexterity. As Sherlock, Jr., his realization on the bike is the first time he wavers and becomes frightened by the dangerous stunt he has unwittingly performed (and not just casually concerned, as he is earlier in the scene, when he offhandedly warns the absent driver to be more careful). As the projectionist, he awakens abruptly when his dream-inspired movements cause him to fall off his stool in the projectionist's booth. Once he "wakes up" from his dream/fantasy, he looks back up at the movie playing in the theater and is genuinely puzzled over the cut from the hero kissing his heroine to the shot of the hero bouncing twins on his knees. How does one get from the first situation to the other, the projectionist wonders. The answer is by editing, at which he had been adept while dreaming but is not now. When he falls from his stool, he loses his ability to understand and "fit into" cinematic time and space. Both these scenes are examples of the instant of "re-cognition" that Wile E. Coyote experiences in the seconds before he plummets to the ground and what we experience when we become embarrassed at having been startled by something on screen.

More typical of the filmgoer's experience, though, is the lack of self-consciousness exhibited during another telling scene in *Sherlock, Jr.*, in which Keaton first attempts to jump into the space of *Hearts and Pearls*. The wakeful Keaton, who has ventured into the theater while his alter ego sleeps, is ejected from the film and thrown back into the theater by the film's villain. As he lands unceremoniously on his head, the film cuts to the Keaton sleeping in the projection booth, whose body jerks violently. The sleeping Keaton has been startled and moved by the experience, but he *doesn't wake up*. In other words, that jolt is not followed by a moment of self-consciousness that pulls him out of the fictive world. He is still very much "in the film" at that point.

That both sleeping and wakeful Keatons feel a similar jolt echoes our own experience of shock in the film experience. Taken aback by a startling or violent moment in the film, we jump in our seats. Our seated body has not been touched or violated in any way, of course, but *in the film* we have been shocked, and that shock manifests itself right "here," in our bodies, seated a safe distance away from the events on screen. Like Keaton is at that moment, we are in two places at once, living and moving and being thrown about "there," in the world of the film and, at the same time, feeling those very sensations "here," in the safety of our seats.

Some might attribute this experience of physical shock to the filmgoer's imagination, but the jolt we feel is too palpable and corporeal an experience to be considered a solely mental event. Keaton's commitment to the film's world involves his whole body, not just his mind; the same goes for us. We and Keaton ultimately succeed in being in two places at once, in the film and outside it, in our own place and elsewhere. He expresses literally the phenomenon that we experience sensually and intuitively. We feel the film's world—its particular configurations of gravity, speed, depth, for example—because we have thrown ourselves up there, into the film, not just cognitively and emotionally but physically as well, even as we keep a firm grasp on ourselves, here in our seats.

Gilberto Perez takes issue with the reductive equation of films with dreams. "Saying that they both seem 'real' to us just means that in both cases we're caught up in illusion, and there are different degrees and different kinds of illusion, which must be sorted out in order to understand more accurately the points of similarity between films and dreams—and also the points of divergence."[57] For example, he cites Suzanne Langer's point that "the most noteworthy formal characteristic of dream is that the dreamer is always at the center of it. Places shift, persons act and speak, or change or fade. . . . But the dreamer is always 'there.'"[58] Perez points out that comedy poses a problem for any theory that would insist on an imprecise dream/film analogy because, he says, "dreams are not funny. Even when they are happy, they have no sense of humor. Perhaps this is because we are always at their center, and comedy requires a certain distance. We may awaken from a dream and find it funny . . . but by then we have gained distance from the dream." Unlike dreams, then, the film experience involves a delicate oscillation between proximity and distance, illusionism and reality, and perhaps most important, between sensory experience and intellect. That "bewildering equilibrium" (to borrow from Perez) is precisely what makes us laugh and wince simultaneously at the antics of Keaton and Coyote.

APPREHENSION

Action-adventure films that emphasize the experiences of the chase and the escape also make an invitation to us through our bodies, but there's a catch and an element of challenge here that's more explicit than it is in Keaton's films and more antagonistic than it is poignant. The handshake that occurs between Keaton and his world and between his audience and his films is tenuous. But when these action-adventure films extend a hand, it is only to pull it away at the last second, often leaving us to feel foolish. The invitation isn't to a dance or a handshake at all, really; chase and escape films ask us instead to play a tricky game of "follow the leader" in which they entice us to follow, then move in such a way that we can't possibly keep up. Like the handshake, this game is reciprocal in that two parties enter into a relationship of mimicry of sorts. But instead of celebrating the similarities, however tenuous, between the film's and viewer's bodies, these films push the connection to its breaking point, luring us with the similarities between our body and the film's body only to flaunt the differences. They invite us along for a ride, but once we've jumped on, they threaten to outrun us, push us too far or too fast, or throw us off completely. During the most harrowing chase scenes, our bodies tense and swerve, lean forward or jump back, fingers clenching the armrests of our seats as we try to catch up and hang on. A chase film cuts us loose from our moorings altogether for minutes at a time only to return us safely to them at the end, leaving us exhilarated, exhausted, and shaken. Our seduction by these films is both a tease and a thrill, and the feelings of frustration, desperation, and fear they inspire are a primary source of the pleasure we may or may not take in them.

The experience of chase films is one of being seduced, held tight, trapped, and suddenly thrown off, again and again. We are drawn to the film because we share with it certain aspects of our muscular comportment and certain desires and projects in the world, but we're thrust away from it by the considerable muscular differences between us. This constant feeling of being pulled and yet pushed leads to the unique way we experience chase and suspense films, which is with a great sense of *apprehension,* in many senses of the word.

"Apprehension" means not only the anticipation and dread—"the representation to oneself of what is still future, chiefly of things adverse"— that we experience while waiting for the gut-clenching climax of a summer blockbuster. It also means "the laying hold of sensuous or mental impressions," from the Latin "prehension": to seize.[59] We do both when we watch chase films: we *anticipate* frightening events (both in the narrative and in our own experience of the film) and we *seize* the film, taking hold of it by leaning forward in our seats, swerving with a speeding camera, or ducking to avoid "near misses." In police work, to "apprehend" is to catch someone or something, which is just what the viewer of a chase film tries to do: as the hero tries to catch the suspects, we endeavor to "catch" and "catch up with" the film. We throw ourselves at it, trying to hitch ourselves to the film's body. Our behavior is anticipated and encouraged by the film, which, like the helpful passenger on a speeding bus, holds out a hand for us to grab as we run alongside, trying not to miss our ride. But here's the rub: the film is not only the passenger, but also the driver of the bus, who not only refuses to slow down but may actually speed up to make our situation even more dire. A chase film inspires our desire to grasp even as it instills and exacerbates our fear of losing our grasp.

This hitching of our bodies to the film's body is characteristic of our general muscular attitude while watching action films. For "apprehension" means, more generally, "sympathetic perception," such as the kind we feel for a film that often moves in ways and according to purposes with which we can sympathize.[60] When, for example, a film follows its subject from behind with a slow-moving tracking shot, and we the viewers lean forward in our seats in anticipation, we and the film are engaged in an act of curiosity and investigation: we are both "stalking" the object of our attention. When a film moves back suddenly, as by cutting to a long shot after a series of close-ups or by a rapid backward zoom, and we viewers jump backwards in our seats, we and the film are both moving defensively away from something that has taken us by surprise; or perhaps, if our movements were more gradual, we both might be trying to get perspective on things, trying to see "the big picture." The many ways in which we and the film feel and behave alike (and more examples will follow) could thus be called a broader kind of "apprehension."

Finally, to "apprehend" is to have an understanding of something, and indeed, one could argue that to "get" these films, and certainly to enjoy them, is a muscular phenomenon: to "get" them is to "grasp" them, to hang on tight. Taken together, all these forms of "apprehension" provide an accurate description of the experience of an action film, the best examples of which are wild rides "fast enough to drive every thought from your head, make you dig your fingers into the seat in front of you and hang on for dear life."[61]

We have sympathy for the film as it performs its movements in part because we have done them ourselves: we have chased, run, followed, led, swerved, etc. However, in many cases, the actions performed by the film itself are actions we *haven't* done, and can't do, ourselves. We can't really fly at warp speed through space, and we can't fit into the spaces that digital-era movies like *Fight Club* (David Fincher, 1999) or *Wanted* (Timur Beckmambetov, 2008) go with the help of computer-generated imagery. Still, not having had those experiences to draw from, we do manage to feel the film's bodily movements anyway, because we're invested in the film's projects and attitudes, able to imagine ourselves there, chasing bad guys or fleeing attackers, feeling panic or anger in every muscle. The film invites us to share its curiosity, aggression, righteousness, vengeance, fear, delirium, etc. We take up those attitudes, and they in turn manifest themselves in our own movements and gestures. Our movements will be vastly different in shape, but similar in attitude.

Action films are driven by a need to act, to move, to *do something*. That's what the action genre is all about, and it becomes the spectator's project as well (or must, if the spectator is to enjoy the film on its own terms). The worst feeling one can have while watching an action film is that of inertia or immobility: whether the narrative goal is a bank heist or a risky rescue, the primary impetus activated in both the film's body and our own is to *move*. Even when the film teases us by trying to outrun us, we and the film simultaneously feel the need for speed, action, movement, and kinetic power.

Our empathy with the film's body stems not just from our mutual investment in shared projects, but also from the fact that the film performs basic actions with which we are familiar, such as seeking, fleeing, and chasing, though of course, it performs those acts differently than we would. In the most general way, we and the film share a tendency toward forward movement and uprightness, for example, but also other muscular habits and patterns as well. Tracking shots, for example, are the film's muscular means of performing the act of investigation, by tracking its subject as we would do on foot if we were following someone. These shots might suggest subterfuge by having objects placed between the camera and subject, or by being filmed from a low angle, an attitude we might express by hiding behind things or crouching as we follow our subject. Tracking shots can also be a means of perusal: a slow dolly along the storefronts of the main street at the beginning of a film or a scene, for example, is the film's way of "getting the lay of the land" and is not dissimilar from something we would do on foot or from the window of a passing car. A hand-held tracking shot or a quickly edited flurry of shots might express the film's urgency, uncertainty, or loss of control, just as unsteady movements on our part might do. An especially sudden camera movement can express paranoia and panic. A camera that swivels wildly or zooms suddenly to reveal an unexpected presence is responding to a fallibility that we share: the film doesn't have eyes in the back of its head and can't see in all directions at once or forever into the distance (though its peripheral vision might be extensive, as for example in CinemaScope films). We are limited in the same ways, and we empathize.

Muscular movements aren't limited to camera movement and placement, but they will be the main focus of this section simply because the physical movement of the camera is the closest approximation of muscular movement of the human body. All cinematic elements have muscular potential, however: editing, film speed, special effects, and sound also contribute to the film's "body language." Slow-motion cinematography in action films, for example, can express (and elicit the viewer's own) bodily frustration at immobility, paralysis, and helplessness in a genre that celebrates agility and power. SurroundSound technology is a kind of embrace or envelopment, a film's way of drawing us close to its body.

In the case of the gestures involved in chasing and fleeing, so prominent in many action films, the reciprocity of the film's body and our own is especially apparent, because both chasing and fleeing are by definition reciprocal gestures, like the handshake. Both parties are aware of and indeed mimic the other; in doing so, they each perform a similar gesture that becomes half of a whole. In Peter Yates's 1968 film *Bullitt,* the criminals and the cop engage in a wild car chase, during which the camera follows both of them, mimicking every lurch and swerve of the cop's car as he follows the villain's car. The camera moves into the wrong lane or onto the shoulder just when the cop's car does, for example. Viewers are not just watching a chase; we're caught up with the camera in the act of chasing. The camera could remain steady on its path and we'd get the *idea* of the chase, but by swerving behind the car in pursuit, it gives us the *sense* of the chase: we *grasp* it, and the scene exhilarates us.

In chase films, the film is to our bodies like car is to driver: we live through it vicariously, allowing it to shape our own bodily image. It becomes our proxy, our vehicle for movement and action, as well as the thing that provides us a safe haven from which to experience real danger. And yet, despite the lure of safety and vicarious power, the film reminds us that we're *not* as competent, fast, graceful, and powerful as the film's body. It thwarts our grasp in a number of different ways. In this section, I'll discuss films whose own movements mimic our bodies' typical movements but either exaggerate our muscular capabilities to the degree that we cannot "keep up" with the film's body, or exaggerate our muscular limitations to the degree that we feel constrained by our association with it.

A great many action films create in us the "need for speed" and then proceed to exceed our speed limits. These are the films that have us gripping our armrests for anchorage during their chase scenes and pulling back in our seats as if we could slow the films down that way. The wild car chase beneath New York City's elevated train tracks in *The French Connection* (William

Friedkin, 1971) is exemplary of the type of film that careens out of control. This film and its many emulators make extensive use of rapid cutting patterns and point-of-view shots from within speeding vehicles in order to intensify in the muscular register the audience's sense of involvement, which is already encouraged by the narrative. We not only identify with the hero, but also occupy his physical position as he races against the train that speeds along the tracks above him. Camera placement encourages us to want as much as he does—and, more important, as much as the film does—to catch up to the fleeing suspect. And yet, the means to this end are harrowing, and the film moves much faster than we're comfortable with.

Of course action films only exacerbate a contradiction that dates back at least as far as early cinema's *actualités*, panoramas, and exhibitionist displays of arriving trains, elephant electrocutions, earthquakes, and the like. "Films exceed normal observation and yet throw up huge barriers to it," writes David MacDougall. "They give us the privileged viewpoints of the close-up, the enclosing frame, the photographic 'look' of things—their lighted textures, their extended focal lengths, their monochrome range in black and white—indeed, everything that heightens or defamiliarizes everyday perception—yet at the same time they confine us to limited frames, give us limited time to inspect them, and in other ways deprive us of our will. This becomes a gap on a larger scale, of a different order. It can create a compulsion to see, even to see something terrible."[62]

Director Jan de Bont named his first film after the ambivalent desire and fear that drives our fascination with action films. *Speed* (1994), which centers on a runaway bus careening through the streets of Los Angeles, is described by critic Leonard Maltin as an "incredibly kinetic, supercharged action yarn." Likewise, De Bont's next film, *Twister* (1996), is "a wild ride of a movie" memorable as much for its frenetic "stormchaser" scenes, with characters racing impending storms and each another across Midwestern highways, as for the tornado effects themselves. As do most films in this genre, *The French Connection, Speed,* and *Twister* combine fast editing, point-of-view shots, and narrative suspense to "carry you along . . . from one kinetic burst to another."[63] They are exemplary, not unique, in the way they indulge our need to move, to chase, and to flee by exaggerating the sense of speed to the point of discomfort. That is the pleasure we derive from them, and I trust that the reader does not require a wealth of evidence to this effect. For the remainder of the section, I'd like to turn my attention to some specific movements, in addition to fast-moving cinematography and frenetic editing patterns, that elicit our muscular sense of careening out of control.

8.   *Bullitt* (Peter Yates, U.S.A., 1968)

Many a review or advertising tag line will refer to the latest chase film as a "thrill ride" or a "roller-coaster," and that description rings true in many ways. Cameras strapped to speeding helicopters and cars, for example, literally take our bodies along for the ride, which we most often experience from the point-of-view of the driver's or passenger's seat. In *Bullitt*, for example, a majority of the shots in the memorable car chase in downtown San Francisco are taken from the position of the back seat of one car or the other, with the drivers' hands in plain sight as they grip the wheel, their tense facial expressions visible in the rearview mirrors. Though these shots are harrowing, they do give us some small sense of safety and control: as we watch each car swerve, seeing the drivers' hands on the wheel assures us that *someone* is driving the car and is in control. (Reckless though they may be, one of the drivers is even shown to fasten his seat belt, which might bolster our sense of safety.) These shots also mimic something we can imagine experiencing ourselves, because most audience members have been in a speeding car at one time or another, watching nervously (or gleefully) through the front windshield. The speeds may be frightening, but the experience is familiar and feasible, something to which we can relate and of which we are capable, and we are lured into a feeling of relative safety and control by the way we empathize with the film's body in shots like these.

However, at crucial moments during *Bullitt*'s chase scene, the film ousts us completely from the safety of the vehicle. The palpable thrill of that scene stems in part from a recurring pattern of shots that first gives us a sense of security by enclosing us within a speeding car, but then robs us of it by positioning us "as" the car. Repeatedly, following a steady build-up of shots from the point of view of the drivers themselves or from the back seats, the film cuts to a shot from a camera mounted on the front of the vehicle. With these shots, we're pushed out of the car altogether, ejected violently from our spot behind or with the driver and forced to experience a few hair-raising moments of the chase from the vantage point of the car's front grille rather than its back seat. These shots usually occur just as the drivers are taking a particularly sharp turn or risky maneuver, and they're very brief, as are most of the 163 shots in this eleven-minute sequence, whose frenetic editing certainly contributes to the sense of velocity we get from it.

Though *Bullitt* executes it with unusual finesse, this same patterning of shots from inside and outside vehicles is fairly common among chase films. The Death Star attack sequence in *Star Wars* (George Lucas, 1977), for example, situates us for the most part inside the fighter planes with their pilots, but in the final moment of each attack, pilot and plane suddenly disappear from our view and we find ourselves thrust outside the vehicle altogether, riding into the attack without the safety net offered by the window, dashboard, and gun sights that had earlier indicated our safe enclosure inside the plane. Here again, camera placement combines with rapid-fire editing to makes us feel in our muscles every hairpin turn and near miss. By alternating shots taken from *inside* vehicles with those taken from cameras mounted *on* them, these films force us into movements that aren't meant for humans, only for machines. In these moments, we go where not even fearless drivers and pilots would dare to go; we are riding without seat belts, without windshields, without any protection at all. The film throws us out and gives us nothing to hang onto.

As if this editing strategy weren't scary enough, *Bullitt* catapults us into the action even more violently with its use of the zoom. At two critical moments toward the end of the chase, when a fatal mistake sends the villains to their fiery death as their car flips off a freeway, the film cuts to shots taken by a camera mounted on the vehicle itself and, to make matters worse, it also zooms quickly forward. First, as cop Steve McQueen's Mustang rams the bad guys' Charger, the film cuts to a shot from *outside* McQueen's car looking directly at the Charger, which is only a foot or two away from the Mustang. From this vantage point, the film promptly zooms into a close-up of the Charger's driver, who looks back toward both the Mustang and the camera and consequently loses control. A split-second later, there follows a blurry shot taken from the front of the

9. *Bullitt* (Peter Yates, U.S.A., 1968)

Charger itself; the camera is placed low on the vehicle, with none of the framing devices (dashboard, rearview mirror) that had marked interior shots from the car. Immediately following this shot there is another zoom—this one even faster, more reckless, and with exaggerated motion blur—toward the fueling station into which the Charger is crashing. Of course, the car doesn't actually crash into the fueling station: only the film's body does. In these two zooms, we and the film transcend even the machines' bodily movements; we go where the car and its passengers won't go. If most chase scenes "carry us along" at hair-raising speeds, this one unbuckles us and sends us flying.

Though *Bullitt* is a particularly artful example, the chase film generally has a way of "cutting us loose" while we sit safely in the movie theater. I have discussed, earlier in this chapter, moviegoers' ability to feel as if we were in two places at once. More than that, we usually feel *safe* in both places: "here," in our theater seats, and "there," in the place carved out for us by the film. Chase films, however, make us feel doubly *unsafe*. They pull us first *out* of our seats and *into* the film's body (as other films do) by encouraging our empathy with it, but then, once it has us in its grasp, it lets go. It robs us of our feeling of being grounded in *either* place, terrifying and thrilling us at the same time.

If sudden cuts to exterior shots and rapid zooms are basically human-like movements that push us too far and too fast, other styles of camera movement can shake loose our grasp of the film by moving in ways that are altogether impossible for the human body. Steadicam cinematography and computer-generated or -enhanced camera movements (or illusions of camera movements, in some cases) take us beyond our own abilities, moving in ways and to places that no human could reasonably expect to go. Paradoxically, Steadicam shots and some digital movements base themselves on human movement, just as dolly shots do. But in these cases, the film's body takes human movement to illogical, impossible extremes. These shots over-perfect our movements or make them too fast, exaggerating the humanlike tendencies of the film to the point that the movement is no longer remotely human: we can't keep up, we feel out of sorts and dizzy, and we can barely hang on.

Director Tom Tykwer says of his frenetic chase film, "I wanted *Run Lola Run* [1998] to grab viewers and drag them along, to give them a roller-coaster ride. I wanted the sheer, unadorned pleasure of speed."[64] The film does all this, but most of it takes place on foot. Indeed, the only speeding vehicle in this film is its female lead, who races through the streets of Berlin in search of enough cash to save her boyfriend from impending murder or jail time. Without the use of a roller coaster or speeding car, this film employs Steadicam photography to "drag us along" and "take us for a ride."

The Steadicam has an interesting and ambivalent relationship to human comportment because it mimics and transcends human styles of movement at the same time. The Steadicam is a cinematic means of replicating human comportment, in particular our ability to move fluidly in 360 degrees. When the Steadicam circles Lola, it is moving as we might do if we were in the scene, catching up with her and coming around to see her face as she stops momentarily. But the Steadicam is steadier than we are; it takes the intentions of our bodies and enacts them in ways not available to us. A Steadicam doesn't have two legs on which to stumble and doesn't experience vertigo or wavering uncertainty. As the camera follows alongside or ahead of Lola, moving at her speed and watching her as she runs, it doesn't bounce or falter, as we might if we were running alongside her. It is preternaturally smooth. A prosthesis that outdoes its human model, a Steadicam shot moves in ways that are humanlike but at the same time more perfect than human. (Interestingly, Steadicam operators must train their own bodies to move in ways that are not natural to them, in order to remove the traces of human movement from the image.) The effect of this perfection and transcendence of human comportment can, in fact, be dizzying for its viewers. The shot that circles Lola rapidly at the moment that she's gunned down in the street is a good example of the disorienting quality that skilled Steadicam work can produce: beautiful but deliriously daunting.

Run Lola Run walks the line between more traditional types of camera work (and here I'm speaking in relative terms, for Steadicam work is hardly old-fashioned in the larger historical sense) and turn-of-this-century computer-generated imagery. Whereas its Steadicam shots of Lola running through the streets draw upon human modes of comportment and take them to the limit of human feasibility, other shots diverge completely from the human model of muscular comportment: they go places we can't possibly fit and move in ways we can't imagine moving. Tykwer's film exacerbates the difference, at times, between two styles of movement: human and cinematic (including digital). In doing so, the film is its own critique of the action film, making clear that the "action hero" body is an impossible one, and that the action film places impossible demands on the bodies of the characters and its viewers. Not only does Lola have only twenty minutes to collect an awesome amount of cash, but she (and we) can't possibly keep up with the film's hyperkinetic, digitally effected movements, nor can we run as smoothly as a Steadicam.

The opening shot suggests the ambivalence that this film's body feels between human and nonhuman styles of comportment. It begins with a frenzied camera movement through a crowd. The movement is digitally sped up, but the camera slows down to "normal" speed when it comes upon certain people who say a few words before the camera leaves them and speeds on its way again, the rest of the crowd whizzing by in a flurry. This balance between dizzying kinetic movement and the slowness of human interaction is reflected in the film as a whole, which is divided between scenes of Lola racing frantically through the streets accompanied by a pounding technopop score and scenes of still, quiet drama slowly unfolding between Lola and her father, her father and his mistress, and Lola and her boyfriend.

The second scene of the film prepares us for the "unadorned pleasure of speed" of which Tykwer spoke. This scene, which provides our introduction to Lola and her dilemma, begins with a bird's eye view of the city, shot from a helicopter, so far away that parks and streets are discernible merely as graphic shapes. In what might seem like a parody of the opening shot of *Psycho* (Alfred Hitchcock, 1960), the camera swoops down and in a matter of milliseconds reaches Lola's apartment building; there the shot continues as the camera enters the building, races manically down the hallway, and makes a hairpin turn toward Lola's room, where it tracks recklessly into a close-up of Lola's face as she speaks on the phone with her boyfriend. The manic, frenzied speed of these shots is nothing like the way the viewer's body moves in real time and in real space. Tywker has exceeded his own goals, for this shot alone is faster than any human movement, than any roller-coaster—it is unfathomably fast. It has a jostling, hand-held quality to it, unlike the slower and more graceful Steadicam shots, which poses an interesting paradox: the shots that move at something like our speed are smoother than we could hope to be, while the shots that move with an imperfect gait, like our own, move faster than we could ever hope to move.

At one point in *Run Lola Run*, the film's movement loses any semblance whatsoever to human comportment and leaves us behind altogether. When Lola pins all her hopes on the spin of the roulette wheel in a casino, Tywker uses a "snorkel camera" to follow closely behind a roulette ball, which takes up nearly the entire screen as it rolls around the tiny track at the edge of the wheel. This is a place we humans couldn't possibly go, no matter how fast we move or how flexible we are, and the shot exemplifies the drastic differences, rather than the similarities, between our body and the film's body's in the way we relate to space. This shot in particular resembles many of the recent blockbuster action films that draw heavily on digital imagery to flaunt the differences between the film's body and our own. In fact, the roulette ball shot is very like two digitally effected close-ups in the remarkable *Fight Club*, one of which begins inside an office wastebasket and moves outward through the trash, like a spaceship weaving through a galaxy of stars, and another of which winds its way inside and around a gas stove-top burner and down the back of a refrigerator while an off-screen voice describes the events of a gas explosion.

Recent action films that make generous use of computer effects exacerbate our sense of awe at the movie that moves so much faster than we can and our terror and thrill at barely being able to hold on for the ride. Often, they transcend the world of human bodily potential for minutes at a time, simply leaving us in the dust. *Spiderman I* and *Spiderman II* (Sam Raimi, 2002 and 2004) fling their hero through the skies of Manhattan, and we follow, swinging deliriously above traffic and between skyscrapers at speeds no helicopter or hang-glider could afford us; these are speeds we can't have experienced ourselves, and yet we feel them in our muscles in a way that exhilarates us. *Minority Report* (Steven Spielberg, 2002), *The Matrix* series (The Wachowski Brothers, 1999–2003), *Live Free or Die Hard* (Len Wiseman, 2007), *Wanted* (Timur Beckmambetov, 2008), and many others capitalize on computer imagery to mark an insurmountable difference between film's body and viewer's body, leaving us slack-jawed and amazed. Perhaps this is why digital-effect-laden action films are so thrilling to some viewers and so unsettling to others (perhaps even thrilling and unsettling at the same moment for some): these shots don't correspond to our body's experience at all. These dizzying digital effects leave us feeling anything but steady and make "old-fashioned" tracking shots involving dollies and Steadicams feel positively pedestrian.

This isn't to say that all action films' bodies move faster and more gracefully than we can. While some films or scenes are superhuman in their speed and agility, others are all *too* human in their muscular movements; they are slower, less mobile, less competent, and less flexible than our own bodies. These scenes might use slow-motion cinematography, hand-held camerawork, and certain types of camera placement, for example, to exaggerate their own muscular *limitations*, limitations we're forced to share as we watch. Tethered to the film's body, we may be slowed down or even immobilized by it, kept from getting where we need to be. Like the faster-moving scenes, these scenes thrill and terrify us with the discrepancies between our body and the film's, but here, the discrepancies are not in the film's favor. Whereas high-octane and digital-effect-laden chase scenes push us faster and in more directions than we could go ourselves, these other types of scenes remind us that, for example, we can only move so fast and cannot see in every direction at all times, whether because of the limits of our peripheral vision or because our body isn't flexible enough.

The use of slow motion in a chase film, for example, goes against the need for speed that such films both borrow from and encourage in us. *Run Lola Run* contains a slow-motion shot in which Lola races toward her boyfriend, Manni, in the last seconds before he has told her he will stop waiting for her and take matters into his own hands. As Manni turns toward the store he's sworn to rob in order to get the cash he needs, Lola races toward him, just around the corner now but still unseen by him. The shot goes to split screen, with Manni in one third of the screen, Lola in another, and an enormous ticking clock in the bottom third. Long moments pass between each movement of the clock's second-hand, as Manni turns away from the corner Lola is about to turn, and both characters move in very slow motion. Viewers are already anxiously invested in Lola's mad race across town, and the slow-motion cinematography ratchets the tension even higher: we want both Lola and the movie to *go faster*, and we may lean forward in our seats, in hopes of spurring the images on to a speed that will appease us. Chase films that use slow-motion cinematography in this way play upon our fears of inertia and powerlessness by making us want to run and holding us back at the same time.

Camera placement, too, can give a sense of immobility or inflexibility, by thwarting a desire (inspired by the film) to look in certain directions. In moments where, if it were our own body in the picture, we would adjust our bodies for a better view, the film refuses to turn, twist, or crane its neck to see what we want to see. In *Bullitt*, for example, hero and villain race through the notoriously hilly streets of San Francisco. In several shots, as the villains' car soars over the crest of a hill, the camera maintains its position at the level of the driver's shoulder, so that all we see before us is the dashboard and blue sky. The driver himself stretches up in his seat to see further ahead, as we would do if we were his passenger, but the camera refuses to angle its body for a better view, and we are left hanging in mid-air for a moment before the car reaches the summit and points down again, with the bottom of the hill in its (and our) sights. The way the film's body briefly mimics our own bodies' limits is terrifying.

If emotion is motion, and if emotions emerge and are shaped by the material (and, I have argued, muscular) contact between bodies, the muscular ambivalence I've described on the part of action films may give us a way to discuss to discuss viewers' feelings toward the genre that is in keeping with existential phenomenology's emphasis on pre-personal subjectivity. As Mazis writes, "the term 'feeling' points to the lived body as prior to such distinctions and fragmentations: the etymology in its root in the Icelandic *falma* means 'to grope.' Through 'feeling' in its emotional sense, the body moves forward gropingly into the world, not as self-sufficient, not as holding a meaning already to be signified, not even with the kind of 'having beforehand' that thinkers as diverse as Plato and Heidegger have sensed about reflective understanding, but rather as touching things in order to be touched back."[65] Perhaps, then, the ambivalence felt by certain viewers toward the action film is structured by the muscular contact with these films themselves, which is itself ambivalent. Confronted with a viewing body that reaches toward them, the films refuse to "touch back."

These disparate examples serve to demonstrate the complexity of the kinaesthetic empathy that exists between our bodies and the film's body. It is not merely a one-to-one relationship of simple and successful mimicry. Rather, the handshake or chase in which we and the film engage together can express a wide range of attitudes toward the world and toward each other. The muscular mimicry at work here contributes to a dynamic of repulsion and attraction, push and pull, between the films and their viewers that leaves us hanging in the balance between them. It is within this dynamic, indeed because of it, that we fully grasp the films' comic poignancy, gripping excitement, or even their lack of emotional "pull" and intellectual "weight." The meaning and impact of the films makes itself felt in our muscles and tendons just as strongly as in our minds. The contact does not end there, however, for the exhilarating adrenaline-pumping exchange between our bodies is not only muscular but also visceral.

3. Viscera

You will never persuade my heart that it is wrong to tremble
or my viscera that they are wrong in being moved.
DENIS DIDEROT

HEART-STOPPING

The tenuous connection between the film's and viewer's muscular bodies,
which is variously terrifying, reassuring, and exhilarating, finds its way as
well into the depths of the film's and viewer's body, where a similar
dynamic of attraction and repulsion, similarity and difference, is at play.
This chapter shifts the focus from the activities and responses of the external body—goose bumps, shivers, hands gripping the arms of one's seat, and
the like—to the internal body, where the pulse and the rhythmic filling and
emptying of the lungs can enact and express attitudes and emotions such
as desire, fear, anticipation, and relief. In short, we have moved now to a
discussion of the murky, mysterious interior, the viscera of the spectator
and the cinema, whose vital organs share a remarkable capacity for expression and perception.

Earlier I discussed *Run Lola Run* (Tom Tykwer, 1998) in terms of its exag-
geration of machinelike speed and flexibility in comparison with our human,
pedestrian slowness. The trailer even dares us with this tag line: "Keep up or
pay the price." With its use of digital effects, three-part narrative structure,
and frenetic editing, *Run Lola Run* seems to encourage in its viewer the fantasies of being able to defy the passage of time and the pull of gravity.

But unlike most action films, it doesn't *flaunt* those differences so much
as cop to them. It reminds us that action-film speed is an illusion, that "getting there faster" is an effect of narration, editing, camera movement. In
subtle ways, it exposes the gap between cinematic and human bodies and
even, occasionally, lets us rest there for a moment. *Run Lola Run* is an action
film that's as much about inaction as about action, as much about stillness as
about speed, as much about "stop" and "yield" as it is about "go."[1]

Reviewer Janet Maslin notes the film's "altered sense of emotion and meaning in the face of breathless forward momentum."[2] The film and its heroine both seem to straddle the gap between motion and emotion, focusing their energies not only on movement but also on "breathlessness" and breathing, on moments of stillness that mark the journey. Within the need to *do something* and *get somewhere*, there is also the necessity of being still, neither here nor there, neither now nor then.

Lola runs, Lola walks, Lola leaps, Lola races. Lola does all these things, but not smoothly or perfectly. Lola also stumbles, misses, crashes, gets emotional, gets winded, has to stop to think and catch her breath. She gets shot, even, and she starts over. The film, like Lola, is fallible: it falters, it runs out of breath, it recognizes its limits and gathers strength from them. It paces itself, it pauses, it breathes. These behaviors are performed primarily, but not exclusively, through editing. In a film that makes such tight, deliberate use of cross-cutting, it is worth noting several jump cuts that do *not* work to propel the narrative or heighten the speed of an action sequence. As Lola walks down a hallway pleading with her father, and as Manni collects himself during the armed robbery, barely noticeable jump cuts appear, perhaps as a reflection of the scenes' emotional friction. That they are so subtle makes them feel less like purposeful ratcheting-up of the excitement of the chase and more like tiny hitches in the forward motion of the film's body.

The gaps marked by these jump cuts are barely noticeable, but others are more apparent, including those marked by the credit sequence's stop-motion "mug shots" and Lola's mental tally of potential benefactors, whose faces appear one by one in short, percussive inserts. Camera speed, as well, makes the gap between motion and stillness momentarily palpable. Although the film often shifts to a slow-motion sequence before resuming normal speed in the next, particularly interesting are those moments when it disrupts continuity with a noticeable shift in speed *within* a very short sequence. This happens when Lola recounts the theft of her bike—the scene unfold in a series of shots that alternates between slow and fast motion—and again at the moment Lola is shot. Here, her dramatic collapse is shot in slow motion, but the reaction shots of the cop who pulled the trigger are in "real time." In these and other examples, it is unclear at what speed Lola and other people are moving.

At key moments the film plunges further into these gaps to rest in the moments "in between." In a long sequence that, like the two previous examples, shifts between slow motion and real time, Lola runs along a city street and we hear her thoughts on the soundtrack: "I'll just keep running, ok? I'm waiting. I'm waiting. I'm waiting." In a film that seems to be about "getting there faster," it is surprising how often the act of "waiting"—the lingering in the spaces between here and there, now and then—is its focus. In all three "versions" of Lola's visit to her father's bank, for example, Lola stops outside to think for a long moment. Time is of the essence, but taking one's time seems somehow more important than defying it.

Lola's most vulnerable and powerful moment, and the film's as well, is the moment when she takes a bullet and says, simply, "Stop." In this moment before the cops would arrest her, we are all—Lola, the film, and the viewers—*arrested* in time and space. As she lies in the ground gasping for breath, the pulse of the movie slows to a near stop before opening up into the first of two interstitial sequences that occur at near-death moments and mark, structurally, the transitional points of the narrative's triptych. These scenes, infused by a blood-red filter and set off by dissolves (rarely used in this film), are moments out of time. Their stillness, quiet, and timelessness make it impossible to know where *or when* we are. In this sense, they function exactly according to the quotation at the beginning of the film from soccer coach Sepp Herberger: "After the game is before the game."[3] They *are* the time in between literal acts of breath-taking. In that sense, they constitute the emotional and visceral, muscular heart of the film. Through them, and through the subtler patterns of editing and camera speed and movement already noted, *Run Lola Run* draws our attention away from muscular, goal-oriented momentum to something we rarely notice: the intermittence that underpins and makes possible our own human movement through the world.

The phenomenological ambivalence between stillness and motion played out by *Run Lola Run* is not unique to this film experience. It defines the very nature of cinema, where that tension is experienced and expressed viscerally through what Andrey Tarkovsky described as the "time that pulsates through the blood vessels of the film."[4]

HICCUPS

When we speak of viscera, we're usually speaking about one of two things. Either we use the term in its specific, medical sense to refer to the internal organs, including, for example, the heart, lungs, and pancreas, or we use the term more vaguely, to refer to a general area—the insides, the depths, the guts—that describes not organs but feelings, emotions, and intuition. By our "visceral" reaction to a film we often mean our "gut reaction," a general feeling that begins deep inside but makes its way to the surface. In the first sense, the medical one, we hardly notice our viscera under normal circumstances: they do their business without our direct attention or involvement. In the second sense, though, our viscera overpower everything else. Nervousness, excitement, dread, passion—these things are felt deeply but affected and inflected by sensations and behaviors at the body's surface. Not only that, but these visceral feelings also rise to the forefront of our experience, where they shape and color our entire bodily experience, in such forms as flushed skin, nausea, and facial expressions that allow others to read us like an open book.

This chapter delves into the depths of the body to understand how the viscera—both human and cinematic—exhibit and inhabit a particular temporal structure that, in combination with the material/textural structures of the skin and the spatial structures of the musculature, forms the elements of our embodied experience of film. It begins with descriptions of the "viscera" in medical phenomenology and quickly moves on to discuss the ways in which the deepest, most secretive rhythms of the body resonate between film and viewer in such a way as to intensify what is already an intimate relationship between the two. I will describe an eroticism and empathy similar to but even deeper than the sort described in the previous two chapters, a visceral resonance between film and viewer that is closer than that which occurs at the skin and the musculature, because it moves *through* the skin and the musculature to get here. As I will show, the viscera are awakened precisely through the film's appeal to those more accessible dimensions of the body. We and the film open onto each other completely, "denuding and dispossessing" ourselves to the other so that we are absorbing/absorbed through our skin and holding/held close in a muscular embrace; once there, the similarities and differences between our visceral rhythms deepen the connection in a way that's both startling, unsettling, and seductive.

The descent of touch into the body's depths necessitates its reconfiguration as a less volitional, less accessible sense than I have described thus far. We no longer witness touch when it occurs in the inner organs, nor do we control the particular forms it takes. This is touch as it is experienced and enacted in a dimension of the body that we rarely if ever see for ourselves. The inner body is a secret, hidden by layers of muscle and flesh, our attention diverted from it by our daily engagement with the "world at hand." The visceral body makes itself known to us only in the most dramatic situations, of which, this chapter argues, the film experience is one. Although the viscera rarely factor into our perceptual field, they are awakened and summoned through the surface body's engagement with the shapes and textures of cinema. Like the surgeon who cuts through the surface in order to "palpate the palpitating masses enclosed therein [and] . . . share in those turbulent internal rhythms of surging intermittencies and peristaltic unwindings," and like the doctor who reads the surface body as an outward sign of internal disease, our access to the viscera begins at the surface.[5]

Why employ such an archaic and vague term at all, rather than using the more specific names for individual organs—spleen, pancreas, kidney, esophagus? Precisely because of its vagueness, the "viscera" is phenomenologically an accurate word for the internal organs as we experience them: "viscera" is as specific and descriptive as we can get in our daily, immediate experience of our own body's insides. The word captures the indistinct impression we have of our internal organs and our inability to distinguish among them in their daily actions by experience alone.

Though this chapter concerns the viscera more as a phenomenological region than a medical one, we can begin with Drew Leder's useful scientific definition: "The category of the 'visceral' understood broadly includes not only the organs of the digestive system but of the respiratory, cardiovascular, urogenital, and endocrine systems, along with the spleen."[6] Leder's is a broad definition, and I also use the term in a purposefully broad sense to refer to the collective insides of the body: the vital organs in their entirety. Taken together, these are the structures that underlie other, more immediately apparent, aspects of bodily action and sensation. These structures enable the perception of and action upon the outside world, and they are directly involved in that perception and action, even though we may not ordinarily perceive or think of them that way. The region's fundamental inaccessibility makes it an "anonymous strata," writes Leder, "a prenatal history, the body asleep."[7]

Our experience of our inner bodies is not the experience of clearly distinguishable organs but of a mass of organs interacting to produce sensations we describe in general terms. When one feels nausea, for example, one says that one is sick to the stomach, not that one suffers from an ailment of the pancreas or the spleen. Nervousness is not necessarily attributed to a specific production of a specific substance by a specific organ; it is just called "the jitters." What person without some knowledge of science and medicine can assign any given sensation—a pang, a cramp, or the fluttering of "butterflies," for example—to a particular organ? General practitioners nearly always begin by asking their ailing patients "where does it hurt?" and for good reason. We can only begin to attribute sensations to specific organs by first locating the pain in a certain region where anatomical charts tell us that certain organs reside. The lived experience of the internal organs is that of a murky, viscous, pulsing system in which organs work in tandem to yield an overall effect, be it nausea, tension, aches, or jitteriness.

The mysterious, murky impression that we have of the internal organs has much to do with our lack of conscious control over their actions. While I can orchestrate my movements at the muscular level, instructing myself—whether automatically or habitually—to walk forward, duck to avoid a flying object, or pull back on the knob of a particularly sticky door as I turn the key in the lock, I have no such authority over the daily activities of my viscera. In describing this lack of mastery over the internal organs, Leder cites a digestive example: although I can walk in search of food when hungry and can pick up and bite into an apple, after that, the guts are in control and arrange for the apple's passage through the complex digestive system. That the visceral activities of digestion, as well as respiration and circulation, are not a matter of my volitional control is a good thing, of course, for it allows me to direct my attention elsewhere, to projects for which I am better suited. Lewis Thomas describes the relief he feels at being free of responsibility for the viscera's ongoing processes: "If I were informed tomorrow that I was in direct communication with my liver, and could now take over, I would become deeply depressed. For I am, to face the facts squarely, considerably less intelligent than my liver. I am, moreover, constitutionally unable to make hepatic decisions, and I prefer not to be obliged to, ever. I would not be able to think of the first thing to do."[8]

The difficulty of thinking about one's liver in concrete terms, much less exerting control over it, indicates the essential absence from conscious life of the lived body, which "is rarely the thematic object of experience."[9] This absence figures differently at various levels of the body:

> Experience attests to a certain forgetting of the body in general. Yet the causative factors at play differ at different physical/phenomenal levels. If we were to imagine ourselves descending through corporeal layers, we would see a gradual shift from those modes of disappearance characteristic of the sensorimotor "I" to that form which typifies the anonymous depths. Surface organs are forgotten via their structural role, focal or background, in the ecstatic arc, while the viscera recede beneath the reach of this arc. The body disappears both as a seat of consciousness and as the site of an unconscious vitality.[10]

The surface body, which is available to our intentional will and closely aligned with our sense of autonomous selfhood, is ecstatic, which is to say that it disappears from our consciousness as we direct our attention *through* our enabling limbs and muscles *toward* the world around us. "The hand is no longer a hand when it has taken hold of the hammer," writes

Michel Serres; "it is the hammer itself, it is no longer a hammer, it flies transparent, between the hammer and the nail, it disappears and dissolves, my own hand has long since taken flight in writing. The hand and thought, like one's tongue, disappear in their determinations."[11] The sensorimotor organs are the tools with which we perceive and act in the world, the medium but not ordinarily the object of our intentional project, and as such they become transparent in their usefulness.

The internal body, however, is absent by virtue of its recessive, rather than ecstatic, tendency. Whereas the surface body is caught up in an "intentional arc [whose] telos . . . carries attention outward, away from its bodily points of origin, . . . the viscera disappear precisely because they are displaced from this arc. They are that part of the body which we do *not* use to perceive or act upon the world in a direct sense. . . . My visceral organs, not constructed for ecstatic perception, disappear from the ranks of the perceived. I do not perceive *from* these organs; hence, they can hide beneath the body surface such that I do not perceive *to* them either."[12]

The body's degree of absence is not an anomaly, nor is it something we must regulate by consciously remembering to forget; it is the natural state of affairs. "As these disappearances particularly characterize normal and healthy functioning, forgetting about or 'freeing oneself' from the body takes on a positive valuation."[13] Without this degree of absence, we would be unable to concentrate on the world around us, obsessed with what would become a body-as-world rather than a body-in-the-world.

It is instructive to point out Sara Ahmed's contention with this notion of the "absent" body, which, she argues, is too suggestive of an "either/or" dynamic that does not accord with the lived experience of the body. "I would not use the terms 'absent' and 'present' to describe embodiment as Leder does," she writes, "as it implies that bodies *can* simply appear or disappear. Rather, I would point to the economic nature of intensification, and suggest that one is more or less aware of bodily surfaces depending on the range and intensities of bodily experiences. The intensity of pain sensations makes us aware of our bodily surfaces, and points to the *dynamic nature of surfacing itself* (turning in, turning away, moving towards, moving away)."[14]

As with the skin and the musculature, the idea of the viscera as something common to both viewer and film hinges more on function than on biology or mechanics, and if the film can be said to have a body, it can be said to have viscera, too. The viscera, be they cinematic or human, serve a similar function: they sustain life, animate us, and regulate themselves without our notice in order to maintain the continuity of our movement and activities at the middle and surface of the body. For us, this role is played by the heart, lungs, liver, and other vital organs.

The film's viscera consists of those "organs" or structures that enable its conscious activities but are not, except in extraordinary circumstances, under its direct control. The movement of celluloid through sprocket holes in a certain rhythm, for example, and the taking in and the subsequent projection of light through a lens—these things go without saying, in most cases. The power source, light source, sprocket holes, projector's gate, and other parts of the mechanism keep light and celluloid moving through the camera and projector in the same way that our viscera keep blood and other vital fluids moving through our bodies. And just as we cannot ordinarily control the rhythm of our heartbeat or circulation, the film doesn't have access to these things except in a few cases (film projection speed, for example) and special circumstances, as when experimental filmmakers turn their attention inward, meditating on the inner mechanisms of cinema like yogis who seek conscious control over their heartbeats and body temperature. Like the lungs expanding and collapsing, the heart filling and emptying, and the pancreas doing whatever it does, sprocket holes and optical soundtracks are parts of the apparatus that usually escape the film's notice and our own, and that very rarely come into play in the telling of a story.

Despite the fact that the viscera are fundamentally recessive and absent from conscious life, it is possible to argue that the viscera come into play during the conscious act of watching the movies. Leder's concept of "dys-appearance" lays the groundwork for such an argument. Although the viscera's recessiveness stems from "an innate resistance," and they "cannot be summoned up for personal use, turned ecstatically upon the world," the internal body is occasionally brought to our immediate attention, quite drastically in some cases. In certain situations, it is made an object rather than a medium of our attention and action. Leder terms that reversal "dys-appearance," from the Greek prefix "dys-," signifying "bad," "hard," or "ill." As opposed to what he describes as the quiet and ordinary "dis-appearance" of the healthy body from our conscious attention, "dys-appearance" is the *reappearance* of the body into conscious life under conditions of disease, pain, or other extreme circumstances. In those moments, we take notice of the body's internal functions, its rhythms and sounds, which seem alien by virtue of their appearing to our attention at all. "At moments of breakdown," Leder writes, "I experience *to* my body, not simply *from* it. . . . It is as if a magnet had reversed poles, reorganizing the experiential field inward."[15] Moments of dys-appearance are the exceptions that prove the rule of the internal body's ordinary reticence.

Though Leder's examples of dys-appearance run along the lines of heart failure, pregnancy, disablement, and advanced age, I would characterize the film experience itself as one of those extreme circumstances yielding dys-appearance. The experience of films draws our attention inward, toward the viscera, indirectly by way of the external body. Films appeal to the more immediately accessible musculature and skin, inviting their participation in a way that evokes the temporal rhythms of the viewer's viscera, which in many ways match those of the film's viscera.

This chapter focuses on the temporal structures of the viscera, because often that's how the viscera most likely announce themselves on the rare occasions when they do come to our attention. Specifically, both viewer's and film's bodies exhibit a structure of intermittence that is scarcely perceptible until it is evoked at the deepest recesses of the human and cinematic form. We find a film's rhythms riveting, perhaps even eerily human, because they are, in fact, founded on and perpetually indebted to our own imperceptible human rhythms. The illusion of "motion pictures," which are in fact a series of still images, corresponds to the way human movement proceeds, which is by fits and starts, though we hardly ever notice them.

Though we perceive our bodies' movement through the world to be smooth and continuous, human movement actually consists of a series of intermittent and separate motions. Every move we make involves the contraction and subsequent release of individual muscles, for example, and "the lungs fill and collapse before they fill again. The valves of the heart open and shut, and both respiration and heartbeat are not continuous, but segmented, rhythmic activities. Yet, we do not consider ourselves in 'intermittent motion.' Similarly, we do not visually experience our attentive gaze as intermittently disrupted by the blinking of our eyelids," Vivian Sobchack writes.[16] To suggest that as human beings we move through life feeling this intermittence and discontinuity of movement in any tangible way would be simply contrary to fact. The discontinuity on which our movement is essentially predicated recedes from consciousness along with the other internal functions and rhythms of the viscera and reveals itself only sensually and experientially, in unusual circumstances. Heart palpitations, asthma, and a case of the hiccups are all capable of shifting our attention suddenly to the rhythm of the internal body. In the case of the hiccups, the sudden awareness of one's breathing patterns brought about by their disruption can be funny, frustrating, and when the hiccups go on too long, a little frightening.

This tension between the perceived continuity of our bodies' lived movement and the discontinuity that underlies it asserts itself sensually, though rarely explicitly, in the cinematic viewing experience. Motion pictures posit a disjointed type of temporality much like our own. Sobchack reminds us of the similarities: "We could liken the regular but intermittent passage of images into and out of the film's material 'body' to human respiration or circulation—the primary bases for what we deem animation."[17] Sitting in the movie theater and caught up in the events on screen, we are no more aware of the film's intermittence than we are of our own. And yet, as I have argued in previous chapters, one of the reasons we respond so passionately to cinema as an art form is because of a deep, and not uncomplicated, affinity between our bodies and the film's body. The affinity between our visceral rhythms may be subtle and barely perceptible, but it is also palpable. Cinema gives us a feel for our own deep rhythms, reminding us what we're made of.

Most of Leder's examples of dys-appearance seem to involve dysfunction, disease, and trauma, and the cinematic experience does have its occasional crises, which can remind us of the discontinuity at the heart of our body and the film's, when our perceptual attention is so clearly directed away from it. A random fiber caught in the projector's gate diverts attention from the images to the frantic movement of this stray speck; it leaps wildly across the screen at every frame advance, reminding us of the flurry of activity that accompanies even the most languorous long take as the images race through the gate. An accidental slippage of the celluloid from the projector's sprocket holes gives us a sudden glimpse at an optical soundtrack and destroys the illusion of real human bodies walking and talking in real time. A projectionist's error in the choice of lens necessitates a quick change that robs the on-screen space of the integrity our minds and bodies had imparted to it. In all these cases, the cinema's internal body comes hurtling forward to our conscious attention (and its own) in a moment of crisis. Each of these mechanical failures is like a heart palpitation, but it is not *our* heart that's fluttering: it is the heart of the film.

Of course, there is also a kind of purposely reflexive, intentional dys-appearance, wherein the film itself directs its attentions inward, willingly disrupting the flow of things. Ingmar Bergman's *Persona* (1966), for example, highlights the essential fallibility of the apparatus when it pictures the melting of a piece of film in the projector's gate, and *Fight Club*'s Tyler Durden literally points out the presence of the "cigarette burns" at the screen's edge that function as projectionist's cues (David Fincher, 1999). Consider, also, the moment in *La Jetée* (Chris Marker, 1962) when a woman's blinking eyes disrupt a quiet rhythm of successive, extended still images.[18] If these instances stem from the film's intentional, self-conscious gaze upon its own (ordinarily) hidden recesses, the inadvertent, unselfconscious moments of dys-appearance are even more startling and genuinely disruptive. Consider those moments when, during a film's screening, the celluloid really does burn up in the projector's gate: the film is stopped and the projectionist must rush to rescue the print and set it in motion again. Even the audience turns back to look at the projection booth, as one might press one's hand against one's chest when the heart skips a beat.

These moments—both accidental and purposeful—are relatively rare, however. More often the film's body and the spectator's body express and perceive their shared rhythms indirectly and very subtly. While the viscera keep us in motion and enable all our conscious activities, they are not usually accessible to our control, and so film and spectator express and perceive their rhythms to one another indirectly, through the dimensions of the body that we do notice and control (like skin and muscle). These ecstatic parts of the body are appealed to first, and they lead us to the recessive ones. This is a matter of shifting our attention, or having it shifted for us, from the outside to the inside.

By way of example, I'd like to offer the prologue of the Quay Brothers' *Street of Crocodiles* (1986), a blend of lyrical live-action cinematography and stop-motion animation that evokes with haunting silence and a hazy blue-toned image the specter of early cinema. Appropriately titled "The Wooden Oesophagus," this short prologue dramatizes and literalizes the way that cinema awakens us to the internal body by means of an invitation extended first to the surface body. This sequence will be the catalyst for the chapter's subsequent discussions of early cinema and stop-motion animation as cinematic forms that make the connection between surface and depth palpable.

The prologue begins with a museum caretaker entering a silent, cavernous auditorium, its chairs empty and its stage populated with lifeless machinery. His footsteps echoing throughout the room, the man whistles as he steps onto the stage, carrying with him a stage light. He sets the light on the floor next to one particular machine and walks off screen. A series of camera movements follows, in which the camera glances quickly down the surface of this machine, giving us glimpses (in black and white) of bits and pieces of the contraption: an eyepiece, a tiny crank, a small porcelain bowl of screws.

The man returns and peers through the viewfinder. Another jerky camera movement follows that takes us down into the machine's inner workings and then rapidly back up (this time in color rather than black and white). The caretaker adjusts a magnifying glass that is attached to the machine and perched above a detailed map. He stands upright and, after a pause, spits slowly into the innards of the machine. There is a cut to a color image of the machine's interior, where the saliva falls slowly from the top of the frame and sets into frantic motion a series of gears, pulleys, and unidentifiable mechanisms.

Amidst the mechanical whirrings, a little manlike puppet appears who will be our protagonist. His hand is attached by a thread to a pulley hanging above a doorway, and he tugs at the thread but is unable to move. The film cuts to a black-and-white image of the caretaker's hand reaching slowly into an opening in the side of the machine, holding a pair of scissors. As the puppet-protagonist continues to pull his arm to no avail, the caretaker reaches his scissors further into the machine and snips. Inside the machine, the scissors appear, enormous now and in color, emerging from the top of the screen to cut the thread holding the protagonist. A quick animated camera movement shows the pulley spinning out of control. Finally the protagonist moves jerkily out of the frame, free to wander the murky and mazelike space of this strange mechanical inner world.

This opening sequence establishes a metaphor for the viewer's intensely intimate relationship with the film's innards and with the objects and spaces that constitute that inner world. The caretaker brings the machine to life through his muscular and haptic body by stepping close to the machine, bending over its eyepiece, and reaching with his hand to cut the strings of the pulley, and through his internal body by spitting into its inner mechanisms. The apparatus not only invites the involvement of the caretaker's body; it cannot, in fact, move without him. His preliminary contact with the apparatus at the surface of the body (both his and the machine's body) parallels a contact that occurs even deeper within him and the machine, a contact involving the muscular, mechanical workings and internal rhythms of each. That the prologue evokes both early cinema viewing machines (to which the machine depicted bears a strong resemblance) and stop-motion animation (which constitutes the remainder of the film, and whose purposefully jerky movements here evoke the flicker effect of early cinema itself) seems felicitous, for in both these forms, the disjointed temporality that is successfully hidden in most film experiences is not only barely concealed, but a celebrated part of their charm as well.

However, only indirectly do viewers get caught up in the temporal structures of early cinema and stop-motion animation. The primary appeal of these cinematic styles or modes is not to the viscera, but to the musculature and skin, respectively. The descriptions that follow will examine how exactly the "surface" impact of early cinema and stop-motion animation makes its way into the viscera to establish a deeply intimate intertwining between the film and viewer.

LA PETITE MORT

Cinema's deep connection to the human body is borne out by the fact that the medium first emerged in the context of the amusement park, fairground, and penny arcade. The pleasures of the commercial amusements that drew crowds to New York's Coney Island, Chicago's Riverview, and other amusement parks were unabashedly physical: each and every concession and attraction, from the dancing pavilions to the food stands to the moving picture concessions, invited patrons to indulge in some form of physical stimulation. Kinetoscopes and mutoscopes stood in the penny arcades and amusement parks alongside coin-operated scales, hobby horses, fortune-telling machines, "lung-testers," and even machines that allowed couples to measure the ardor of their kiss for the modest price of 25 cents.[19] A fascination with the human body pervades all the various arcade entertainments, which tested physical skill, measured physical sensations, and offered patrons a moment of physical thrill for the price of a few coins. In some cases the common physiological interests of noncinematic amusement machines and kinetoscope film subjects were made explicit, as in the case of the coin-operated punching bags by which patrons could compare the force of their punches with those of "Gentleman Jim" Corbett, James J. Jeffries, and Bob Fitzsimmons, whose boxing matches were among the most popular of kinetoscope subjects.[20] The physical body was even more explicitly the subject of early medical imaging technologies available in the arcades. These included the X-ray machine and the fluoroscope, which used X-ray technology to provide patrons a glimpse of their own skeletal systems in real time: amusement-seekers could drop a nickel in the slot, place a hand in the designated spot, and behold the movements of their own bones.[21]

The fact that moving pictures grew up in such close proximity to the roller coaster and other physical attractions suggests that it offered a similar kinetic thrill. At the risk of stating the obvious, I want to emphasize that very early cinema featured above all the body *in motion*. The muscular movements of the human body are precisely what constituted not only the novelty of cinema, but, more important, its impact and appeal. The choice of subject matter of the earliest films underscores the fascination (of its makers and its audiences) with the body. Violence and sexuality, in the forms of boxing matches and titillating dance numbers, were extraordinarily well represented in early exhibition programs. The first kinetoscope programs featured flexing demonstrations by the famed bodybuilder Eugene Sandow, performances by a female contortionist, abbreviated wrestling matches, acrobatics, cockfights, and exotic dances by performers like Annabelle Whitford (Moore), whose *Annabelle Butterfly Dance* and *Annabelle Serpentine Dance* (both 1894) were particularly popular. The public desired to see more than anything else images of the human body in various states of pain or pleasure and, above all, frenetic movement.[22]

Tom Gunning calls the cinema prior to the development of narrative that occurred around 1906 the "cinema of attractions," that is, "a cinema of instants, rather than developing situations."[23] At this historical moment in cinema's evolution, he suggests, pure spectacle is the *raison d'être* of the medium. Spectators took pleasure in the thrill of merely seeing the body in motion on screen and had no need for a narrative to make sense of the images; the films "made sense" sensually, as pure stimulation. Trains hurtled toward the spectator, their cargo and destination unidentified, and Annabelle twirled with dizzying speed before the camera, unbound by any story of struggle and success in the footlights of Broadway. In some cases it was enough for film subjects to stand and look at the camera: Gunning cites a whole genre of films dedicated to facial expressions, in which characters simply stare and make faces at the camera.[24] In the cinema of attractions, human bodies simply *did* things, performed acts ranging from muscle-flexing to dancing to sneezing, for no other reason than the sheer delight in seeing them done.

"Primitive" cinema's muscularity was not limited to on-screen performers, but also involved the relation between viewers and the viewing machines themselves. Prior to being projected on large screens, of course, motion pictures were exhibited individually in self-contained imaging apparatuses such as Thomas Edison's kinetoscope, which premiered publicly in 1894, and Biograph's mutoscope, launched for entertainment purposes in 1897.[25] Rather than cast their images over rows and rows of passive spectators, these machines insisted on the immediate presence and proximity of the spectator's body to the apparatus and the film itself at every level. "Step right up," they seemed to say, and individual viewers took that invitation literally. In order to see the image, one had to stand close and lean into the machine; one might put one's elbows and arms against it or place one's hands around its viewfinder to block out light. These early cinema viewing machines required an *investment* on the part of the viewer—not merely a financial investment of a few coins, but a physical and bodily investment perhaps manifested most literally by the act of dropping one's coin into the machines' coin slot. This single act marks not only a monetary exchange between patron and industry, but also, more important, the contribution of the spectator's bodily movement and action to the event, which precipitates the motion of the film itself.[26] Without the motion of the viewer depositing the coin, there could be no "motion pictures."

It is early cinema's involvement of the viewer's muscular body that awakened the viewer to the temporal patterns of the viscera, and nowhere is that more explicitly demonstrated than in the case of the mutoscope. More than the kinetoscope, the mutoscope insists on an even more continuous, extended form of active participation and bodily contribution on the part of its patron, and it is the mutoscope that gives us the sharpest example of the musculature's evocation of the viscera. Whereas electrified machines (including some later models of the mutoscope) propelled a strip of film past the lens of the viewfinder, most mutoscopes featured a set of flip-cards propelled past the viewfinder by the spectators themselves, who continuously cranked a handle on the side of the machine. A spectator's movements of the hand initiated, maintained, and determined the speed of the movement of the image past the viewfinder.[27]

The temporal connection foregrounded here is a broad one, to be sure, having to do with the speed of the viewer's conscious muscular movements rather than with heartbeat and breathing. However, this kinetic interrelation of human and machine in the realm of the musculature begins in a very subtle way (to be made more explicit further on) to evoke a deeper, temporal connection between the film's body and the human body in the realm of the visceral.

The situation presented by early cinema viewing machines, in which the spectator seeks entertainment through a medium that cannot operate without his or her continuous participation, and in which, in the case of the mutoscope, the speed of spectators' bodily movements determines the speed of the images, demonstrates the remarkable extent to which the human body is figured as an intimate and integral component of the cinema. Cinema's defining characteristic is the movement of discontinuous images in space and time at a prescribed rate of frames per second, and this intrinsic form is derived from the temporal structures of the human body, whose actions are also made up of discontinuous movements (the contraction and release of muscles that move the arm that move the crank handle, for example) that seem smooth and uninterrupted. The contrast between continuity and intermittence is ordinarily blurred in our experience of human movement and of the cinema, but when brought to our attention it can induce a sensation that is at once pleasurable and discomfiting.

This confluence of spectators' bodies, subjects' bodies, and the early cinema viewing machines complements what is already an intimate—often even sexual—overtone to the experience of these films. Consider the filmed performances of scantily clad dancing women, among the most popular films with the mutoscope parlors' predominantly male clientele. The popularity of the Annabelle films suggests an intriguing convergence of pleasure derived from on-screen bodily display and pleasure derived from the viewer's own physical contribution to the spectacle. Human bodies, filmed bodies, and the cinema's body come together in a startlingly intimate moment of physical thrill.

The thrill of *Annabelle Serpentine Dance* and other films like it lay partly in the sheer frenzy of movement as Annabelle spins across the tiny screen, the sort of muscularity characteristic of early cinema. However, another pleasure in watching Annabelle was the spectacle of sex, which had everything to do with temporality. As viewers cranked the handle that set these images into motion, there existed (at least in viewers' minds) the teasing possibility of glimpsing the unseen: patrons could slow the rotation of the images to a stopping point just at the moment when those billowing skirts reached their most titillating height, at which point they might, theoretically at least, reveal flesh. Annabelle's sexuality was expressed as movement, muscularity, and vitality, yet her patrons' desire may have been to *stop* her movement at the crucial moment. Men (and her fans were predominantly men) could slow these images down in at attempt to catch that moment, "pause" it and, by doing so, tame the relentless movements of both Annabelle and the apparatus.[28]

This elusive glimpse of sexuality and stillness are, of course, closely related. *La petite mort* is, after all, the height of sexual pleasure and a moment of pure, sudden stillness wrapped up in one. In fact, all films do implicitly what *Annabelle Serpentine Dance* does explicitly: they tease us with passionate, frenetic, relentless movement at twenty-four frames per second, which thrills us but also entices us to want to slow them down or stop them altogether. Knowing that the film is based in intermittence and knowing that it could break down at any time contribute, however subtly, to the drama of the film experience, just as the knowledge of the fundamental fragility of our own bodies is always with us, however suppressed, as we move through life. The film reminds us of our own tenuousness, bringing us with it as it teeters on the precipice between life and death, movement and stillness. The experience is ambivalent to say the least, at once titillating and terrifying.[29]

In those moments when a film's movement is slowed or stopped (as in the mutoscope films or a mechanical breakdown of a projected film), we get an intimate look not only inside the film but also inside ourselves, for cinema's inner mechanisms are a mirror image of our own. We may think nothing of our heartbeat as we go about our daily business, but when we suddenly become aware of it for some reason, we momentarily feel, in the space between two heartbeats, the frailty of the system on which we are built. This intimate affinity between film and viewer is particularly well exhibited by early cinema, whose very forms of exhibition exacerbate the tenuous balance between stillness and movement. Early cinema expressed human forms of movement by incorporating those forms into its own body, rendering them visible on its screens and viewfinders and in the flicker of darkness between frames.[30] As such, it seems truly to have been designed as a metaphor for the human body.

CHILD'S PLAY

If it can be said that cinema is a technological metaphor for the body—that is, drawing its forms from the human body and expressing them back to us in cinematic form—then animation, in its product and its very process, is a metaphor for cinema itself. If cinema is the illusion of continuous motion, animation is the illusion of the illusion, and as such it provides a unique opportunity to study this passionate liaison between the body and the cinema. It indulges our fascination with how things work by inviting us to lay our hands on the machine itself, take it apart, and peek inside. It reveals to us the deep-seated intermittence at the heart of the movies and human motion, an experience that can be fascinating and even scary, but always exquisitely intimate.

Stop-motion animation takes the underlying principle of cinema—the construction of movement from individual still images—literally as its own mode of production and presentation. It exaggerates the discontinuity according to which motion pictures work and in the process renders even more obvious the discontinuous nature of movement, both cinematic and human. Whereas the earliest films and exhibition technologies allowed spectators a fleeting glimpse of moments of stillness and cessation in the viewer's body and film's body, stop-motion animation offers a lingering look at an *extended* arrest of movement.

Animation still works like live-action, of course, with the illusion of smooth and continuous movement achieved through the projection of separate images at such a speed that the gaps between them become imperceptible to the "naked" eye. Animation, however, incorporates the smallest of cinematic units—the frame—into the tangible process of production.

Camera movements, for example, are not real camera movements, but animated, simulated camera movements: the camera is moved a fraction of an inch, one frame at a time, to create a sometimes jerky, slightly imperfect illusion of a single camera movement. The delicacy and intricacy of the process are heightened, and the essential characteristic of cinema—its ability to represent apparently fluid movement through a process based on intermittent, discontinuous motion—is exaggerated and intensified. In this sense, animation could be called cinema *par excellence.*

Stop-motion animation, even more so than cel animation, draws our body's attention to the discontinuity inherent in cinema and in our own body, in large part because it appeals to the sense of touch, though in a different way than the hand-cranked mutoscopes and muscular films of early cinema did. Although it could easily be argued that early cinema has a haptic quality to it because of the flatness and graininess of the images, stop-motion animation even more so is a haptic art form, one that addresses itself first and foremost to the fingertips, provoking our desire to touch, caress, squeeze, and scrape the images before us. It is through the fingertips that stop-motion animation entices us to feel the stops and starts in our own physical "animation."

That so many stop-motion animated films address themselves to an audience of children (and childlike adults) should come as no surprise, because, even more than cel and computer animation, stop-motion animation's *modus operandi* is hands-on play, at which every child is an expert. The animator's touch sets these creatures, bodies, and films in motion, in a more literal way than in any other kind of filmmaking. One can even see the occasional fingerprint on the clay figures in Aardman Studios' Wallace and Gromit shorts *The Wrong Trousers* and *A Close Shave,* "and we're proud of them," says the man who left some of those traces, creator Nick Park. "The Wallace and Gromit films have a very handmade feel to them and I think that's part of the charm."[31] The tactility of stop-motion animated films like these taps into the sensuality (and perhaps revolutionary potential) of child's play, including the itch some of us have to take our toys apart and find out how and why they work, and how they might work differently.[32]

Stop-motion animation entices the viewing body with materiality and textures that beg to be touched. This marks the key difference between stop-motion animation and cel animation, whose "objects" are not as tangibly familiar to us from our own experience. Instead, they are flat representations of lived three-dimensional objects, their rough surfaces polished until smooth as celluloid. The Quay Brothers' *Street of Crocodiles,* Jan

Svankmajer's *Dimensions of Dialogue* (1982), and Ladislas Starewicz's *Revenge of the Cameraman* (1912), for example, are filled with objects that, beyond carrying any narrative or symbolic value (although some do that), address viewers primarily as organic objects of the world, reminding us of our own embodied existence in that world. Even the mechanical objects in *Street of Crocodiles*, and there are many, seem significant only by virtue of the dust particles and rust that accumulate on them, the saliva that propels them, and the dirt that surrounds them.

Street of Crocodiles takes very little in the way of narrative from Bruno Schulz's novel of the same name, but it does borrow its keen focus on materiality and the sense of touch. In the novel, the narrator's father asks, "Can you understand the deep meaning of that weakness, that passion for colored tissue, for *papier mâché*, for distemper, for oakum and sawdust? This is . . . proof of our love for matter as such, for its fluffiness or porosity, for its unique mystical consistency. . . . We . . . love its creaking, its resistance, its clumsiness. We like to see behind each gesture, behind each move, its inertia, its heavy effort, its bearlike awkwardness."[33]

The scene in the film that corresponds to this passage revels in texture. The puppet-protagonist meets a tailor, a doll with a head of porcelain, who choreographs the movements of three other porcelain dolls as they welcome the protagonist into their shop. The dolls fawn over and fondle their guest, running their tiny porcelain hands over his wiry hair and cracked, bewildered-looking features. He becomes the object of some strange ritual in which they drape carefully selected fabrics over his body and replace his head with one like their own, stuffing it with cotton and then pulling tufts of that from the empty top, ears, and eye sockets.

At one point, the tailor stands at a table where he runs his hands over an exquisitely detailed map of Poland and magically produces from his fingertips a piece of raw meat that he lays over the map. He reaches into a drawer and pulls out a sheet of tissue paper, the kind used for dress patterns, and smoothes it over the meat. The moisture of the meat's surface seeps through the tissue paper as the tailor runs his hands over the length of it. An army of pins marches up the surface of the meat, sinking themselves into the glistening flesh as they fasten the tissue pattern to it. As the dolls continue to dress the now barely recognizable protagonist, the tailor cradles the protagonist's detached head in his arms, running his tiny fingers through the coarse gray hair. He sets the head on the map table and covers it carefully with tissue paper.

The tailor and his worker-dolls escort the protagonist, intact now, to another room in the tailor shop. Another bodily organ, looking like meat, lies on a table in front of a wall covered with pencil sketches of other vaguely human, vaguely sexual organs. A porcelain hand caresses the surface of the organ slowly. Meanwhile, the tailor invites the protagonist to gaze through a window into a darker room beyond the tailor shop. Flanked by two dolls who caress his backside through his rough tweed coat, the protagonist peers through the grimy window. On the other side of the glass, a small porcelain doll-child sits on a dirt floor and cradles in his arms a light bulb that is nearly as big as he. As the protagonist and dressmakers look on, the child pulls a woolen hat from his head and gently covers the light bulb with it. In an extreme close-up, tiny screws surrounding the little boy rise up, twirl deliriously through a layer of dirt so porous and dry that one can feel it under one's fingernails, and scamper off.

One cannot help but be engrossed in *Street of Crocodiles*, not by virtue of its intriguing plot or characters, if those terms can even be applied here, but by virtue of the materiality of its objects. The textures in this sequence, for example—the cold hardness of the pins against the warm and slimy surface of the meat, the thick textures of the tweed coat and woolen hat, the fragility of dry, crackling tissue paper—speak to the viewer's fingertips, awakening the senses and an awareness of the viewer's own tactility. The world described in *Street of Crocodiles* is in every sense a tactile one: a world of dirt, dust, flesh, fabric, and textures that are familiar to us but which the film invites us to see for the first time. The tailor shop sequence is characteristic of the haptic quality of the experience of this film. The dolls' hands caress every available surface voluptuously, and the film invites us to do the same. Even the sonorous violins of Leszek Jankowski's score elicit a tactile sense of friction, of horsehair bows moving gently, then roughly, over delicate, quivering strings.

Just as the surface sensuality of the film's objects, spaces, and sounds engages us physically and emotionally in the world of the film, so the scale of those objects and spaces impels us to watch with keen and attentive eyes. Objects that are at first glance unrecognizable and meaningless reveal themselves, through the viewer's concentrated gaze and the film's use of extreme close-up, to be eminently familiar objects of daily life—straight pins, doorknobs, a leather shoelace—the sorts of things that escape our notice in daily life.

Cinematic units and gestures themselves, too, are miniaturized here: the frame becomes the relevant unit of measure, as in stop-motion animation generally. Perhaps the most dynamic example are the film's animated "camera movements." I set the term in quotation marks to indicate that at least some of these movements are probably fabricated in the stop-motion mode, while others move in real-time over their objects, and it is difficult to tell how any given movement is made.

The camera movements are not only ontologically ambiguous but also thematically ambivalent: they express, in muscular terms, the simultaneous but contradictory experiences of curiosity and claustrophobia, freedom and restriction, vitality and death. The pans and tilts and tracking shots are as tiny as the objects they explore: each one moves very quickly, sliding across intricate, richly textured surfaces like fingertips across Braille. This rapid movement, combined with the camera's extreme proximity to the objects of its attention, expresses an intense curiosity, a desire to explore the world of the film closely and intimately, and to "take in" as much detail and information as possible with each fleeting instant. At the same time, though, the camera movements underscore a sense of restless and uneasy confinement. No camera movement lasts more than a second or two, and each one ends abruptly, so that the restless energy of the camera is constantly snuffed out. The camera moves almost obsessively in tiny increments as if struggling to work itself free from a cramped space. Ultimately, it fails: like the protagonist who is set free from his tether in the prelude only to wander endlessly through the small and twisted spaces of this cave-like world, the moving camera is paradoxically perpetually constrained.

The film's amplification of the essence of cinema—the use of intermittent motion to create the illusion of motion as smooth and continuous—raises interesting questions about temporality as it is co-constituted by the film, by the objects represented on screen, and by the viewer. Whereas movement in live-action cinema manages, for the most part, to convince us of its smooth continuity, we're constantly aware of the intermittent nature of movement in stop-motion animation, of the fact that the smooth motion of the objects on screen is an illusion. This aspect of the viewing experience is especially fascinating in the films of the Quay Brothers. Because they're so good at what they do, the illusion of smooth and continuous movement is always almost perfect; in fact one has the sense that it could be flawless and utterly convincing if the animators so desired.

But the illusion is not quite perfect; there's always some reminder in the motion that it is an illusion (we know that screws don't just get up and roll away of their own volition), that the movement of these objects is, in actuality, intermittent, discontinuous, disjointed. Even the music reminds us muscularly of the intermittent motion at the core of the film's structure. Jankowski's haunting violins sing out throaty, ominous, low notes one moment and higher-pitched staccato notes the next. Though the slow and melodic sections seem to wash over the soundtrack without a pause, one must remember the nature of the instrument on which they are played. How does one play a violin, except by back-and-forth, intermittent motion of the bow across the strings? The units and segmentation of time here, as in the animation itself, are infinitesimal; nevertheless, the basic structure of the music is of discrete movements making up the auditory illusion of continuous sound.

This constant awareness of the intermittent nature of the objects' real movement in *Street of Crocodiles* would be unremarkable, no more interesting than our occasional awareness of it in live-action cinema, if it weren't for the deep involvement of our bodies in this viewing experience, an involvement achieved through the tactility and miniaturization of the film's objects, movements, and production process. Because we feel a material and muscular investment in the film world and the film's body, our bodies are implicated in its temporality as well, just as our investment in Buster Keaton's projects leads us to invest ourselves in the film's space. If we react viscerally to this film, it is in part because the nature of our own physical motion is, like that of the film, inherently (although rarely perceptibly) discontinuous and intermittent. For the duration of the film experience, we simultaneously inhabit, whether painfully or pleasurably, the temporal structures both of ceaselessly flowing "real life" and of the lurching irregularity of the film-world. By actively engaging us in two simultaneously and inherently opposed modes of temporality, the film reminds us of our carnal embeddedness in both those temporal planes.

Ladislas Starewicz made this case even more poignantly, by populating his films with the dead bodies of birds, frogs, and insects that formerly flew, hopped, and crawled. In *Revenge of the Cameraman* and his other works, Starewicz chose once-living creatures and, by animating them one discrete movement at a time, dissected their movement and revealed the unstable, disjointed basis for what had, in life, seemed effortless and graceful. More than a lesson in animal biology, the films force a recognition of our own basis in inconsistent movement as well as the tenuousness and fragility of our bodies. Despite the sense we have of them as competent and coherent, they can surprise us and betray us by succumbing to death and stillness in a fleeting instant. The effect would not have been the same if Starewicz had drawn his figures on animation cels: the familiar surface textures of these animals and insects establishes the intimate connection between the creatures and the viewer that resonates deeply, viscerally, between the film's body and the viewer's body.

The conflict between these two vastly different temporalities—graceful movement and utter discontinuity—could prove too much for the viewing

10.   *Street of Crocodiles* (The Quay Brothers, U.K., 1986)

body that must, if the viewer would engage with the film at all, inhabit them simultaneously. This ambivalence is not unlike the discomfort some people feel while reading in a moving vehicle. In both situations, the body is required to concentrate on minuscule things and movements (dust particles and frame-by-frame motion in *Street of Crocodiles,* for example, and individual letters and minuscule movements of the eye from one letter to the next while reading), while at the same time the body is engaged in continuous movement on a much larger scale (the movement of the body as we consciously perceive it through daily life, and the movement of the body in a vehicle speeding along a highway), which the body perceives as smooth rather than based on discrete units, as stop-motion animation and the act of reading are.

The unease that some viewers feel watching *Street of Crocodiles* may arise from the inability of the lived body to reconcile itself with the inter-mittence of the movement that characterizes this film and other stop-motion animation. (Not inconsequentially, that discomfort on the part of the viewer also recalls the irritation experienced by spectators during a faulty projection of a film, where the "continuous" images are revealed to consist of separate, still images. Here, too, the viewer is reminded of an

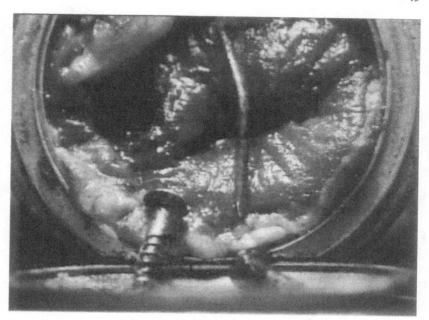

11. *Street of Crocodiles* (The Quay Brothers, U.K., 1986)

alternate temporality that one would prefer to forget.) Other viewers, however, may be bewitched by stop-motion animation precisely because it makes sensible to the viewing body, in cinematic form, a temporality that is not ordinarily sensible. The stop-motion film as product and process serves to remind us of our own physical basis in intermittent bodily movement. The intense attraction to these films, the experience of getting caught up in their rhythm, may well invoke a feeling of sensual harmony.

Street of Crocodiles winds up with a particularly striking image that reveals the complexities and subtleties of this textural and temporal affinity between the viewer and the film. Toward the end of the film, the tiny screws that appear in the prologue and throughout the film have unscrewed themselves from the floorboards of a small, decrepit space behind the tailor shop and now scurry along its corridors. There is a cut to a small table on which lies a dusty and tarnished pocket watch. At the right of the screen, the screws appear at the edge of the table in extreme close-up and wiggle themselves toward the watch. When they reach it, they leap up and disappear inside the watch, pushing themselves forcefully, almost violently, into its cracked and dirty face (which, interestingly enough, features letters rather than numbers, further destabilizing our ordinary sense of time). The watch shuts tight and spins around on the table, then falls open to reveal its inner workings, which consist entirely of glistening raw meat. The screws emerge again from these shockingly organic innards, wriggling their way out of the meat to fall onto the table again and scurry away.

This segment echoes the entire film in its attention to minuscule detail (the tiny letters on the watch face are large enough to read) and the astonishingly material quality of the watch's innards. More significant, however, is that this meaty sequence articulates the overall effect of the film, which is to remind us as embodied viewers of our carnal, visceral embeddedness in time itself. By engaging our fingertips and skin with images of meat, dust, metal, and the like, the film entices us into a deeper relationship with it, by which we come to a palpable recognition that the inner clockwork of our bodies and the film's body are surprisingly similar. Our tactile, visceral body grasps the implication immediately: like the cinema itself, our own robust vitality is an illusion, and our vital rhythms mark with every breath the perpetual possibility of stillness and death.

The meatiness of the watch's innards evokes carnality and sexuality, as does the tailor-shop sequence, with its porcelain dolls lasciviously fondling pieces of raw flesh and caressing the protagonist's backside. Just as *Annabelle Serpentine Dance* does, this sequence makes a palpable connection between temporality and sex. However, the image also suggests, more generally, a relationship of sensuous intimacy that is at once physical and emotional, and which characterizes both early cinema and stop-motion animation. The intimacy established between the film and the viewer contains the possibility of a sexual aspect: the film invites our fascination with the border between movement and stillness, between life and death, in a way that evokes sexual desire and *la petite mort*. But the intimacy also recalls the relationship between children and their favorite toys, something explicitly evoked by the little doll-child playing tenderly with a light bulb in *Street of Crocodiles*. Child's play is as complex as adult passion: it is a combination of tender affection for the toy in question and also, simultaneously, the desire to take one's toy apart to see how it works. Within the intimate relationship they establish with us, early cinema and stop-motion animation indulge both our passionate tenderness and morbid, destructive curiosity about the nature of the machine, both cinematic and human.

Conclusion

Inspiration

The image is indivisible and elusive, dependent upon our consciousness and the real world which it seeks to embody. . . . We cannot comprehend the totality of the universe, but the poetic image is able to express that totality.
ANDREY TARKOVSKY

BREATHTAKING

Now we find ourselves on the other side of this study, but we have not come full circle, for that implies circumvention. Rather, we have moved *through* skin, musculature, and viscera to arrive at a place or a plane where depth becomes surface again, and everything is turned inside out. This chapter's focus is the site of convergence and emergence wherein all the dimensions of sensual, tactile experience—on the part of the human body and the film's body—contribute to and co-constitute the fully embodied cinematic experience.

Merleau-Ponty describes the irrevocable and intimate connection between the subject and the object as the thing that makes vision possible. "The body *stands* before the world and the world stands upright before it, and between them there is a relation that is one of embrace. And between these two vertical beings, there is not a frontier, but a contact surface."[1] His language is evocative, as always, of the tactility inherent in this connection, a tactility that descends even into the body's depths. This connection is a mutual possession without which there can be no perception at all: "He who sees cannot possess the visible unless he is possessed by it, unless he *is of it*."[2]

In the previous chapters, I have elucidated a few of the tactile structures—material/textural, spatial, and temporal—shared by the film's and viewer's body that enable us not only to see but also to feel the film as an embodied subject who is like us but also different in fundamental ways. That we and the film share these tactile modes of being in the world is what allows for communication to occur in the fleshy spaces between us. The contiguity between subject and object, and between film and viewer specifically, is present not merely in the press of skin to skin, muscle to muscle, and vital organs to vital organs. The relationship is also a full-bodied opening into and suffusion of one with the other that goes beyond surface, middle, and depth. I will call this relationship *inspiration,* bearing in mind Merleau-Ponty's suggestion that "we speak of 'inspiration,' and the word should be taken literally. There really is inspiration and expiration of Being, action and passion so slightly discernible that it becomes impossible to distinguish between what sees and what is seen, what paints and is painted."[3]

A literal, embodied act of inspiration involves all three dimensions traced through previous chapters, and, like touch in these other registers, it begins at the surface (we encounter a breeze on our skin, breathe it in through lips or nose) and proceeds through the muscles (throat, chest, and stomach expand as we draw it in) into the depths (our lungs, ventricles, and even the bloodstream fill up with oxygen). It reverses direction as well, to be exhaled through lips and nose again and to appear as vigor or lassitude in the muscles and perhaps a blush on the cheek. Thus, inspiration is transitive (both objective and subjective, inward- and outward-moving), and it is pervasive and diffuse (involving the surface, middle, and depth of the body). It vacillates in the space between immanent and transcendent: it is embodied by a single subject, but at the same time it constitutes the bond between that subject and all others, as well as that subject's immersion in a world of materiality.

Drew Leder's discussion of "absorption" bears crucially on my description of inspiration as an expression of the reversibility between surface and depth and between self and other that is at play in the cinematic experience. Describing a landscape as one might experience it during a walk through a forest, Leder says, "it is as if we were swallowed into a larger body. At the same time, this landscape is swallowed into our embodiment, transforming it from within."[4] He refers to this experience of mutual incorporation as "a mode of one-body relation," in which we converge with the world around us, becoming a part of the living chiasmus. "I open feelingly such that the world can penetrate my senses, my muscles, my consciousness. The temporality of the landscape transforms my temporality. . . . The spaciousness of the outdoors becomes my space. . . . I feel *inspired,* 'breathed in' as if from the wind and trees. . . . The boundaries between inner and outer thus become porous. . . . This is an experience of bi-directional incorporation; the world comes alive empathically within my body, even as I experience myself as part of the body of the world."[5] This incorporation "is by no means restricted to experiences of nature," writes Leder. "It is there when we enter deeply into a work of art. We may skim past a hundred canvases before we become *absorbed* in one. Its mood then starts to saturate our being, its sense of space and time, of rhythm and beauty."[6] The film experience is conducive to this kind of mutual absorption, perhaps even more so than the experience of a painting or landscape, because of the circumstances that surround it (and surround us): the darkness of the theater enshrouds us; the screen stretches bigger than life before our eyes and bathes us in light; and carefully placed speakers throw voices, music, and ambient sound around our shoulders.

The cinema in-spires us, literally and metaphorically; the hyphen may help to maintain both these senses of the word as well as the reversibility of the act itself. When a film has captured our attention completely, we are drawn in (in-spired) by it. Its body opens onto ours and invites, even inhales, us; we might even feel its pulse and breath as our own. The film takes in our forms of being-in-the-world, and at the same time fills us up and animates us with sensations and attitudes. Not only does the film "breathe in" distinct tactile behaviors, as previous chapters have shown; it also breathes in styles of sensitivity to the world around us.

A "breathtaking" film not only makes us gasp in astonishment at what we're watching; it also takes our breath in and gives it back to us in cinematic form. We take in its color, light, movement, drama, music, violence, eroticism, grandeur, intimacy, or immensity, for example. At the same time and in the same, bi-directional movement, we express these qualities back to the film in our own human form, and the film draws these things from us. The sumptuousness of color in Douglas Sirk's melodramas, the violent barrage of Alfred Hitchcock's *Psycho* shower scene (1960), the pensive languor of Andrey Tarkovsky's slow-motion sequences, the exuberant vitality of a Buster Keaton comedy: all of these things, along with our embodied responses to them, are performances of attitudes, affects, and sensations that move between and through both us and the film. We take in the film's vitality and the style of its experience of the world, and we adopt and express those things back to it. We in-spire in both directions at once, infusing the film with our own particularly human version of those qualities.

In the presence of very intense sadness or joy, for example, we might experience a swelling of tears and a swelling in the throat; the film adopts these reactions and transforms them into a swelling of violins and voices in the musical score in *The Sound of Music* (Robert Wise, 1965), for example, or a bursting intensification of the color palette in *Written on the Wind* (Douglas Sirk, 1956). A subtle presence until that moment, music and color rush to the surface of these films in the same way that our emotions rise up and make themselves visible.

To take another example, the film might in-spire our embodied experience and expression of fear and horror. We perceive fear in the way that our heart races and our nerves are "rattled"; we might respond by losing our calm, our composure, and even control over ourselves. We may shut our eyes against the thing that terrifies us, or even, if the fear gets to be too much, lose consciousness altogether. The film, too, experiences and expresses fear in similar albeit distinctly cinematic ways. Jacques Tourneur's *Cat People* (1942), for example, "shuts its eyes" against the horrible as we might do. By allowing the menace to lurk largely unseen in dark, shadowy corners of its sets and its frame, the film not only scares us but expresses fear and trepidation in its own terms, in the embodied language of light, shadow, and movement. Jean Rouch's *The Lion Hunters* (1965) borrows from its viewers a sensitivity and responsiveness to unsettling, paralyzing fear, but the film expresses its panic in cinematic form. When Rouch himself is attacked by lions while shooting a segment, the sound of the attack and the shouts of Rouch and his crew continue over the soundtrack, but the sound is the only consistent element. The scene as a whole loses its composure, devolving into a flurry of blurred images shot by a camera that falls to the ground before the screen goes black.

This is not to say that the film hears us crying and then feels a similar response itself. We *cause* the film to erupt in sound and music in a given moment in the same way that we inspire a close-up with our desire for a closer look or provoke an action film's aggressive tracking shot with our desire to catch up to the fleeing villain. It is not that we laugh or cry too hard that makes the film explode into music or color; rather, the film borrows our ability to feel things deeply and the style with which we express our feelings tactilely and emotionally. It in-spires in our passion, sorrow, lust, joy, hysteria, terror, and panic, just as it fills itself with our movements, agility, tension, softness, uprightness, sensitivity, and intermittence. It *feels* our emotions and our vitality so strongly that its experience overflows the boundaries of its body, not in the form of shrieks, laughter, and tears but in shockingly vibrant color, musical crescendos, and extreme close-ups.

These expressive, affective qualities of the film and the viewer's affective responses to those qualities are, in fact, two sides of a single structure that exists in the space between film and viewer, which we discover by making ourselves vulnerable to the film. Dufrenne describes it as

> something in the object that can be known only by a sort of sympathy in which the subject opens himself to it. Indeed, at the limit, the affectively qualified object is itself a subject and no longer a pure object or the simple correlate of an impersonal consciousness. Instead of being

determined from without, affective qualities involve a certain way of relating themselves to each other, a manner of constituting themselves as a totality—in short, a capacity for affecting *themselves*. As a consequence, the affective qualities into which the atmosphere of an aesthetic object is resolved become anthropomorphic. The horrible in Bosch, the joyful in Mozart, the mocking in Faulkner, the tragic quality in *Macbeth* all designate an attitude of the subject as well as a structure of the object, which are in each case complementary.[7]

This anticipation and awakening is a full-bodied tactile echo between two bodies mutually inspired by one another, though never confused or made identical to each other. In using the term "inspiration," I hope to underscore existential phenomenology's insistence on the intersubjectivity of viewer and the viewed, as well as the way tactile contact between film and viewer moves *through* the body and opens onto something larger than either film or viewer. I will return here to Merleau-Ponty's notion of the flesh, or chiasm, as well as to Tarkovsky's *Mirror*, which seems "inspirational" in many ways, not least in the way that it invites viewers to dwell momentarily in the act of breath-taking that makes palpable the oscillation between surface and depth, motion and emotion, self and other, visible and invisible, and being and Being.

THE WIND IN THE TREES

The flesh is not matter, is not mind, is not substance. To designate it, we should need the old term "element," in the sense it was used to speak of water, air, earth, and fire, that is, in the sense of a *general thing*, midway between the spatio-temporal individual and the idea, a sort of incarnate principle that brings with it a style of being wherever there is a fragment of being. The flesh is in this sense an "element" of Being.

MERLEAU-PONTY, *The Visible and the Invisible*, 139.

Earlier I discussed the shot in Tarkovsky's *Mirror* that introduces us to the narrator's mother as a young woman, seated on a fence overlooking the field that surrounds the house in which so many childhood memories are lodged. In that earlier shot a man could be seen approaching in the distance while, in voice-over, the narrator recalls the way he and his sister would anxiously await the rare visits from their father, hoping that every approaching stranger might be him. This man, a stranger, arrives at the fence and strikes up a playful conversation with the woman. She is cool to his flirtatious banter, but the exchange seems to affect them both, however fleeting it might be. The emotional impact of the scene registers not only in the performances of both actors but also, more profoundly, in the movement of wind through

12. *Mirror* (Andrey Tarkovsky, U.S.S.R., 1975)

the trees that separate them as he begins his journey back to town. The scene is breathtaking in the most literal, embodied sense of that word.

In the first of four shots that depict his departure from the scene, the stranger walks back across the field into the distance as the woman watches. She calls out to him to point out matter-of-factly a smudge of dirt on his face, from a fall he'd taken while sitting on the fence with her. He turns toward her (and us) very briefly, brushes first one cheek, then the other, and turns away again to continue his journey. He walks for several seconds before a gust of wind rises in the distance and begins to sweep across the field. The grass in the distance ripples as the wind travels toward the man, and he pauses momentarily before it reaches him. As it sweeps over and around him, he slowly turns back toward the woman and the camera. His body and his attention seem pulled by the wind itself, in the direction of the woman he is leaving behind. He stares intently as the breeze travels all the way to the camera, where it whips noisily through a row of small trees in front of the fence.

The man continues to stare, unmoving, for a long moment, even after the wind passes and the trees settle. The woman isn't in this shot, but we return to her in the next, a close-up in which she stares impassively toward screen-left, toward the field and the stranger. Her face reveals nothing, but

13. *Mirror* (Andrey Tarkovsky, U.S.S.R., 1975)

the profound, if ambiguous, connection between these two people is unmistakable. It is conveyed not only by the shot/reverse-shot pattern that links her with the man she watches, but also by the movement of the tall trees behind her, which blow gently in the breeze that had already come and gone in the previous shot.

She begins to walk toward screen-right, away from the field and back toward the house. Her movement is interrupted by a cut to the third shot of the sequence, where the stranger has also turned away but has not yet resumed walking. There is no delay this time as a second gust of wind bends the grass ahead of him and quickly sweeps over his body. He turns back again, even more slowly this time, both perceiving and expressing (to us and the woman who watches him) the uncanny nature of this repeated event. (In fact, this shot could easily be mistaken for the shot of the first breeze, repeated but differently cut, were it not for the different pattern of the wind's movement through the trees.) After a long, contemplative gaze toward the woman and the camera, he gives a jaunty wave and turns to walk away again. In another close-up, she pauses briefly as a pensive expression passes over her face, and turns away.

There are two openings here, a temporal fissure between the first and second shots and another between the second and third, that bear remarking. As the stranger stares back toward the woman, the wind seems to pass through and out of the first shot, so that the trees become calm and still for a very long moment before the cut to her first close-up. Despite the lag time between the two shots, however, the breeze seems *not* to have dissipated, for the trees behind her sway in its force. It lingers, apparently, circulating in the space around her and in the space between cuts.

Likewise, when a straight cut returns us to the stranger in the field, we see that a second gust of wind has *already* reached him and is already blowing toward the camera. We don't see the genesis of this breeze, as we had the first: it seems to have been blown into existence by the previous shot. (Tarkovsky takes such special care to show us the rising of that first strong wind in the distant grasses that it seems jarring not to see where this second gust "comes from.")

The wind, then, moves not only through the spaces marked by his body and hers, or by field and fence, but between the shots themselves, and between film and viewer. It seems to swirl in the gaps created by the editing, in a time and space that are beyond and beneath but also within the time and space made visible in each shot and inhabited by our viewing bodies, by the camera, and by the characters.[8]

The sweep of the wind through these trees is a breathtaking moment, to be sure. It is one of many instances in which, as Petr Král writes, "the director's vision literally breathes life into the material mass of objects, awakens life in them, and shows us their secret existence, or their hidden essence."[9] However, it is also an act of *breath-taking*, in which we both take in and *are taken in* by something larger. What is at stake here are not only the stranger's body, the woman's body, or even viewer's body and film's body, but also the larger system of which each of these is only one part, and which brings us all into being.

Maya Turovskaya writes of Tarkovsky's films that "the 'subject time' into which is fitted this or that aspect of an individual's or a people's history is always, in his work, synchronous with the *whole* of Time, stretching away in all directions, untrammeled by limitations. . . . And if the 'subject' time in Tarkovsky's films is synchronous with the whole of human time, so is the 'subject' space in which the action takes place commensurable with the whole of human space. And this is what gives the events recounted in Tarkovsky's films their quality of *everywhere* and *always*."[10] This experience of the "everywhere and always" emerges often through the use of slow-motion cinematography. Indeed, several other instances of wind moving through trees are shot this way, most notably the image of a very young boy running into his grandmother's house as blossoms fall from trees like rain during a gust of wind.

Although the stranger's departure across the field is shot in real time and with a still camera, the movement of wind across the field has the effect of slow motion, which, in Gilles Deleuze's words, "frees movement from its moving body to make a sliding of the world."[11] The sweeping of the wind through grass and trees opens up the image onto a field of time and space that surrounds and sustains the individual events, actions, movements that emerge within it. Král writes that "Tarkovsky's images . . . break free of their narrow limits and reach beyond them to infinity, in time and space. In this sense, fixed-camera sequences are just as evocative as those shot with a moving camera."[12]

Indeed, when trying to ascertain whether the first and third shots of the sequence were in fact identical (they are not), I found myself having to concentrate solely on the edges of the frame and the movement of the wind, rather than the movement of the human figure. Of course, it is difficult to trace the movement of something that is only visible in its effect on bodies; I had to deduce from the movement of man and trees the force and direction of this invisible presence, the wind. It is telling, this requisite shift of attention from figure to ground (literally, to the *ground* on which the man walks and trees sway, as well as to the background and edges that bring figures—man and trees alike—into relief, rendering them visible). The shift of attention to the edges and the in-between spaces reflects or, perhaps, cues a shift of attention from the visible to that which makes the visible possible. In this regard, what Elena del Río has written of Jean-Luc Godard might also be said of Tarkovsky: that "the filmmaker's gaze turns its activity of seeing back on itself, looking not to *what appears* as visible, but to the visible's *mode of appearing*."[13] Like Godard's, Tarkovsky's work generally and this sequence in particular "undertakes an involvement with the visible as a mode of constant becoming, where figures come into being from a latent ground of visibility and virtuality."[14]

EVERYWHERE AND ALWAYS

D. W. Griffith claimed, late in life, that what the cinema needed was "the wind in the trees." While Griffith sought a degree of naturalism missing, he thought, from modern cinema, the wind in Tarkovsky's trees carries a sense of a world greater than any individual but that subtends and makes possible all individual, embodied sensations and actions. "What makes then

of the flesh a seer and of being a visibility is not the production of a clear-
ing by nihilation," writes Alphonso Lingis, perhaps referring to Sartre's
notion of "nothingness," "but an elemental event by which the flesh captures the lines of force of the world, brings itself up to the levels about
which visibility is modulated, rises upright before vertical being."[15]

In the stranger's departure across the field, the wind becomes a tangible
thickness, rising up between us and the field and events taking place in it.
The trees are in the wind, of course, but also the wind is "in" the trees. The
wind is a current that flows in, through, and between everybody and every
body in this encounter: man, woman, trees, camera, microphone, celluloid,
and spectator. The wind is the "stuff" of the world that makes perception
possible and yet distinguishes us from the things we would see and touch.

> We understand then why we see the things themselves, in their places,
> where they are, according to their being which is indeed more than
> their being-perceived—and why at the same time we are separated
> from them by all the thickness of the look and of the body; it is that
> this distance is not the contrary of this proximity, it is deeply conso-
> nant with it, it is synonymous with it. It is that the thickness of flesh
> between the seer and the thing is constitutive for the thing of its visi-
> bility as for the seer of his corporeity; it is not an obstacle between
> them, it is their means of communication.[16]

That "thickness" is exactly the wind in the trees. Our look and the returned
gaze of the man, the trees, the field, the grass—all of them haptic, muscular, and visceral at once—are carried, literally conveyed, in and *as* the thickness of the air, which erupts as movement of the man and the trees turning
and swaying in the breeze.

Earlier I described the meeting that occurs between self and other in the
interactions between skin, musculature, and viscera as an embrace, a handshake, and an intimate perception of one another's rhythms. The kinds of
engagement expressed and discovered in these meetings become more profound in the context of this notion of flesh or chiasm. Surrounding and
suffusing all the dimensions of the body, it is the place in which communication and exchange—including acts of vision and touch—become possible. It is the medium in which specific embodied sensations, movements,
and behaviors are commuted not only from one sense to another and from
depth to surface and back again, but also to others we encounter in the
world. The connection between viewer's body and the film's, and between
our human and cinematic bodies and the world at large, is at once intimate
and immense, involving surface and depth. It is a mutual inspiration in and
of the world.

"The existence of the transcendental," writes Gabrielle Hezekiah, "may presuppose, not a masterful and controlling subject but a subject cognizant of its own object-ness in the broader scheme of things. It may presuppose a subject willing to release its own intentions and to allow its being to serve as a medium for the passage of being."[17] This focus on the "broader scheme of things" is in keeping with Merleau-Ponty's description of perception, maintained throughout his career, as an act that is subjectively, intentionally lived and, at the same time, an act by which we are immersed in a world of bodies, things, and other subjects. Anne Rutherford calls this "a movement of the entire embodied being towards a corporeal appropriation of or immersion in a space, an experience, a moment. It is a movement away from the self, yes, but away from the self conceived as the subject, in so far as this concept is a cognitive or disembodied one—a movement out of the constraints of the definable, knowable—a groping towards a connection, a link-up with the carnality of the idea, the affect of the body, the sensible resonances of experience."[18]

The very act of perception moves us into the space *between* ourselves and others in the world. "'To be moved' means to come to a different position *in regard* to one's situation," writes phenomenologist Glen Mazis. "It is to experience a change in one's 'Being-towards' something or someone or to things in general: the relationship as suddenly burst forth, or perhaps slowly blossomed forth, into some significance, in such a way that a distinctive quality of that relatedness has come forward into manifestness, whether for a moment or for quite a time."[19]

In *Emotion and Embodiment,* Mazis notes that by its very nature, emotion operates in this space of intersubjectivity and reversibility, described by Merleau-Ponty as the basic structure of perception. Mazis points out that we often say we're wracked by, overwhelmed by, gripped by emotion, but, he asks, who or what does the "wracking," the "overwhelming," the "gripping"? Where does that power reside? Some would answer that it originates in the object that provokes such feelings; others would answer that it comes from within the emotional person. Mazis disagrees, saying that the power of emotion emerges and exists precisely in the meeting of perceiver and perceived, or feeling and felt. His idea that emotion is constituted in and by the encounter between subject and object is clearly informed by Merleau-Ponty's phenomenology: "Let us try to see how a thing or a being begins to exist for us through desires or love and we shall thereby come to understand better how things and beings can exist in general."[20]

Mazis resolutely insists on maintaining the hyphen in "e-motion" in order to emphasize the reversibility, the two-way movement, involved in emotion. "E-motion seems to entail both the motion away from the person to his or her world and away from the world to the person," he writes. "In the etymologies of words used as synonyms for the emotions, one finds terms indicating literally a movement 'into the subject' *and* 'away from the subject.'. . . . The motion of e-motion undercuts any division into 'subject' and 'object,' 'active' and 'passive.' There is an indeterminacy in e-motion which is really an interconnectedness that is a mutually enriching circularity: an expression of the subject and an impression of the object, or actually, rather, a *circulation* of meaning *within the circuit of both.*"[21]

Phenomenologist Sue Cataldi likewise argues that emotions by nature exist in the space of reversibility, in the plane of the flesh. "Just as we may extend the circle of touched and touching hands (in shaking or holding hands with another)," she writes, "so our body can 'annex' or 'incorporate' the emotional body of another."[22] Emotions are a source of reversibility in themselves, for to recognize an emotion in another is to recognize it in oneself. "Through curiosity, the significance of the novel or the odd is apprehended," Cataldi writes. "Through serenity, the significance of peace or tranquility is grasped. Through grief, I perceive, emotionally, the significance of loss; just as through boredom, I apprehend the significance of monotony."[23] Cataldi's description resonates nicely with those of Mazis and Sara Ahmed, who goes one step further to argue that bodies themselves do not "enter into" emotional encounters but are constituted and shaped by them.[24]

In their irrepressible reversibility, emotions not only complicate the division of subject from object and self from other, but also of any one dimension (skin, musculature, viscera) from another. Cataldi makes this point as well. She takes as an example the notion of having "butterflies" in one's stomach as a way of describing a feeling of apprehension. This feeling isn't containable within the stomach, but relates to the surface body and the world at large: "The fluttering of butterfly wings must be felt on the skin for this feeling to be felt 'inside.' We may then 'reverse' this feeling— turn it 'inside out,' so that what is 'outside' becomes 'inner' and what is inner becomes outer."[25] In Cataldi's phenomenology of emotions, she argues that the "deeper" or more intense the emotions, the more dramatically apparent is the reversibility: "Deeper emotional experiences expand, if you will, our 'personal' horizons beyond that of our own body, our own living flesh. We tend in these experiences to lose or to expand our sense of 'self' or 'subjectivity.' . . . The 'deeper' the emotional experience, the more . . . we experience ourselves as belonging to or caught up in the Flesh of the world."[26]

Although I have focused here on the four shots in *Mirror* in which the emotional weight of the stranger's departure is carried on and through the wind in the trees, the dizzying, breath-taking quality of that scene does echo in many ways the disorientation provoked by scenes I discussed in the introduction: two shots of this same field in which the camera simultaneously dollies in one direction while zooming in another, and the scene in which a hypnotherapist attempts to cure a boy of his stutter. In all four of these examples, we viewers have no human anchor, nor are we allowed to hitch ourselves to the film's body in a simple one-to-one relationship. In all cases, we experience a fully embodied suffusion that moves through and *beyond* looking at (the mother, the stuttering boy), listening to (the narrator, the therapist), moving as (the stranger, the wandering camera). By movement of the film's body or bodies and things on screen, we are made to reckon with our perpetual immersion in and *inspiration by* something that moves beyond, beneath, and within us all. In these moments, our tactile engagement with the cinema allows us to recognize *through* embodied, perceptive and expressive acts our situation in something larger, "to move through the body to an experience of its possibility."[27]

THE BIG SWALLOW

The full-bodied, mutual inspiration between film and viewer that *Mirror* so palpably evokes is illustrated even more graphically and literally by *The Big Swallow* (James Williamson, 1901). The film begins with a medium-long shot of a gentleman gesturing angrily and shouting (silently, of course) at the camera, presumably because he does not want to be photographed. He moves aggressively closer and closer to the camera until his wide-open mouth blocks the view entirely, seeming to swallow up the camera. An invisible cut to a black background creates a void, into which the flailing cinematographer and his old-fashioned camera pitch forward and disappear. Another invisible cut brings us back to the gentleman's open mouth, and he retreats from the camera, chewing and laughing at his clever triumph over the cinematographer and the apparatus.

The film's provocative premise suggests that while cinema has an astonishing ability to "draw us in" to its spectacle, the positions of film subject, viewer, and filmmaker are tenuous at best in this exchange. The film appears to engulf not only the cinematographer and the apparatus but also, by extension, the viewer. The cinematographer is at first unseen, as the gentleman being photographed walks toward the camera, but as the gentleman opens his mouth, the cameraman tumbles with his equipment into the

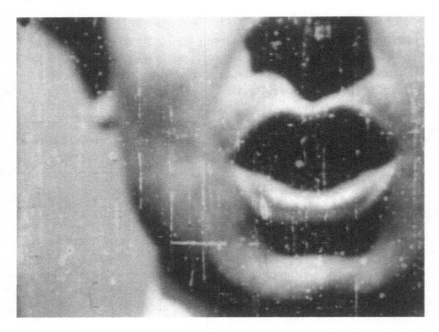

14. *The Big Swallow* (James Williamson, U.K., 1901)

gaping mouth of what had been, just a moment before, the filmed image of the gentleman. Because of the cinematographer's absence from the first image, we the viewers share his position: we initially view the filmed gentleman from the same position that the cinematographer does. Thus, when the cinematographer is swallowed up, so must we be. But we are left alive to see the swallowing up, now *outside* the relationship we'd been part of a moment before, and in the final shot the gentleman grins smugly at the camera despite the fact that he has just been seen to devour said camera in a single bite. The film turns inside and outside itself and back again, swallows itself up and spits itself back out, in the space of a few seconds. The film is a comic visualization of Merleau-Ponty's notion of the chiasmatic "intertwining," in which "there is not identity, nor non-identity, or non-coincidence, there is inside and outside turning about one another."[28]

   The Big Swallow forces the question: where are we in this picture? In this sense, perhaps the most interesting moment in the film comes *after* the gentleman approaches the camera and *before* the cinematographer pitches forward into the void. Those few frames of blackness play the same role, ontologically speaking, as the infinitesimal, imperceptible gap between a backward-dolly and a forward-zoom in *Mirror's* first and last

15. *The Big Swallow* (James Williamson, U.K., 1901)

shots of the field and the wind that blows through the field and between the edits during the stranger's departure. As Merleau-Ponty elegantly states, "the perceived contains gaps which are not mere 'failures to perceive.'"[29] These momentary gaps and reversals are expressions of the chiasm that permeates and makes possible every sensible thing, every tangible movement within it. They are not "voids," however, for as Alphonso Lingis explains, "[W]hat inaugurates touch in a tangible thing is not the production of the absolute untouchable void (for we cannot conceive of a being itself intangible that could touch, just as, after all, the only seer known to us is visible), but rather the capture in a hand of that movement and tempo that 'effect the forming of tactile phenomena, as light delineates the configuration of a visible surface.'"[30]

The ambiguity of Williamson's film suggests the corporeal, reversible contact between film and spectator, who inspire one other—in both directions—and yet do not disappear into one another entirely. In her analysis of the reversibility of emotions, Cataldi points out that their intentional structure requires some distance, however slim. "We are never *so* enamored 'of,' or so physically en-grossed 'in' another person, that we are *completely* identified with—or actually do become (coincide with)—them.

This is impossible; if this were to happen, we could no longer be enamored 'of' them at all. At best, we coin-*side*."[31] *The Big Swallow* depicts quite literally and imaginatively the crossover of the inside and the outside; indeed, the film makes me want to move Cataldi's hyphen: not only do we coin-*side* with the film, we also co-*inside* with it. We and the film inspire and are inspired; we take in and are taken in. The film's final return to the smiling gentleman at the end of the film places the emphasis squarely on the film *experience* taken as a whole, rather than on subject *or* object, viewer *or* viewed. The reversibility of the inspiration echoes the ambivalence, discussed in the introduction with regard to *Mirror*, between being drawn toward and pulled away from the film. That ambivalent but sensuous tactile contact between film and viewer moves all the way through the skin, musculature, and viscera, so that we are inside the film and outside it at the same time.

The embodied, chiasmatic aspects of the film experience are sensible and accessible by the same means that Merleau-Ponty offers for the understanding of hallucinations and myths, to which they bear a slight resemblance: "What brings about both hallucinations and myths is a rooting of things in our body, the overwhelming proximity of the object, the oneness of man and the world, which is, not indeed abolished, but repressed by everyday perception or by objective thought and which philosophical consciousness rediscovers. In order to realize what is the meaning of mythical or schizophrenic space, we have no means other than that of *resuscitating in ourselves, in our present perception, the relationship of the subject and his world* which analytical reflection does away with."[32]

In allowing myself to be deeply touched and inspired, quite literally, by the films I have studied here, I hope to have resuscitated in my own perception and in my analysis the sensuous, tactile relationship between spectator and cinema. Phenomenological analysis affords us a glimpse at embodied, tactile structures that slide, bleed, vibrate, and circulate between film and viewer, moving all the way through the body; it is by means of these structures and their reverberation between cinematic and human bodies that, in Sobchack's words, "the film has the capacity . . . to not only *have* sense but also to *make* sense. . . ."[33]

Dufrenne wrote that "meaning itself must traverse the body. Meaning can be read by feeling or elaborated upon by reflection only if it is first received and experienced by the body, that is, if the body is intelligent from the beginning."[34] This corporeal intelligence involves not only the body of the viewer but also the body of the film, with which we are caught up in this material, tactile embrace and mutual inspiration.

With this notion of meaning *traversing* the body, I'd like to draw to a close with a fragment of a poem read by Andrey Tarkovsky's father midway through *Mirror*. The scene takes place during one of the film's wartime segments, in which we meet a young boy orphaned by the war. The boy is making his way home from an emotionally fraught session of military target practice. He climbs to the top of a snowy hill, eventually stepping into an extreme close-up, as Arseniy Tarkovsky reads this line from his poem "Life, Life": "I would readily pay with my life / For a safe place with constant warmth / Were it not that life's flying needle / leads me on through the world like a thread."[35]

That poetic image evokes not only the complex relationship between past and present, with which the film is explicitly concerned, but also the complexity of the relationship between film and viewer. The line may recall, albeit indirectly, film theory's notion of "suture," which is used to suggest that, by mechanisms such as camera movement, framing, editing, and the configuration of on- and off-screen space, viewers are "sewn" into the film like a button, fixed in place. But the father's poetic line and the mesmerizing, perplexing patterns of cinematic movement in his son's film convey quite a different idea, having to do with the embodied, intimate, ambivalent, and sometimes discomfiting reversibility in which film and viewer are mutually enmeshed. Rather than being "stitched into place," we are neither "here" nor "there." We are caught up in a constant oscillation, drawn like a thread back and forth, through the fabric of the film experience.

Notes

INTRODUCTION

The epigraph (by Vsevolod Pudovkin) is quoted from Siegfried Kracauer, *Theory of Film: The Redemption of Reality* (Princeton: Princeton University Press, 1997), 160.

1. Maurice Merleau-Ponty, *Phenomenology of Perception*, trans. Colin Smith (London: Routledge, 1962; reprint, 1994), 317.

2. James J. Gibson, *The Ecological Approach to Visual Perception* (Boston: Houghton Mifflin & Co., 1979), 183, cited in Anne Rutherford, *Cinema and Embodied Affect* (2002), available from www.sensesofcinema.com/contents/03/25/embodied_affect.html.

3. Glen Mazis, "Matter, Dream, and the Murmurs among Things," in *Merleau-Ponty: Difference, Materiality, Painting*, ed. Veronique M. Foti (Atlantic Highlands, N.J.: Humanities Press International, Inc., 1996), 76.

4. Paul Stoller, *Sensuous Scholarship* (Philadelphia: University of Pennsylvania Press, 1997), xv.

5. Vivian Sobchack, *The Address of the Eye: A Phenomenology of Film Experience* (Princeton: Princeton University Press, 1992).

6. Vivian Sobchack, "What My Fingers Knew: The Cinesthetic Subject, or Vision in the Flesh," in *Carnal Thoughts: Embodiment and Moving Image Culture* (Berkeley: University of California Press, 2004), 60 (emphasis in the original).

7. Gilles Deleuze, *Cinema 2: The Time-Image*, trans. Hugh Tomlinson and Robert Galeta (Minneapolis: University of Minnesota Press, 1986), 75.

8. Deleuze, *Cinema 2*, 69.

9. David MacDougall, *The Corporeal Image: Film, Ethnography, and the Senses* (Princeton and Oxford: Princeton University Press, 2006), 29–30.

10. For an elaboration of the "film's body," see Sobchack, *The Address of the Eye*, 203–5.

11. Sobchack, *The Address of the Eye*, 10.

12. Sobchack's analysis is a reading of Merleau-Ponty's system of four terms—one's inner psyche, one's interoceptive image, the visible body of the other, and the subjective aspect of the other—as described in Maurice Merleau-Ponty, "The Child's Relations with Others," trans. William Cobb, in *The Primacy of Perception*, ed. James M. Edie (Evanston, Ill.: Northwestern University Press, 1964). For an extended discussion of how this four-term system applies to the film experience, see Sobchack, *The Address of the Eye*, 123–43.

13. Gabrielle Hezekiah, "Being, Consciousness and Time: Phenomenology and the Videos of Robert Yao Ramesar" (PhD diss., University of Toronto, 2007), 55.

14. Sobchack, *The Address of the Eye*, 4.

15. That gap between human vision and a film's vision is precisely the reason many filmmakers make use of daily rushes: viewing footage as it appears when projected is a means of reconciling the difference between what the filmmaker saw through the camera's viewfinder and what the camera saw itself.

16. Indeed, a film can have an attitude toward the world distinct from that of its director, writer, or camera-operator. For example, in Michelangelo Antonioni's *Chung Kuo China* (1972), the film's complicated relationship with its Chinese subjects undermines the authority of its own voice-over narration. The narration would have us believe that the Chinese people are intimidated by the Western film crew and its technology, but the editing and mise-en-scène clearly demonstrate that if anyone is intimidated, it is the film itself, unhinged by its *lack* of difference from the ethnographic "others" it investigates. For a fuller discussion of this film, see my essay "Bodily Irruptions: The Corporeal Assault on Ethnographic Narration," *Cinema Journal* 34, no. 3 (1995): 57–76.

17. Alfred Hitchcock's *Rear Window* (1954), Frederick Wiseman's *High School* (1968), and Jean Rouch's *The Lion Hunters* (1965) are all fine examples of a film's explicit reflection upon its role as a perceiving subject. The camera that meanders through the main character's apartment in the opening scene of *Rear Window* obviously distinguishes the film's vision from that of its (sleeping) hero. *High School*'s use of zooms and extreme close-ups accentuates its critical gaze at the institution it depicts, a criticism not guided by any one "character's" viewpoint. In *The Lion Hunters*, Rouch himself is endangered by an attacking lion while operating the camera. The camera shuts down and we see only a black screen, while Rouch's voice continues to narrate the events on the soundtrack. Rouch's own panic is shared by the film itself, which expresses "panic" in the complete unraveling of the continuity between sound and image. In these examples, the film reflexively acknowledges its own acts of perception and expression and experiences itself as an autonomous subject in the world. It declares itself an "I," separate from the "I" of the characters or even the filmmaker. See Barker, "Bodily Irruptions."

18. Mikel Dufrenne, *The Phenomenology of Aesthetic Experience* (Evanston, Ill.: Northwestern University Press, 1973), 461.

19. Andrey Tarkovsky, *Sculpting in Time,* trans. Kitty Hunter-Blair (Austin: University of Texas Press, 1987), 12–13.

20. Hezekiah, "Being, Consciousness and Time," 20.

21. Existential phenomenology's focus on the lived body makes any easy alignment between this approach and a Deleuzian one impossible, but my interest in the liminality of this contact between film and viewer, combined with Merleau-Ponty's notion of the "pre-personal," might allow this kind of analysis to intersect in certain ways with Deleuze's idea of "the fold." Gilles Deleuze, *The Fold: Leibniz and the Baroque* (Minneapolis: University of Minnesota Press, 1993).

22. Jennifer Deger, *Shimmering Screens: Making Media in an Aboriginal Community* (Minneapolis: University of Minnesota Press, 2007), 89.

23. Rutherford, *Cinema and Embodied Affect.*

24. Tarkovsky, *Sculpting in Time,* 108–9.

25. Sara Ahmed, *The Cultural Politics of Emotion* (New York: Routledge, 2004), 4.

26. The quoted passages appear, respectively at pages 139 (emphasis in the original), 130, and 8 of Ahmed, *The Cultural Politics of Emotion.*

27. See Ahmed's discussion of *fort-da* in relation to embodied contact and orientation. *Cultural Politics of Emotion,* 50.

28. Glen Mazis makes a similar argument about emotion being a kind of circuit or conduit, not something that resides in the perceiver or perceived. Mazis goes so far as to insist on a hyphen—"e-motion"—to emphasize and preserve the intersubjectivity of the one who feels and the one who is felt, the subject and the world, and the inward and outward movements simultaneously involved in any given experience of emotion. Glen Mazis, *Emotion and Embodiment: A Fragile Ontology. Studies in Contemporary Continental Philosophy* (New York: Peter Lang Publishing, 1993).

29. Ahmed, *The Cultural Politics of Emotion,* 10.

30. Hezekiah, "Being, Consciousness and Time," 14.

31. Merleau-Ponty, *Phenomenology of Perception,* 203.

32. "Meaning-giving" and "sense-bestowing" are Elizabeth Grosz's terms for this aspect of Merleau-Ponty's conceptualization of the body. Elizabeth Grosz, *Volatile Bodies: Toward a Corporeal Feminism* (Bloomington: Indiana University Press, 1994), 87.

33. Hezekiah, "Being, Consciousness and Time," 14.

34. M. C. Dillon, *Merleau-Ponty's Ontology* (Evanston, Ill.: Northwestern University Press, 1988), 55.

35. Maurice Merleau-Ponty, "Eye and Mind," trans. Carleton Dallery, in *The Primacy of Perception,* ed. James M. Edie (Evanston, Ill.: Northwestern University Press, 1964), 167.

36. The quoted passages appear, respectively, in Dufrenne, *The Phenomenology of Aesthetic Experience,* 337 and 471.

37. Maurice Merleau-Ponty, "The Film and the New Psychology," ed. Claude Lefort, in *Sense and Non-Sense,* trans. Hubert L. Dreyfus and Patricia

Allen Dreyfus, ed. James M. Edie (Evanston, Ill.: Northwestern University Press, 1964), 58.

38. Merleau-Ponty, *Phenomenology of Perception*, 93.

39. Maurice Merleau-Ponty, *The Visible and the Invisible*, ed. Claude Lefort, trans. Alphonso Lingis (Evanston, Ill.: Northwestern University Press, 1968), 147–48.

40. There may be productive intersections between Merleau-Ponty's notions of reversibility and the flesh with the Heideggerian notion of "presencing" and "technē," and with Deleuze's ideas of the fold, becoming, and the BwO. For an elaboration of the possible convergences, see, for example, Deger, *Shimmering Screens;* Elena del Río, "Alchemies of Thought in Godard's Cinema: Deleuze and Merleau-Ponty," *SubStance*, issue 108, vol. 34, no. 3 (2005): 62–78; Hezekiah, "Being, Consciousness and Time"; Laura U. Marks, *Touch: Sensuous Theory and Multisensory Media* (Minneapolis: University of Minnesota Press, 2002); Vivian Sobchack, "'Susie Scribbles': On Technology, Technē, and Writing Incarnate," in *Carnal Thoughts: Embodiment and Moving Image Culture* (Berkeley: University of California Press, 2004).

41. Dillon, *Merleau-Ponty's Ontology*, 159, quoting Merleau-Ponty, *The Visible and the Invisible*, 133.

42. Laura U. Marks, *The Skin of the Film: Intercultural Cinema, Embodiment, and the Senses* (Durham, N.C.: Duke University Press, 1999), 255.

43. MacDougall, *The Corporeal Image*, 22; Michael Taussig, *Mimesis and Alterity: A Particular History of the Senses* (New York: Routledge, 1993), 30 (emphasis added).

44. Taussig, *Mimesis and Alterity*, 31. Taussig refers here to the analogy made between the surgeon and the cinematographer in Walter Benjamin, "The Work of Art in the Age of Mechanical Reproduction," in *Illuminations*, ed. Hannah Arendt, trans. Harry Zohn (New York: Schocken Books, 1969).

CHAPTER ONE: SKIN

The epigraph (by Norman MacLaren) is quoted from Herman G. Weinberg, *Saint Cinema: Writings on the Film, 1929–1970*, 2nd ed. (New York: Dover Publications, 1973), 173.

1. Kate Haug, "An Interview with Carolee Schneemann," *Wide Angle* 20, no. 1 (1998): 46.

2. Caroline Koebel, "From Danger to Ascendancy: Notes toward Carolee Schneemann," *Wide Angle* 20, no. 1 (1998): 52.

3. Marks, *The Skin of the Film*, 170.

4. Haug, "An Interview with Carolee Schneemann," 43.

5. Merleau-Ponty, "Eye and Mind"; Richard Shiff, "Cézanne's Physicality: The Politics of Touch," in *The Language of Art History*, ed. Salim Kemal and Ivan Gaskell (Cambridge: Cambridge University Press, 1991); Steven Connor, *The Book of Skin* (Ithaca, N.Y.: Cornell University Press, 2004), 27–28.

6. James Elkins, "Marks, Traces, Traits, Contours, *Orli*, and *Splendores:* Nonsemiotic Elements in Pictures," *Critical Inquiry* 21 (1995): 834.

7. Siegfried Kracauer, "Marseille Notebooks" (1940), 2:6, Kracauer Papers, Deutsches Literaturarchiv, Marbach am Neckar, quoted in Miriam Bratu Hansen, "'With Skin and Hair': Kracauer's Theory of Film, Marseilles 1940," *Critical Inquiry* 19 (1993): 462.

8. Antonin Artaud, *Selected Writings*, ed. Susan Sontag, trans. Helen Weaver (New York: Farrar, Straus, and Giroux, 1976), 151.

9. Kracauer, "Marseille Notebooks," 1:23, quoted in Hansen, "'With Skin and Hair,'" 458.

10. Merleau-Ponty, *The Visible and the Invisible*, 132. This sense of flesh resonates with *chora*, a term that can be traced from Plato to Jacques Derrida to Luce Irigaray to Elizabeth Grosz. *Chora* is the unseen and ungraspable potentiality around, behind, below, and above the visible and tangible thing. It is easy to see from this example, ripe with the color red and with nourishing tissues, why Irigaray might have drawn the conclusion that Merleau-Ponty's concept of flesh is inherently and inescapably feminine and maternal, though he never described it in those terms explicitly. Irigaray herself develops a theory of tactility that describes it in even more "elemental" as well as explicitly feminine terms. She insists that the tactile is most closely defined by and associated with the female body, in which the womb is the most obvious site of the "plenitude, enfolding and infinite complexity of the tactile and the tangible" (Grosz, *Volatile Bodies*, 106). For a discussion of the analysis of *The Visible and the Invisible* that Irigaray makes in *An Ethics of Sexual Difference*, ed. and trans. Carolyn Burke and Gillian C. Gill (Ithaca, N.Y.: Cornell University Press, 1993), see Grosz, *Volatile Bodies*. For a study even more keenly focused on this topic, see Catherine Vasseleu, *Textures of Light: Vision and Touch in Irigaray, Levinas, and Merleau-Ponty* (London: Routledge, 1998).

11. Merleau-Ponty, *The Visible and the Invisible*, 131.

12. Ibid., 127.

13. Merleau-Ponty does not claim that human skin and "flesh" are identical, but Steven Connor does find a suggestion to this effect in Didier Anzieu's work, and dismisses it: "It will be hard to investigate the effects of this apprehension of spatial duplicity [that is invited by the skin] without seeming to be identifying the skin, as Anzieu tends to do, as the ground of grounds, or the form of forms, from which all conceptions and transformations of space, place, and shape derive, and to which they all invariably devolve. Under such conditions, when everything is the skin, and the skin is everything, when, in short, there is no alternative to or outside to the experience of skin, there would be little point in undertaking the work of differentiating its functions." Connor, *The Book of Skin*, 39. Connor refers here to Didier Anzieu, *The Skin Ego*, trans. Chris Turner (New Haven: Yale University Press, 1989).

14. Merleau-Ponty, *The Visible and the Invisible*, 138.

15. Ibid., 147–48.

16. David C. Lindberg, *Theories of Vision: From Al-Kindi to Kepler* (Chicago: University of Chicago Press, 1976), 2.

17. Gilberto Perez, *The Material Ghost: Films and Their Medium* (Baltimore: Johns Hopkins University Press, 2000), 28.

18. Roland Barthes, *Camera Lucida: Reflections on Photography*, trans. Richard Howard (New York: Hill and Wang, 1981), 80–81, quoted in Perez, *The Material Ghost*, 32. Barthes refers here to Susan Sontag, *On Photography* (New York: Farrar, Strauss, and Giroux, 1978).

19. Barthes, *Camera Lucida*, 40.

20. Ibid., 26–27.

21. Shiff, "Cézanne's Physicality." See also Connor, *The Book of Skin*, 27–28; Elkins, "Marks, Traces, Traits, Contours, *Orli*, and *Splendores*"; Merleau-Ponty, "Cézanne's Doubt," in *Sense and Non-Sense*, ed. James M. Edie, trans. Hubert L. Dreyfus and Patricia Allen Dreyfus (Evanston, Ill.: Northwestern University Press, 1964); Merleau-Ponty, "Eye and Mind."

22. See, for example, Tarja Laine, "Cinema as Second Skin: Under the Membrane of Horror Film," *New Review of Film and Television Studies* 4, no. 2 (2006): 93–106; Anne Rutherford, "What Makes a Film Tick? Cinematic Affect, Materiality, and Mimetic Innervation" (PhD diss., University of Western Sydney, 2006). The latter includes the essay *Cinema and Embodied Affect* on this topic.

23. Antonia Lant, "Haptical Cinema," *October* 74 (1995): 68. Lant refers here to a passage from Virginia Woolf, "Movies and Reality," *The Nation* (1926), reprinted as "The Cinema" in *The Captain's Death Bed and Other Essays*, ed. Leonard Woolf (New York: Harcourt Brace Jovanovich, 1950).

24. *The Oxford English Dictionary*, compact edition (Oxford: Oxford University Press, 1971), s.v. "contingency."

25. Christian Keathley, *Cinephilia and History; or, The Wind in the Trees* (Bloomington: Indiana University Press, 2006), 8.

26. Giuliana Bruno, *Atlas of Emotion: Journeys in Art, Architecture, and Film* (London and New York: Verso, 2002), 254.

27. Elena del Río, "The Body as Foundation of the Screen: Allegories of Technology in Atom Egoyan's *Speaking Parts*," *Camera Obscura* 38 (1996): 102.

28. Ibid., 101.

29. Ibid.

30. Alphonso Lingis, "Sense and Non-Sense in the Sexed Body," *Cultural Hermeneutics* 4 (1977): 355, quoted in del Río, "The Body as Foundation of the Screen," 100.

31. This mutuality is precisely what Schneemann intended with the making of *Fuses:* "I wanted to put into that materiality of film the energies of the body, so that the film itself dissolves and recombines and is transparent and dense— like how one feels during lovemaking. . . . It is different from any pornographic work that you've ever seen—that's why people are still looking at it! And there's no objectification or fetishization of the woman." Andrea Juno, "Interview with Carolee Schneemann," *RE/Search* 13 (1991), quoted in David Levi Strauss, "Love

Rides Aristotle through the Audience: Body, Image, and Idea in the Work of Carolee Schneemann," in *Imaging Her Erotics: Essays, Interviews, Projects,* ed. Carolee Schneemann (Cambridge, Mass.: MIT Press, 2002), 323.

32. Marks, *The Skin of the Film*, 183.

33. Ibid.

34. Ibid., 184.

35. Ibid.

36. Laura U. Marks, "Video Haptics and Erotics," *Screen* 39, no. 4 (1998): 338 n. 24.

37. Marks, *The Skin of the Film*, 183.

38. *Merriam-Webster's Seventh New Collegiate Dictionary* (Springfield, Mass.: G. & C. Merriam Company, 1967), s.v. "haptic."

39. Harry F. Malgrave, ed., *Empathy, Form, and Space: Problems in German Aesthetics, 1873–1893* (Santa Monica, Calif.: Getty Center for the History of Art and Humanities, 1994), 63. Malgrave is summarizing Alois Riegl, *Late Roman Art Industry* (*Spätrömische Kunstindustrie,* 1927), trans. Rolf Winkes (Rome: Giorgio Bretschneider Editore, 1985).

40. Noël Burch, *Life to Those Shadows,* ed. and trans. Ben Brewster (Berkeley and Los Angeles: University of California Press, 1990); Lant, "Haptical Cinema." Giuliana Bruno gives a concise history of "haptics" in theories of art and cinema that includes Burch and Lant as well as Benjamin and Étienne de Condillac but was published too early to address Laura Marks's contribution to that history. See Bruno, *Atlas of Emotion: Journeys in Art, Architecture, and Film,* 247–59.

41. Marks, *The Skin of the Film,* 162, 163.

42. Ibid., 169.

43. Steven Shaviro, *The Cinematic Body* (Minneapolis and London: University of Minnesota Press, 1993).

44. Marks, *The Skin of the Film,* 151.

45. Laine, "Cinema as Second Skin," 99.

46. Ashley Montagu, *Touching: The Human Significance of the Skin,* 3rd ed. (New York: Harper and Row, 1986), 193.

47. Noelle Oxenhandler, "The Eros of Parenthood," *New Yorker,* 19 February 1996, 48–49.

48. Anzieu, *The Skin Ego,* 30.

49. Marks, *The Skin of the Film,* 184.

50. Bill Brown, "How to Do Things with Things: A Toy Story," *Critical Inquiry* 24, no. 4 (1998): 955.

51. Ibid., 952.

52. Brown's essay offers an incisive and playful analysis, informed by Benjamin's work on child's play, of the film's attitude toward toys and material things in relation to materialist history.

53. Laura Marks offers a detailed discussion of the haptic qualities specific to video and digital media in chapter 3 of *The Skin of the Film* and the chapter titled "Video's Body, Analog and Digital" in Marks, *Touch,* 147–59.

54. Shaviro, *The Cinematic Body,* 133.

55. William Ian Miller, *The Anatomy of Disgust* (Cambridge, Mass.: Harvard University Press, 1997), 89.

56. Walter Benjamin, "One-Way Street," trans. Rodney Livingstone, in *Walter Benjamin: Selected Writings,* vol. 1, *1913–1927,* ed. Michael W. Jennings, Howard Eiland, and Gary Smith (Cambridge, Mass., and London: The Belknap Press of Harvard University Press, 1999), 448.

57. Shaviro, *The Cinematic Body,* 95.

58. Ahmed, *The Cultural Politics of Emotion,* 65.

59. Miller, *The Anatomy of Disgust,* 55.

60. Benjamin, "One-Way Street," 448.

61. Julia Kristeva, *Powers of Horror: An Essay in Abjection* (New York: Columbia University Press, 1982), quoted in Sue Cataldi, *Emotion, Depth, and Flesh: A Study of Sensitive Space: Reflections on Merleau-Ponty's Philosophy of Embodiment* (Albany: State University of New York Press, 1993), 142.

62. Iris Marion Young, *Justice and the Politics of Difference* (Princeton: Princeton University Press, 1990), 136–37, quoted in Cataldi, *Emotion, Depth, and Flesh,* 142.

63. Merleau-Ponty, *The Visible and the Invisible,* 263–64.

64. Marks, *The Skin of the Film,* 162.

65. Ibid.

66. The only haptic images in the sequence consisting of documentary footage of the bomb's effects are two shots of dirt, from which an earthworm and a fly emerge. I find it interesting that, although the landscape of dirt could, in a film where light and dark are often misleading, be mistaken for a body badly burned, the only bodies actually represented in these haptic images are those of the nonhuman creatures that rise from the ruins of Hiroshima. When human bodies are shown, it is from a considerably greater distance, whether because of their size or because of some need for the documentary photographers to keep their distance, perhaps out of horror or out of respect for what these victims have experienced.

67. Notably, the very first shot of the film, the one that appears under the credits, is also a haptic image of a sort. It depicts a sprouting of weeds from a sidewalk. However, this opening shot is in fact a reverse (i.e., negative) image of a shot that appears later. That later shot is bright with daylight, but here, the sidewalk is completely black, so that it might be sky, or ground, or water, or nothingness. Against this murky background, the weeds are unrecognizable as such: they might be stars, or flowers, or insects, or pure design. The indistinct imagery here anticipates the amorphous quality of the images that follow this shot.

68. Marks, *The Skin of the Film,* 163.

69. Marks, "Video Haptics and Erotics," 342. Marks refers here to Stanley Cavell, *The World Viewed: Reflections on the Ontology of Film* (Cambridge, Mass.: Harvard University Press, 1979).

70. Marks, "Video Haptics and Erotics," 344–45.

71. Ahmed, *The Cultural Politics of Emotion*, 25.
72. Marks, *The Skin of the Film*, 163.

CHAPTER TWO: MUSCULATURE

The epigraphs (by Henri Bergson and Chuck Jones) are quoted, respectively, from Henri Bergson, "Laughter" (1900), in *Comedy*, ed. Wylie Sipher (Baltimore: Johns Hopkins University Press, 1980), 71; and Chuck Jones, *Chuck Reducks: Drawing from the Fun Side of Life* (New York: Warner Books, 1996), 207.

1. This is not the "view from everywhere" that Vertov's *kino-eye* promised, for example, but a fragmented and incoherent view that leaves us unable to make any bodily "sense" of the space. McCarey's scene seems to stumble over the 180-degree rule, whereas Vertov is playing on a different field altogether.

2. Linda Williams, "Film Bodies: Gender, Genre, and Excess," *Film Quarterly* 44, no. 4 (1991): 2–13.

3. Marks, *The Skin of the Film*, 183 (citations omitted). Marks makes reference here to Walter Benjamin, "On the Mimetic Faculty," in *Reflections: Essays, Aphorisms, Autobiographical Writings* trans. Edmund Jephcott, ed. Peter Demetz (New York: Schocken Books, 1986); Roger Caillois, "Mimicry and Legendary Psychasthenia," *October* 31 (Winter 1984): 16–32; and Paul Stoller, *The Taste of Ethnographic Things: The Senses in Anthropology* (Philadelphia: University of Pennsylvania Press, 1989).

4. Benjamin, "On the Mimetic Faculty." My argument about mimesis and the cinema is indebted to discussions of the topic by Miriam Hansen and Laura Marks. Miriam Hansen, "Benjamin, Cinema and Experience: 'The Blue Flower in the Land of Technology'," *New German Critique* 40 (1987): 179–224; Marks, *The Skin of the Film*.

5. Hansen, "Benjamin, Cinema and Experience," 195.

6. Taussig, *Mimesis and Alterity*, 21.

7. Deger, *Shimmering Screens*, 85.

8. Robert Frost, "Perfect Day—A Day of Prowess," in *Baseball: A Literary Anthology*, ed. Nicholas Dawidoff (New York: The Library of America, 2002), 260.

9. The etymology of the word contains many relevant connotations: Middle English *extasie*, from Old French, from Late Latin *extasis*, terror, from Greek *ekstasis*, astonishment, distraction, from *existanai*, to displace, derange. "Ecstasy. From the Greek word *ekstasis:* to stand outside of oneself, or to stand outside of place." *The American Heritage Dictionary of the English Language*, 4th ed. (Boston: Houghton Mifflin, 2000), s.v. "ecstatic."

10. Robert Vischer, "The Aesthetic Act and Pure Form: An Anthology of Changing Ideas," in *Art in Theory, 1815–1900*, ed. Charles Harrison, Paul Wood, and Jason Gaiger (Malden, Mass.: Blackwell Publishers, 1998).

11. These examples come from James Elkins, *Pictures of the Body* (Stanford, Calif.: Stanford University Press, 1999), 24.

12. Dufrenne, *The Phenomenology of Aesthetic Experience.*

13. Eugène Minkowski, *Vers une cosmologie* (Paris: Aubier, 1906), quoted in Gaston Bachelard, *The Poetics of Space*, trans. Maria Jolas (Boston: Beacon Press, 1969), xii–xiii n. 1.

14. Barker, "Bodily Irruptions."

15. Dufrenne, *The Phenomenology of Aesthetic Experience*, 339.

16. The "pause" button in our home video/DVD player serves as an extension of the viewer's body when it is used to hold the film on these elusive images in a way that's not possible in the theater. This is just one example of the ways in which tactile forms and behaviors can differ in the experience of moving pictures experienced at home versus those seen in theaters.

17. In one of many echoes between the two films, Alfred Hitchcock would employ a similar spinning camera effect on the glassy eye of Janet Leigh at the end of *Psycho*'s shower scene (1960).

18. Hugo Münsterberg, *The Photoplay: A Psychological Study* (New York: Dover, 1916).

19. Hubert L. Dreyfus, "The Current Relevance of Merleau-Ponty's Phenomenology of Embodiment," in *The Electronic Journal of Analytic Philosophy* 4 (Spring 1996) (originally hosted by Indiana University; transferred in 2001 to the University of Louisiana at Lafayette: http://ejap.louisiana.edu).

20. Siegfried Kracauer, *Theory of Film: The Redemption of Physical Reality* (Princeton: Princeton University Press, 1997), 159.

21. Alexander Sesonske, "Cinema Space," in *Explorations in Phenomenology*, ed. David Carr and Edward S. Casey (The Hague: Martinus Nijhoff, 1973), 403.

22. Vivian Sobchack has written astutely on the phenomenological structure of the dolly-zoom in this and other films. See Vivian Sobchack, "The Active Eye: A Phenomenology of Cinematic Vision," *Quarterly Review of Film and Video* 12, no. 3 (1990): 21–36.

23. For an extended discussion of these issues, see especially the section entitled "Space," in Merleau-Ponty, *Phenomenology of Perception.*

24. *The Oxford English Dictionary*, compact edition (Oxford: Oxford University Press, 1971), s.v. "ecstatic."

25. Sesonske, "Cinema Space," 399–400.

26. Merleau-Ponty, *Phenomenology of Perception*, 251.

27. Ibid., 106.

28. Ibid., 109.

29. My reference to such projects as "catching the criminal" and "getting the girl" are purposely problematic. I aim here to qualify the notion of "empathy" in a way that opens up onto a line of thought not explored here but certainly ripe for study, which has to do with embodiment and race, class, gender, and sexual orientation, for example. When I say we and the film "share" certain attitudes and projects, I do not mean to suggest we necessarily share them comfortably or easily, much less complaisantly. Empathy between film and viewer is, as I've suggested throughout, rife with tension and ambivalence and

subject to resistance, sources of which may certainly include one's personal history and identity, embodied in very specific ways, especially when they are "other" than what the film assumes.

30. Merleau-Ponty, *Phenomenology of Perception*, 250.

31. Ibid.

32. Ibid., 251.

33. Münsterberg, *The Photoplay*, 36–37.

34. Merleau-Ponty, *Phenomenology of Perception*, 103–5.

35. Ibid., 105.

36. Ibid., 108.

37. Ibid., 109 (emphasis added).

38. Sesonske, "Cinema Space," 403–4.

39. Merleau-Ponty, *Phenomenology of Perception*, 105.

40. Bergson, "Laughter" (1900), in Sipher, *Comedy*, 71.

41. Richard Thompson, "Meep Meep," in *Movies and Methods*, vol. 1, ed. Bill Nichols (Berkeley and Los Angeles: University of California Press, 1976), 133.

42. Ibid.

43. Ibid., 132.

44. *The Oxford English Dictionary* defines "estrange" as "to remove . . . from an accustomed abode, haunt, association, or occupation. To keep apart from experience of or acquaintance with anything. To put away from oneself; eschew. To render 'foreign' or dissimilar in character. To alienate in feeling or affection. *To make unlike oneself*." *The Oxford English Dictionary*, compact edition (Oxford: Oxford University Press, 1971), s.v. "estrange" (emphasis added). Thus the word contains in it the possibilities that exist in the film/viewer relationship, which is based in similarity and difference.

45. These were lines from the national newspaper advertising campaigns for *Twister* (Jan de Bont, 1997) and *Deep Blue Sea* (Renny Harlin, 1999).

46. Jean-Paul Sartre, *Being and Nothingness: A Phenomenological Essay on Ontology*, trans. Hazel E. Barnes (New York: Washington Square Press, 1993).

47. For a discussion of the difference in these two philosophers' attitudes toward subjectivity and vision, see Martin Jay, *Downcast Eyes: The Denigration of Vision in Twentieth-Century French Thought* (Berkeley and Los Angeles: University of California Press, 1993).

48. Perez, *The Material Ghost*, 96.

49. Ibid., 121.

50. Ibid., 103.

51. Peter F. Parshall, "Houdini's Protégé: Buster Keaton in *Sherlock, Jr.*," in *Buster Keaton's Sherlock, Jr.*, ed. Andrew Horton (Cambridge and New York: Cambridge Press University, 1997), 72.

52. Merleau-Ponty, *Phenomenology of Perception*, 198.

53. Andrew Horton, "Think Slow, Act Fast," in Horton, *Buster Keaton's Sherlock, Jr.*, 5.

54. Parshall, "Houdini's Protégé," 73.

55. See, for example, Stephen Bottomore, "The Panicking Audience? Early Cinema and the 'Train' Effect," *Historical Journal of Film, Radio, and Television* 19, no. 2 (1999): 177–216; Tom Gunning, "An Aesthetic of Astonishment: Early Film and the (in)Credulous Spectator," in *Viewing Positions: Ways of Seeing,* ed. Linda Williams, 114–33 (New Brunswick, N.J.: Rutgers University Press, 1989); and Isabelle Morissette, "Reflexivity in Spectatorship: The Didactic Nature of Early Silent Films." *Off-screen* (2002), available from www.horschamp.qc.ca/new_offscreen/reflexivity.html.

56. Garrett Stewart, "Keaton through the Looking Glass," *The Georgia Review* 33, no. 2 (1979): 364–65.

57. Gilberto Perez, "The Dream Life" (review of Colin McGinn, *The Power of the Movies: How Screen and Mind Interact*), *The Nation*, 27 March 2006.

58. Perez refers here to Suzanne Langer, *Feeling and Form: A Theory of Art Developed from Philosophy in a New Key* (New York: Charles Scribner's Sons, 1953), 413.

59. *The Oxford English Dictionary,* compact edition (Oxford: Oxford University Press, 1971), s. v. "apprehension."

60. Ibid.

61. Hal Hinson, "Speed" (review of *Speed*) *Washington Post,* 10 June 1994.

62. MacDougall, *The Corporeal Image,* 26.

63. Leonard Maltin, "Speed," in *2001 Movie and Video Guide* (New York: Penguin Putnam, Inc., 2001); idem, "Twister," in *2001 Movie and Video Guide* (New York: Penguin Putnam, Inc., 2001).

64. Notes for *Run Lola Run,* Columbia/Tri-Star DVD-04014(1999).

65. Mazis, *Emotion and Embodiment,* 29–30.

CHAPTER THREE: VISCERA

The epigraph (by Denis Diderot) is quoted from "Essay on Painting" (1765), in Denis Diderot, *Selected Writings,* ed. Lester G. Crocker, trans. Derek Coltman (New York: Macmillan, 1968), 166.

1. Tykwer's description (and the language of film reviewers) sells it as a nonstop, relentlessly mobile, all-out action film, a roller coaster of a film. And it *is* a roller coaster, but it is not nonstop. Few roller coasters are. A roller coaster always hangs suspended for a moment at the top of its arc, a momentary pause that allows passengers to catch their breath and gather strength for the rest of the ride. *Run Lola Run* takes its time at the top of that arc.

2. Janet Maslin, "Film Festival Review; A Dangerous Game with Several Endings" (review of *Run Lola Run*), *New York Times,* 26 March 1999.

3. Tom Whalen identifies the source of that quotation in his essay on the gamelike structure of the film. Tom Whalen, "*Run Lola Run*" (review), *Film Quarterly* 53, no. 3 (2000).

4. Tarkovsky, *Sculpting in Time,* 114.

5. Taussig, *Mimesis and Alterity,* 31. Taussig's reference is to the analogy between the surgeon and the cinematographer in Benjamin, "The Work of Art in the Age of Mechanical Reproduction."

6. Drew Leder, *The Absent Body* (Chicago: University of Chicago Press, 1990), 37.

7. Ibid., 62.

8. Lewis Thomas, *The Lives of a Cell* (New York: Bantam Books, 1974), 78, quoted in Leder, *The Absent Body*, 43.

9. Leder, *The Absent Body*, 1.

10. Ibid., 55.

11. Michel Serres, *Les cinq sens* (Paris: Hachette, 1998), 30, 34–35, cited in Steven Connor, *Michel Serres's* Five Senses (Centre for Interdisciplinary Research in Culture and the Humanities Birkbeck College, University of London, 29 May 1999), available from www.bbk.ac.uk/english/skc/5senses.htm. The translation is Steven Connor's.

12. Leder, *The Absent Body*, 44, 53.

13. Ibid., 69.

14. Ahmed, *The Cultural Politics of Emotion*, 26 (emphasis in the original).

15. The quoted passages are from Leder, *The Absent Body*, respectively, 55, 84, and 73.

16. Sobchack, "The Active Eye," 23.

17. Ibid. See also Sobchack's discussion of the intermittence-appeal of "new" media in "Nostalgia for a Digital Object: Regrets on the Quickening of Quicktime," *Millennium Film Journal* 34 (1999): 4–23, reprinted in *Future Cinema: The Cinematic Imaginary after Film*, ed. Jeffrey Shaw and Peter Weibel (Cambridge, Mass.: MIT Press, 2003).

18. For an insightful discussion of stillness and the "in between" in Marker's film, see Reda Bensmaïa, "From the Photogram to the Pictogram: On Chris Marker's *La Jetée*," *Camera Obscura* 24 (1990): 139–61.

19. Kathy Peiss, *Cheap Amusements: Working Women and Leisure in Turn-of-the-Century New York* (Philadelphia: Temple University Press, 1986), 146.

20. David Nasaw, *Going Out: The Rise and Fall of Public Amusements* (New York: Basic Books, 1993), 157.

21. Lisa Cartwright, *Screening the Body: Tracing Medicine's Visual Culture* (Minneapolis and London: University of Minnesota Press, 1995), 109. Other imaging technologies, too, celebrated the body in motion, including the Vitascope, the Bioscope, the Choreutoscope, the Eidoloscope, the Fregoligraph, the Iconograph, the Phantascope, the Polyscope, the Tachyscope, and the Thaumatograph, to name but a few. See Emmanuelle Toulet, *Birth of the Motion Picture* (New York: Harry N. Abrams, 1995).

22. For a wealth of examples, see Jonathan Auerbach, *Body Shots: Early Cinema's Incarnations* (Berkeley and Los Angeles: University of California Press, 2007); Charles Musser, *The Emergence of Cinema: The American Screen to 1907* (Berkeley and Los Angeles: University of California Press, 1990); and Gordon Hendricks, "History of the Kinetoscope," in *The American Film Industry*, ed. Tino Balio, 43–56 (Madison: University of Wisconsin Press, 1985).

23. Gunning, "An Aesthetic of Astonishment," 122.

24. Tom Gunning, "'Primitive' Cinema—A Frame-up? or The Trick's on Us," *Cinema Journal* 28, no. 2 (1989): 5.

25. Musser, *The Emergence of Cinema.*

26. Linda Williams discusses the physical and social ramifications of these early cinema (and pre-cinema) viewing machines in "Corporeal Observers: Visual Pornographies and the 'Carnal Density of Vision'," in *Fugitive Images,* ed. Patrice Petro, 3–41 (Bloomington: Indiana University Press, 1995).

27. Of course, pre-cinematic devices, too, are founded on this convergence of human motion and motion pictures, the flipbook being perhaps the most basic example.

28. It might be possible to do a similar analysis that focused on female viewers' experience of films featuring Eugene Sandow the body-builder, for example.

29. For a discussion of the significance of cinema's intermittence for the viewer, see Sobchack, "Nostalgia for a Digital Object."

30. Of course, the human fascination with the dynamic of stillness and movement set in motion the history of film technology. Eadweard Muybridge's photographic analysis of a horse's gait inspired Étienne-Jules Marey to develop photographic apparatuses specifically to record images of the irregular and disjointed movements made by animals and humans alike. Anson Rabinbach writes that, for Marey, "the central feature of all work—whether of humans or machines—was the suppression and transformation of irregular, inconsistent, and jarring shocks into regular and uniform activity." Thus, the earliest cinematic machines were modeled after living, breathing bodies. Anson Rabinbach, *The Human Motor: Energy, Fatigue, and the Origins of Modernity* (New York: Basic Books, 1990), 118.

31. BBC News, *Ask Wallace and Gromit Creator Nick Park* (BBC, 2002), available from http://news.bbc.co.uk/1/hi/talking_point/forum/2314009.stm.

32. See for example, Walter Benjamin, "The Cultural History of Toys," trans. Rodney Livingstone, in *Walter Benjamin: Selected Writings,* vol. 2, part 1: *1927–1930,* ed. Michael W. Jennings, Howard Eiland, and Gary Smith (Cambridge, Mass., and London: The Belknap Press of Harvard University Press, 1999); idem, "On the Mimetic Faculty"; idem, "Program for a Proletarian Children's Theater," trans. Rodney Livingstone, in *Selected Writings,* vol. 2, part 1; Brown, "How to Do Things with Things"; Miriam Bratu Hansen, "Room-for-Play: Benjamin's Gamble with Cinema," *October* 109 (2004): 3–45.

33. Bruno Schulz, *The Street of Crocodiles,* trans. Celina Wieniewska (New York: Penguin Books, 1977), 62.

CONCLUSION

The epigraph (by Andrey Tarkovsky) is quoted from Andrey Tarkovsky, *Sculpting in Time,* trans. Kitty Hunter-Blair (Austin: University of Texas Press, 1987), 106.

1. Merleau-Ponty, *The Visible and the Invisible,* 271 (emphasis in the original).

2. Ibid., 134.

3. Merleau-Ponty, "Eye and Mind," 167.

4. Leder, *The Absent Body,* 165.

5. Ibid., 166.

6. Ibid.

7. Dufrenne, *The Phenomenology of Aesthetic Experience*, 442.

8. Anne Rutherford describes a gust of wind blowing through the climactic scene of Terrence Malick's *Days of Heaven* (1978) in terms that could as easily be applied to the scene in Tarkovsky's film. She suggests that the wind is an iteration of the film's larger structure, which "is conceived as an energetic charge that cycles through the sensorium of the spectator. The narrative cannot be separated out from this action as the film is made up moment by moment of sensory intensities." Rutherford, "What Makes a Film Tick?" 13.

9. Petr Král, "Tarkovsky, or the Burning House," part 1, *Slavic and East European Performance* 15, no. 3 (1995): 52.

10. Maya Turovskaya, *Tarkovsky: Cinema as Poetry*, ed. Ian Christie, trans. Natasha Ward (London and Boston: Faber and Faber, 1989), 90, 92 (emphasis in the original).

11. Deleuze, *Cinema 2*, 59.

12. Král, "Tarkovsky," 54.

13. Elena del Río, "Alchemies of Thought in Godard's Cinema: Deleuze and Merleau-Ponty," *SubStance*, issue 108, vol. 34, no. 3 (2005): 65 (emphasis in the original).

14. Ibid., 63.

15. Alphonso Lingis, "Translator's Preface," in Merleau-Ponty, *The Visible and the Invisible*, lv.

16. Merleau-Ponty, *The Visible and the Invisible*, 135.

17. Hezekiah, "Being, Consciousness and Time," 77.

18. Rutherford, *Cinema and Embodied Affect*, unpaginated, available from www.sensesofcinema.com/contents/03/25/embodied_affect.html.

19. Mazis, *Emotion and Embodiment*, 20.

20. Merleau-Ponty, *Phenomenology of Perception*, 154, quoted in Mazis, *Emotion and Embodiment*, 20.

21. Mazis, *Emotion and Embodiment*, 29 (emphasis in the original). On the cultural and historical analysis of emotion *as* motion, see also Ahmed, *The Cultural Politics of Emotion*; Bruno, *Atlas of Emotion*.

22. Cataldi, *Emotion, Depth, and Flesh*, 115.

23. Ibid., 113.

24. Ahmed argues in *The Cultural Politics of Emotion* that bodies do not enter into the encounter with the other as fully gendered, racialized, and nationalized, for example, but are in fact *constituted* in these ways by specific forms of contact with others.

25. Cataldi, *Emotion, Depth, and Flesh*, 130.

26. Ibid., 115–16.

27. Hezekiah, "Being, Consciousness and Time," 78. This notion of the viewer and film being in a relation of *inspiration* substantially unsettles traditional subject/object relations in a way that is in keeping with Merleau-Ponty's reversibility thesis described in *Phenomenology of Perception*, but also opens

onto another plane of being that became a focus later in *The Visible and the Invisible.* "In the later work, Merleau-Ponty no longer conceives being as subject, but rather as infinity. . . . Merleau-Ponty seems to recognize an immanent plane where all forms of life, intelligence, and meaning are simultaneously created as differential strands of *élan vital* that form by internal differentiation and division. Merleau-Ponty's positive infinite may be regarded as a pure plane of immanence that 'expresses itself without end . . . '" (del Río, "Alchemies of Thought in Godard's Cinema," 77–78.) It may be, as well, an opportunity to entertain the possible overlap between Merleau-Ponty's "intertwining," Deleuzian "becoming," and Heideggerian "presencing," all of which reflect an interest in seeking out the precise terms of the coexistence of immanence and transcendence, and in meaning and being as not fixed but circulating, moving, dynamic, embodied (though in different ways). Elena del Río, Gabrielle Hezekiah, Laura Marks, and Jennifer Deger are among the scholars currently exploring these intersections. Deger, *Shimmering Screens;* del Río, "Alchemies of Thought"; Hezekiah, "Being, Consciousness and Time"; Marks, *Touch.*

28. Merleau-Ponty, *The Visible and the Invisible,* 264.

29. Merleau-Ponty, *Phenomenology of Perception,* 11.

30. Lingis, "Translator's Preface," lv. The quoted material is from Merleau-Ponty, *Phenomenology of Perception,* 315.

31. Cataldi, *Emotion, Depth, and Flesh,* 112.

32. Merleau-Ponty, *Phenomenology of Perception,* 291 (emphasis added).

33. Sobchack, *The Address of the Eye,* 55–56.

34. Dufrenne, *The Phenomenology of Aesthetic Experience,* 341.

35. Tarkovsky, *Sculpting in Time,* 143. The translation that appears on the Kino DVD differs slightly from Hunter-Blair's: "I'd gladly give my life / For a safe corner of warmth / If life's swift needle / did not draw me on as though I were a thread."

Bibliography

Ahmed, Sara. *The Cultural Politics of Emotion*. New York: Routledge, 2004.

Anzieu, Didier. *The Skin Ego*. Translated by Chris Turner. New Haven: Yale University Press, 1989.

Artaud, Antonin. *Selected Writings*. Translated by Helen Weaver; edited by Susan Sontag. New York: Farrar, Straus, and Giroux, 1976.

Auerbach, Jonathan. *Body Shots: Early Cinema's Incarnations*. Berkeley and Los Angeles: University of California Press, 2007.

Bachelard, Gaston. *The Poetics of Space*. Translated by Maria Jolas. Boston: Beacon Press, 1969.

Barker, Jennifer M. "Bodily Irruptions: The Corporeal Assault on Ethnographic Narration." *Cinema Journal* 34, no. 3 (1995): 57–76.

Barthes, Roland. *Camera Lucida: Reflections on Photography*. Translated by Richard Howard. New York: Hill and Wang, 1981.

BBC News. 2002. "Ask Wallace and Gromit Creator Nick Park." *Talking Point*, available from http://news.bbc.co.uk/1/hi/talking_point/forum/2314009.stm.

Benjamin, Walter. "The Cultural History of Toys." Translated by Rodney Livingstone. In *Walter Benjamin: Selected Writings*, vol. 2, part 1: *1927–1930*, edited by Michael W. Jennings, Howard Eiland, and Gary Smith, 113–16. Cambridge, Mass., and London: The Belknap Press of Harvard University Press, 1999.

———. "On the Mimetic Faculty." Translated by Edmund Jephcott, edited by Peter Demetz. In Walter Benjamin, *Reflections: Essays, Aphorisms, Autobiographical Writings*, 333–36. New York: Schocken Books, 1986.

———. "One-Way Street." Translated by Rodney Livingstone. In *Walter Benjamin: Selected Writings*, vol. 1: *1913–1927*, edited by Michael W. Jennings, Howard Eiland, and Gary Smith, 444–88. Cambridge, Mass., and London: The Belknap Press of Harvard University Press, 1999.

———. "Program for a Proletarian Children's Theater." Translated by Rodney Livingstone. In *Walter Benjamin: Selected Writings*, vol. 2, part 1: *1927–1930*, edited by Michael W. Jennings, Howard Eiland, and Gary Smith,

201–6. Cambridge, Mass., and London: The Belknap Press of Harvard University Press, 1999.

———. "The Work of Art in the Age of Mechanical Reproduction." In Walter Benjamin, *Illuminations*, edited by Hannah Arendt, translated by Harry Zohn. 217–52. New York: Schocken Books, 1969.

Bensmaïa, Reda. "From the Photogram to the Pictogram: On Chris Marker's *La Jetée*." *Camera Obscura* 24 (1990): 139–61.

Bergson, Henri. "Laughter" (1900). In *Comedy*, edited by Wylie Sipher. Baltimore: Johns Hopkins University Press, 1980.

Bottomore, Stephen. "The Panicking Audience? Early Cinema and the 'Train' Effect." *Historical Journal of Film, Radio, and Television* 19, no. 2 (1999): 177–216.

Brown, Bill. "How to Do Things with Things: A Toy Story." *Critical Inquiry* 24, no. 4 (1998): 935–64.

Bruno, Giuliana. *Atlas of Emotion: Journeys in Art, Architecture, and Film*. London and New York: Verso, 2002.

Burch, Noël. *Life to Those Shadows*. Edited and translated by Ben Brewster. Berkeley and Los Angeles: University of California Press, 1990.

Caillois, Roger. "Mimicry and Legendary Psychasthenia." *October* 31 (1984): 17–32.

Cartwright, Lisa. *Screening the Body: Tracing Medicine's Visual Culture*. Minneapolis and London: University of Minnesota Press, 1995.

Cataldi, Sue. *Emotion, Depth, and Flesh: A Study of Sensitive Space: Reflections on Merleau-Ponty's Philosophy of Embodiment*. Albany: State University of New York Press, 1993.

Connor, Steven. *The Book of Skin*. Ithaca, N.Y.: Cornell University Press, 2004.

———. "Michel Serres's Five Senses." In *Michel Serres Conference*, Centre for Interdisciplinary Research in Culture and the Humanities, Birkbeck College, University of London, 29 May 1999, available from www.bbk.ac.uk/english/skc/5senses.htm.

Deger, Jennifer. *Shimmering Screens: Making Media in an Aboriginal Community*. Minneapolis: University of Minnesota Press, 2007.

del Río, Elena. "Alchemies of Thought in Godard's Cinema: Deleuze and Merleau-Ponty." *SubStance*, issue 108, vol. 34, no. 3 (2005): 62–78.

———. "The Body as Foundation of the Screen: Allegories of Technology in Atom Egoyan's *Speaking Parts*." *Camera Obscura* 38 (1996): 92–115.

Deleuze, Gilles. *Cinema 2: The Time-Image*. Translated by Hugh Tomlinson and Robert Galeta. Minneapolis: University of Minnesota Press, 1989.

———. *The Fold: Leibniz and the Baroque*. Minneapolis: University of Minnesota Press, 1993.

Diderot, Denis. "Essay on Painting" (1765). In Denis Diderot, *Selected Writings*, edited by Lester G. Crocker, translated by Derek Coltman, 161–68. New York: Macmillan, 1966.

Dillon, M.C. *Merleau-Ponty's Ontology*. Evanston, Ill.: Northwestern University Press, 1988.

Dreyfus, Hubert L. "The Current Relevance of Merleau-Ponty's Phenomenology of Embodiment." *The Electronic Journal of Analytic Philosophy* 4 (Spring 1996) (http://ejap.louisiana.edu).

Dufrenne, Mikel. *The Phenomenology of Aesthetic Experience.* Evanston, Ill.: Northwestern University Press, 1973.

Elkins, James. "Marks, Traces, Traits, Contours, *Orli,* and *Splendores:* Nonsemiotic Elements in Pictures." *Critical Inquiry* 21 (1995): 822–60.

———. *Pictures of the Body.* Stanford: Stanford University Press, 1999.

Gibson, James J. *The Ecological Approach to Visual Perception.* Boston: Houghton Mifflin & Co., 1979.

Grosz, Elizabeth. *Volatile Bodies: Toward a Corporeal Feminism.* Bloomington: Indiana University Press, 1994.

Gunning, Tom. "An Aesthetic of Astonishment: Early Film and the (in)Credulous Spectator." In *Viewing Positions: Ways of Seeing,* edited by Linda Williams, 114–33. New Brunswick, N.J.: Rutgers University Press, 1989.

———. "'Primitive' Cinema—A Frame-up? or The Trick's on Us." *Cinema Journal* 28, no. 2 (1989): 3–12.

Hansen, Miriam Bratu. "Benjamin, Cinema and Experience: 'The Blue Flower in the Land of Technology'." *New German Critique* 40 (1987): 179–224.

———. "Room-for-Play: Benjamin's Gamble with Cinema." *October* 109 (2004): 3–45.

———. "'With Skin and Hair': Kracauer's Theory of Film, Marseilles 1940." *Critical Inquiry* 19, no. 3 (Spring 1993): 437–69.

Haug, Kate. "An Interview with Carolee Schneemann." *Wide Angle* 20, no. 1 (1998): 20–49.

Hendricks, Gordon. "History of the Kinetoscope." In *The American Film Industry,* edited by Tino Balio, 43–56. Madison: University of Wisconsin Press, 1985.

Hezekiah, Gabrielle. "Being, Consciousness and Time: Phenomenology and the Videos of Robert Yao Ramesar." PhD diss., University of Toronto, 2007.

Hinson, Hal. "Speed" (review of *Speed*). *Washington Post,* 10 June 1994, D6.

Horton, Andrew. "Think Slow, Act Fast—Keaton's Comic Genius" In *Buster Keaton's* Sherlock, Jr., edited by Andrew Horton, 1–28. Cambridge and New York: Cambridge Press University, 1997.

Irigaray, Luce. *An Ethics of Sexual Difference* (1984). Edited and translated by Carolyn Burke and Gillian C. Gill. Ithaca, N.Y.: Cornell University Press, 1993.

Jay, Martin. *Downcast Eyes: The Denigration of Vision in Twentieth-Century French Thought.* Berkeley and Los Angeles: University of California Press, 1993.

Jones, Chuck. *Chuck Reducks: Drawing from the Fun Side of Life.* New York: Warner Books, 1996.

Juno, Andrea. "Interview with Carolee Schneemann." *RE/Search* 13 (1991): 66–77.

Keathley, Christian. *Cinephilia and History; or, The Wind in the Trees.* Bloomington: Indiana University Press, 2006.

Koebel, Caroline. "From Danger to Ascendancy: Notes toward Carolee Schneemann." *Wide Angle* 20, no. 1 (1998): 50–57.

Kracauer, Siegfried. "Marseille Notebooks," 1940. Kracauer Papers, Dokumente zum Exil in Frankreich und den Vereinigten Staaten, Deutsches Literaturarchiv, Marbach am Neckar.

———. *Theory of Film: The Redemption of Physical Reality*. Princeton: Princeton University Press, 1997.

Král, Petr. "Tarkovsky, or the Burning House," part 1. *Slavic and East European Performance* 15, no. 3 (1995): 51–57.

Kristeva, Julia. *Powers of Horror: An Essay in Abjection*. New York: Columbia University Press, 1982.

Laine, Tarja. "Cinema as Second Skin: Under the Membrane of Horror Film." *New Review of Film and Television Studies* 4, no. 2 (2006): 93–106.

Langer, Suzanne. *Feeling and Form: A Theory of Art Developed from Philosophy in a New Key*. New York: Charles Scribner's Sons, 1953.

Lant, Antonia. "Haptical Cinema." *October* 74 (1995): 45–73.

Leder, Drew. *The Absent Body*. Chicago: University of Chicago Press, 1990.

Lindberg, David C. *Theories of Vision: From Al-Kindi to Kepler*. Chicago: University of Chicago Press, 1976.

Lingis, Alphonso. "Sense and Non-Sense in the Sexed Body." *Cultural Hermeneutics* 4 (1977): 345–65.

———. "Translator's Preface." In Maurice Merleau-Ponty, *The Visible and the Invisible*, edited by Claude Lefort. Evanston, Ill.: Northwestern University Press, 1968.

MacDougall, David. *The Corporeal Image: Film, Ethnography, and the Senses*. Princeton: Princeton University Press, 2006.

Malgrave, Harry F., ed. *Empathy, Form, and Space: Problems in German Aesthetics, 1873–1893*. Santa Monica, Calif.: Getty Center for the History of Art and Humanities, 1994.

Maltin, Leonard. "Speed." In *2001 Movie and Video Guide*, 1312. New York: Penguin Putnam, Inc., 2001.

———. "Twister." In *2001 Movie and Video Guide*, 1483. New York: Penguin Putnam, Inc., 2001.

Marks, Laura U. *The Skin of the Film: Intercultural Cinema, Embodiment, and the Senses*. Durham, N.C.: Duke University Press, 1999.

———. *Touch: Sensuous Theory and Multisensory Media*. Minneapolis: University of Minnesota Press, 2002.

———. "Video Haptics and Erotics." *Screen* 39, no. 4 (1998): 331–47.

Mazis, Glen. *Emotion and Embodiment: A Fragile Ontology, Studies in Contemporary Continental Philosophy*. New York: Peter Lang Publishing, 1993.

———. "Matter, Dream, and the Murmurs among Things." In *Merleau-Ponty: Difference, Materiality, Painting*, edited by Veronique M. Foti, 72–89. Atlantic Highlands, N.J.: Humanities Press International, 1996.

Merleau-Ponty, Maurice. "Cézanne's Doubt." In *Sense and Non-Sense*, edited by James M. Edie, translated by Hubert L. Dreyfus and Patricia

Allen Dreyfus, 9–24. Evanston, Ill.: Northwestern University Press, 1964.

———. "The Child's Relations with Others." Translated by William Cobb. In *The Primacy of Perception*, edited by James M. Edie, 96–155. Evanston, Ill.: Northwestern University Press, 1964.

———. "Eye and Mind." Translated by Carleton Dallery. In *The Primacy of Perception*, edited by James M. Edie, 156–90. Evanston, Ill.: Northwestern University Press, 1964.

———. "The Film and the New Psychology." In *Sense and Non-Sense*, edited by James M. Edie, translated by Hubert L. Dreyfus and Patricia Allen Dreyfus, 48–59. Evanston, Ill.: Northwestern University Press, 1964.

———. *Phenomenology of Perception*. 1962. Translated by Colin Smith. London: Routledge, 1962. Reprint, 1994.

———. *The Visible and the Invisible*. Edited by Claude Lefort, translated by Alphonso Lingis. Evanston, Ill.: Northwestern University Press, 1968.

Miller, William Ian. *The Anatomy of Disgust*. Cambridge, Mass.: Harvard University Press, 1997.

Minkowski, Eugène. *Vers une cosmologie*. Paris: Aubier, 1906.

Montagu, Ashley. *Touching: The Human Significance of the Skin*. 3rd ed. New York: Harper and Row, 1986.

Morisette, Isabelle. "Reflexivity in Spectatorship: The Didactic Nature of Early Silent Film." *Off-screen* (2002), available from www.horschamp.qc.ca/new_offscreen/reflexivity.html.

Musser, Charles. *The Emergence of Cinema: The American Screen to 1907*. Berkeley and Los Angeles: University of California Press, 1990.

Münsterberg, Hugo. *The Photoplay: A Psychological Study*. New York: Dover, 1916.

Nasaw, David. *Going Out: The Rise and Fall of Public Amusements*. New York: Basic Books, 1993.

Oxenhandler, Noelle. "The Eros of Parenthood." *New Yorker*, 19 February 1996, 47–49.

Parshall, Peter F. "Houdini's Protégé: Buster Keaton in *Sherlock, Jr.*" In *Buster Keaton's* Sherlock, Jr., edited by Andrew Horton, 67–88. Cambridge and New York: Cambridge Press University, 1997.

Peiss, Kathy. *Cheap Amusements: Working Women and Leisure in Turn-of-the-Century New York*. Philadelphia: Temple University Press, 1986.

Perez, Gilberto. "The Dream Life" (review of Colin McGinn, *The Power of the Movies: How Screen and Mind Interact*). *The Nation*, 27 March 2006.

———. *The Material Ghost: Films and Their Medium*. Baltimore: Johns Hopkins University Press, 2000.

Rabinbach, Anson. *The Human Motor: Energy, Fatigue, and the Origins of Modernity*. New York: Basic Books, 1990.

Riegl, Alois. *Late Roman Art Industry* (*Spätrömische Kunstindustrie* [Vienna: Österreichisches Staatsdruckere, 1927]). Translated by Rolf Winkes. Rome: Giorgio Bretschneider Editore, 1985.

Rutherford, Anne. 2002. "Cinema and Embodied Affect." In *Senses of Cinema*, www.sensesofcinema.com/contents/03/25/embodied_affect.html.

———. "What Makes a Film Tick? Cinematic Affect, Materiality, and Mimetic Innervation." PhD diss., University of Western Sydney, 2006.

Sartre, Jean-Paul. *Being and Nothingness: A Phenomenological Essay on Ontology*. Translated by Hazel E. Barnes. New York: Washington Square Press, 1993.

Schneemann, Carolee, ed. *Imaging Her Erotics: Essays, Interviews, Projects*. Cambridge, Mass.: MIT Press, 2002.

Schulz, Bruno. *The Street of Crocodiles*. Translated by Celina Wieniewska. New York: Penguin Books, 1977.

Serres, Michel. *Les cinq sens*. Paris: Hachette, 1998.

Sesonske, Alexander. "Cinema Space." In *Explorations in Phenomenology*, edited by David Carr and Edward S. Casey. The Hague: Martinus Nijhoff, 1973.

Shaviro, Steven. *The Cinematic Body*. Minneapolis and London: University of Minnesota Press, 1993.

Shiff, Richard. "Cézanne's Physicality: The Politics of Touch." In *The Language of Art History*, edited by Salim Kemal and Ivan Gaskell, 129–80. Cambridge: Cambridge University Press, 1991.

Sobchack, Vivian. "The Active Eye: A Phenomenology of Cinematic Vision." *Quarterly Review of Film and Video* 12, no. 3 (1990): 21–36.

———. *The Address of the Eye: A Phenomenology of Film Experience*. Princeton: Princeton University Press, 1992.

———. "Nostalgia for a Digital Object: Regrets on the Quickening of Quicktime." *Millennium Film Journal* 34 (1999): 4–23. Reprinted in *Future Cinema: The Cinematic Imaginary after Film*, edited by Jeffrey Shaw and Peter Weibel. Cambridge, Mass.: MIT Press, 2003.

———. "'Susie Scribbles': On Technology, Technë, and Writing Incarnate." In *Carnal Thoughts: Embodiment and Moving Image Culture*, 109–34. Berkeley: University of California Press, 2004.

———. "What My Fingers Knew: The Cinesthetic Subject, or Vision in the Flesh." In *Carnal Thoughts: Embodiment and Moving Image Culture*, 53–84. Berkeley: University of California Press, 2004.

Sontag, Susan. *On Photography*. New York: Farrar, Strauss, and Giroux, 1978.

Stewart, Garrett. "Keaton through the Looking Glass." *The Georgia Review* 33, no. 2 (1979): 345–65.

Stoller, Paul. *Sensuous Scholarship*. Philadelphia: University of Pennsylvania Press, 1997.

———. *The Taste of Ethnographic Things: The Senses in Anthropology*. Philadelphia: University of Pennsylvania Press, 1989.

Strauss, David Levi. "Love Rides Aristotle through the Audience: Body, Image, and Idea in the Work of Carolee Schneemann." In *Imaging Her Erotics: Essays, Interviews, Projects*, edited by Carolee Schneemann, 317–25. Cambridge, Mass.: MIT Press, 2002.

Tarkovsky, Andrey. *Sculpting in Time.* Translated by Kitty Hunter-Blair. Austin: University of Texas Press, 1987.

Tarkovsky, Arseniy. "Life, Life" (1950). In Andrey Tarkovsky, *Sculpting in Time,* translated by Kitty Hunter-Blair, 143. Austin: University of Texas Press, 1987.

Taussig, Michael. *Mimesis and Alterity: A Particular History of the Senses.* New York: Routledge, 1993.

Thomas, Lewis. *The Lives of a Cell.* New York: Bantam Books, 1974.

Thompson, Richard. "Meep Meep." In *Movies and Methods,* vol. 1, edited by Bill Nichols. Berkeley and Los Angeles: University of California Press, 1976.

Toulet, Emmanuelle. *Birth of the Motion Picture.* New York: Harry N. Abrams, Inc., 1995.

Turovskaya, Maya. *Tarkovsky: Cinema as Poetry.* Translated by Natasha Ward; edited by Ian Christie. London and Boston: Faber and Faber, 1989.

Vasseleu, Catherine. *Textures of Light: Vision and Touch in Irigaray, Levinas, and Merleau-Ponty.* London: Routledge, 1998.

Vischer, Robert. "The Aesthetic Act and Pure Form: An Anthology of Changing Ideas." In *Art in Theory, 1815–1900,* edited by Charles Harrison, Paul Wood, and Jason Gaiger. Malden, Mass.: Blackwell Publishers, Inc., 1998.

Weinberg, Herman G. *Saint Cinema: Writings on the Film, 1929–1970.* 2nd ed. New York: Dover Publications, 1973.

Whalen, Tom. "*Run Lola Run*" (review of *Run Lola Run*). *Film Quarterly* 53, no. 3 (2000): 33–40.

Williams, Linda. "Corporeal Observers: Visual Pornographies and the 'Carnal Density of Vision'." In *Fugitive Images,* edited by Patrice Petro, 3–41. Bloomington: Indiana University Press, 1995.

———. "Film Bodies: Gender, Genre, Excess." *Film Quarterly* 44, no. 4 (1991): 2–13.

Young, Iris Marion. *Justice and the Politics of Difference.* Princeton: Princeton University Press, 1990.

Index

Text:	10/13 Aldus
Display:	Aldus
Compositor:	International Typesetting and Composition
Indexer:	Alexander Trotter

CPSIA information can be obtained
at www.ICGtesting.com
Printed in the USA
JSHW022113050620
6038JS00010B/45